Steven Primrose-Smith was born in Darwen, near Blackburn, in 1970. He managed to escape in 1996 and has since lived in Austria, Spain and the Isle of Man. He has a B.A. in English Language and Philosophy, a B.Sc. in Mathematics and an M.A. in Philosophy. His first book, *No Place Like Home, Thank God*, is an Amazon UK Bestseller and described his three-year, 22,000 mile bicycle ride around Europe during which he ate various unsavoury items including a brain, a handful of maggots and a marmot. His first novel, *George Pearly Is A Miserable Old Sod* is also an Amazon UK Bestseller. This is his fifth book.

Also by Steven Primrose-Smith

TRAVEL

No Place Like Home, Thank God: *A 22,000 Mile Bicycle Ride around Europe*

Hungry For Miles: *Cycling across Europe on £1 a Day*

FICTION

George Pearly Is A Miserable Old Sod

Love And Other Complete Wastes Of Time

Route Britannia

Part 1: The Journey South

A Spontaneous Bicycle Ride through Every

County in Britain

Steven Primrose-Smith

Rosebery Publications

First published in 2016 by Rosebery Publications
1 Perwick Rise, Port St Mary, Isle of Man

ISBN-13: 978-1540516374
ISBN-10: 1540516377

Where appropriate, names have been changed.

Table of Contents

Author's Note

I didn't intend this to be a book in two parts. I figured it would easily fit into one. After all, my trip around Europe, the one that spanned roughly seventeen months in total, fit compactly into the 350 pages of *No Place Like Home, Thank God*, and my British tour was only a five-month project.

But on this ride I was entering somewhere new on a near-daily basis and to distil this book to a single volume would have meant omitting entire counties, and that wasn't what this book was supposed to be about. I wanted it to be about the *whole* of Britain, every piece of it.

This book, *The Journey South* and the second part, *The Journey North* are, in a way, badly named. There are "northern" counties in the second volume that are farther south than some of the "southern" counties in the first, but I decided to slice the story in two at roughly the halfway point. Ideally I would have drawn a line from Liverpool to Hull and made it properly North and South, but then the books would have been of unequal lengths. Besides, the date chosen for the end of the first book is quite an important one.

Once again, because the technical details of my bike and what I carried with me are only of interest to die-hard gearheads, I've included this information as a separate appendix at the back of the book.

I hope you enjoy Route Britannia. If you do, I'd greatly appreciate it if you could pop on over to Amazon and give it a review to tell others about it. If you hated it then, er, please forget we even had this little chat.

Route map, the Journey South

Fig. 1: A very approximate route through the first 49 counties of Britain

Chapter 1: The route to Britannia

Ah, Britain. What does it mean to you? I suspect that depends on whether or not you're from Britain yourself and, if so, from which part. Some people's view of Britain is less than positive. The writer Hanif Kureishi described it as "a squalid, uncomfortable, ugly place...an intolerant, racist, homophobic, narrow-minded, authoritarian rathole run by vicious, suburban-minded, materialistic philistines". And the Queen gave him a CBE!

As I came to the end of my all-Europe bicycle ride a few years ago (*No Place Like Home, Thank God*) I met an Australian in a pub, the Aussie's natural habitat.

"England's weird, mate," he said. "The first thing the English always tell me is how shitty the place is."

"Do you like England?" I asked.

"No, it's shit. But Wales and Scotland are nice."

I have to admit to being guilty of this myself. When I moved to Austria in the mid-nineties my British friends and I would refer to home not as England or Old Blighty, but as Mingland or Old Shitey. Then a new lad, Ben, joined us. Ben didn't like our negativity. He told us Britain was great. We dismissed his arguments while continuing to slag off the place.

We were young, and pumped on an exciting new life abroad, but we weren't the only ones knocking the UK. There were plenty of other people to tell us the country was rubbish. An entire industry makes its fortune by dumping on Britain. There was a book called Crap Towns that struck such a chord with its disaffected British readers they complained their own home towns weren't included. There are now three books in the series.

And then there are websites such as ilivehere.co.uk. It allows you to state exactly why your home town is so bloody awful. Television programmes like Rip Off Britain are part of the same dismal scheme, as is nearly every story in nearly every edition of every tabloid newspaper. Even our politicians, the one group you'd expect to stay positive for Queen and country in the face of all reality, have described the place as 'broken'. We've been conditioned to rip ourselves to pieces and to enjoy doing so, like confused cannibals joyfully eating our own limbs.

While I lived in Austria, and later in Spain, if I told someone I was from Britain, they would invariably respond with a tale of some great recent visit and my only response was a genuinely astonished, "Really?" Britain seemed more popular with people who hadn't actually lived there.

And we do have a well-founded reputation for moaning. The Aussies don't call us whinging poms for nothing. We moan about the weather, the government, the NHS, the roads, about, well, everything. It's a national pastime. Why is that? Is it because, as moaners, we see everything as rubbish? Or is it because everything is rubbish that we like to moan? Even as far back as 1758, writer Arthur Murray said the British are "never so happy as when you tell them they are ruined". This probably explains the popularity of the Daily Mail.

The route near the end of my European bike ride had seen me slog from Harwich in Essex to Cardiff, and then up to Holyhead. I was aiming for speed. It was the end of 22,000 miles on the road and I just wanted to get it finished. The Welsh leg of that trip had been enjoyable enough but the south-central strip of England, jumping from one large, nondescript urban area to the next, was as much fun as a head massage from Abu Hamza.

But the following ride, when we tried to survive for £1 a

day (*Hungry for Miles*), took us down the west coast from Liverpool eventually to Poole in Dorset and suddenly actual areas of the country seemed truly magnificent. Hang on a minute, I thought. Maybe these were the amazing places those Spaniards and Austrians had visited. Or maybe they'd actually gone to Brittany for their holidays and just misheard where I was from.

Now, there will be some of you reading this thinking, "Of course Britain is great. What's wrong with you?" Unless you're a Union Flag-tattooed member of the British Nationalist Party, I bet yours isn't one of those towns heavily and – who knows? – perhaps justifiably slated by Crap Towns or ilivehere.co.uk. Like I said, it depends on where you're from. I was from a rubbish bit, Blackburn, but I didn't want to moan any longer. Ben, that ambassador for Britain in Austria, was right. It's all too negative.

I was sitting in The Welkin, a Wetherspoon's in the centre of Liverpool ("more like Live-in-Stool", according to one anonymous poster on ilivehere.co.uk). The city was up to its old tricks again. Three twenty-something Scousers hung around the pub's exit, not doing anything but scanning the place in a menacing manner. Their threat was negated, however, by their high-pitched Liverpudlian whine that only dogs and other Scousers can hear. Then a wasted-looking scally slinked like a jackal from table to table offering a half-open carrier bag to its occupants.

"Want some perfume, mate?" he whispered urgently.

Funnily enough, I didn't.

I've visited Liverpool so many times and I've yet to experience a trip that doesn't involve criminality at some level: a three-way street fight, someone who openly admitted to being smacked off his tits on cocaine, a friend getting his nose broken and, this time, being offered clearly stolen goods. It's almost like they enjoy the stereotype and want to reinforce it.

The whining lads disappeared and the jackal took his unsold wares to another venue. Then in walked three Americans, two women and a man in their thirties. They sat at the table next to mine. Some American tourists take a very unadventurous view of travel. I once saw a stream of them in wonderful Salzburg shuffle past a row of great Austrian restaurants to seek solace in the local McDonald's to eat exactly the same mundane crap they could get back home. Today's Americans weren't like that though.

"I guess we should try *fish 'n' chips*," said one of the women loudly.

The phrase "fish 'n' chips" sounded awkward in her mouth, as though it were a foreign phrase, which I suppose it was. She made the humble battered cod and spuds sound exotic, a delicacy, like deep-fried parrot in a platypus sauce.

Then the bloke chipped in.

"Yeah, an' we should try a," he said, before pausing for a second, "a *lager*."

How could a word associated with fizzy piss suddenly sound so adventurous and desirable? Didn't he know it was exactly the same gassy pop that Budweiser made back home? It didn't matter. Here, abroad, it was sexy.

The reason I was sitting here was because tomorrow I was about to begin another bicycle ride, a very British one. And right now I realised these Americans were experiencing Britain in exactly the way I wanted to see the country. I hadn't lived in the UK for twenty years but I needed to view it as though it were my first time, uncynically and full of mystery. I wanted to witness Britain with the eyes of a foreigner, of a traveller. In some instances this wouldn't be difficult; there was an awful lot of Britain I'd never seen. And just as I'd done while cycling around Europe, I wanted to hunt out the local food, meals and snacks that, for whatever reason, hadn't been adopted by the country as a whole but had stayed local. I wasn't expecting anything as unusual as poo-flavoured sausages from the Ardennes or Turkey's intestine sandwiches but there would surely be something hidden in the dark corners of Britain's delis and takeaways, other than E.coli.

The Americans sat at their table, repeatedly straining their necks to look for passing waiters, who never materialised because of course this was a British pub.

"You need to go to the bar to order," I said.

They looked towards the counter with its beer pumps and its optics and then back at each other, seemingly considering whether such a journey required the use of a car.

In Britain, at least in pubs, we now take it for granted that you hand over your money for your dinner before it arrives. I've always been a bit suspicious of that. You can hardly refuse to pay for an undercooked chicken breast if you've already stumped up the cash. It doesn't happen anywhere else in the world as far as I know. These Americans were learning the weirdnesses of travel in Britain, the things you have to do to operate in this foreign country.

The American man wandered off to the bar and one of the women received a phone call. She told her friend on the other end what they'd been up to today. By the way, please don't think I was earwigging. Everyone this side of the Wirral could hear her.

"We came in on the train from *Manchester*," she said, her accent making the northern city sound as exhilarating as Bangkok, "to *Liverpool*. We got a cab to give us a tour. He charged us £150 and so we tipped £100." Result! Some Scouse taxi driver was living *la vida loca* tonight. Sometimes you import your own country's weirdnesses to a foreign place and no one tells you it's weird. The locals just smile and take your cash.

The phone call ended and my thoughts returned to my

upcoming trip. I don't like planning. It's tedious, all those calculations regarding how far you have to travel each day to reach the next campsite or the hotel you've booked. A bicycle is supposed to represent freedom. But where's the freedom if you've tied yourself to an immutable schedule? From past experience I know the most fun days on the road were always the most spontaneous ones: an invite to an Orthodox Easter party in Ukraine, watching a Preston lass pogo up and down at a country dancing rehearsal in the Czech Republic's Brno, being given a tour of a roofless, wall-less "house" near a lake in Bulgaria by a man who lived under a table. Some people like to know ahead of time exactly where they'll sleep each night of their journey. Not me. There'd be no planning. I didn't want to know where I'd end up. That way, it could be at a beer festival or maybe 'round Billy Piper's gaff.

I wanted to see the whole of Britain and so I decided the best way to do this was to cycle through each and every county. Friends asked me how many counties there are, as though this is a simple fact that everyone should know – like the country's longest river or its tallest mountain – and that had somehow passed them by. But it's not as easy as that. The counties keep changing, merging, splintering and reforming, like an old rock band who hate each other but whose ex-wives have spent all the royalties.

In the case of England, many former counties have become smaller counties, city councils and unitary authorities and this is messy. As a result I decided to ignore these new divisions for England. It has 47 mainland ceremonial counties, the ones everyone has heard of, and that's quite enough, thanks.

Wales was for a long time made up of a few large, clunky counties that have now been smashed into 21 smaller councils, and so for reasons of total inconsistency I was going to visit these new, smaller ones.

This was the case for Scotland too, where I would visit the 29 new, generally trimmer councils. I say "generally" because after the recent changes Highland became one humongous entity, absorbing Caithness, Sutherland and other places and is now approximately the size of Belgium.

So, in total, this added up to a not-nice, not-round 97 counties through which to heave my heavy bike. The only thing I'd planned was where to start, where to finish and the approximate order in which I'd see the counties to make my trip as efficient as possible and, as it turned out, I didn't even manage to do that right. Everything else about the trip would be determined by others and by spontaneity. From the outside I'd give the appearance of a man with an over-arching plan but, in reality, I'd be winging it. Much like David Moyles, but on a bicycle.

I threw my idea out to Facebook as well as a couple of cycling forums and hundreds of suggestions for places to visit came flooding in. Time would prevent me from seeing them all, but I'd try to visit as many as possible. Surely this was the best way to enjoy Britain even if no one had so far provided the date and time of that party at Billy Piper's.

I left Wetherspoon's and wandered around Liverpool's town centre. It was mid-April and a bitter wind blew over Strawberry Field and down Penny Lane and whatever the hell street I was on. The town was rammed. Today had been the Grand National and the winning gamblers were out giving it large. The party atmosphere was a pleasant change from Liverpool's usual feel when darkness descends, that someone is about to knife you in the head for the cost of a packet of Pokémon stickers.

And then I recognized another of Britain's weirdnesses, one of those things that isn't the case elsewhere: Every single bar in Liverpool had a team of bouncers hanging around outside, fat men squeezed into little, black jackets, meaty top halves and tiny legs of string. One guy had a neck as wide as his head and a fat, bald scalp that rippled unattractively. It looked like his brain was on the outside. Why is it possible for residents of other countries' cities to go out for a drink without the need for security staff? Apparently in Britain, for every one hundred people out drinking, one will require medical treatment as a result. Would this figure be higher without the bouncers or are they responsible for the injuries? Maybe we'd be better off with doctors on the door.

I headed into a busy bar. Having noticed a beer called Britannia Navigation on draft, and because I'd decided to call this trip *Route Britannia*, it seemed like the obvious choice, but it was a thin, disappointing drink. Don't worry, at this stage I was still allowed to moan. I wouldn't set off officially until the morning. From then on it would be positivity all the way. Or for as long as I could manage it.

I sat at a table and clocked the menu, quickly realising the pub was part of a chain. I'd already decided that while wending my way around Britain I'd avoid chains wherever possible. I wanted local, not mass-produced rubbish from a business identical no matter where you came across it, whether Dundee, Doncaster or Droitwich. I decided to get my dinner elsewhere.

I bought another beer from an off licence and was given a black carrier bag to put it in. This is what had happened everywhere in Turkey. (If you bought a soft drink there, you won yourself a *white* carrier bag.) I liked this reminder of Europe. It had felt oddly exotic to be treated this way in Ankara. Maybe some of that exoticism could leach into my experience of Britain. Perhaps if enough memories of former foreign rides were triggered as I toured the country then Britain could feel like the whole of Europe rather than what my friends and I had believed it to be before, the Hole of Europe.

I stopped at a kebab shop, one of those with a smooth, grey elephant's leg spinning in the window. I took my dinner and beer back to my room. I'd asked for a small kebab, which was a good choice since even this one was massive. A large one would have contained the entire horse. But I made the mistake of asking for chilli sauce – I bit into it and screamed like a six-year-old girl – forgetting that, in Britain, kebab shop chilli sauce is hot enough to melt your teeth.

My hotel – the cheapest I could find – had an interesting, very British scheme offering you a free drink if you chose not to have your bedding changed each morning. But the killjoys would only allow you to do this for three days in a row so that long-term guests were prevented from lying in their own faeces while the glasses slowly collected around their beds. The hotel's marketeers clearly knew their clientele. Brits in hotels might generally want crisp bed linen but it wasn't a deal-breaker if a free drink was at stake.

Only a few days earlier I'd been down to the jetty near my parents' place on the Isle of Man. On the sea wall there was a fish chart depicting legal catch sizes. Someone had taken the not inconsiderable time to stick googly eyes to each of the many fish and crustaceans displayed upon it, even attaching some to the tiny birds in the Manx government logo. All the creatures of the sea appeared to be lobotomised or drug-addled. It looked wonderfully mental. I took a couple of snaps, put it on Facebook and the post was shared hundreds and hundreds of times. Googly eyes were the future. They brought a smile to people's faces. I'd bought a bag in case something needed sprucing up as I cycled around Britain. On the wall of my tiny room was a grey-brown painting of a horse's head in profile and this image was drabness itself. I added a googly eye to its glass surface and instantly improved the artwork, turning it into a demented nag. I wondered how long it would be before a maid noticed it, probably months if the room's occupants kept choosing alcohol over cleaning services.

I was looking forward to tomorrow. Over the next five months I wanted to celebrate everything Britain had to offer. I wanted to fall in love with the place in a way I'd never managed to do when I lived here. And there was something else. If I ever decided to come back to live in Britain, I wanted to know where I would come back to. I knew it wouldn't be Blackburn, but where was best for me? Where could I live the sort of life I wanted to live?

I drifted off to sleep, ready for the new day's big, Britain-wide push with a crazed stallion watching over me.

I still couldn't feel my tongue.

Chapter 2: Lizzie is a scratter

Merseyside, Greater Manchester, Cheshire and Staffordshire

Day One was here and in front of me sat a bowl of something that could have been baby food or, equally, cat vomit. But let's start as we mean to go on, positively.

The reason Scousers are so named is because of their traditional dish *lobscouse*, or scouse for short, a mixture of potatoes, carrots and onions and, in theory at least, lamb or beef, although I was struggling to find any animal in my dish this morning. The bowl had arrived with a range of cutlery although such a puréed breakfast required only a spoon. It's easy to see why this dish is so popular here in Liverpool. You could still get it down your neck even with all your teeth knocked out. Scouse had originally been brought to Merseyside by Baltic sailors, like VD, only less visually appealing.

I looked around the café. It was 10 a.m. and I was the only one in there. I didn't even know if scouse was the sort of thing you ate for breakfast, perhaps a social *faux pas* akin to ordering a Full English at a midnight supper club or a bowl of Frosties for Sunday lunch.

The café was Maggie May's and it's famous for selling this local dish. The walls of the place were full of illuminated skylines and old Liverpool maps. Uniquely for an establishment dealing in locality around here, I couldn't see a single mention of The Beatles. Since it's mandatory to display the band's logo at least once every square metre from the centre of Liverpool out to a radius of ten miles, I'm sure this oversight has now been rectified.

I gave my scouse a little taste. Mmm, interesting, I thought. Well, I say interesting. It wasn't that it *tasted* interesting. What was interesting was that it didn't taste of anything at all. I added some salt and pepper. Ah, that was better. Now it at least tasted of salt and pepper. I cleared the bowl in ten or so gloopy spoonfuls. Towards the end of my tiny breakfast I did stumble across something vaguely resembling meat, although it may have been something that had accidentally fallen into the pan, but I still took it to be a positive. This was how the ride was going to be, seeking the gold in everything. Onward and upward! Or until I was ground down by reality.

Day One, and only Day One, was devoted to Merseyside. How can you see an entire county in a single day? I hear you ask. Obviously, I couldn't. I'd found the total area of Britain and that of every county and divvied up how long I was allowed to spend in each, given that I'd planned about 150 days for the entire ride. By that measure, some tiny, heavily populated but interesting areas were given almost no time at all while the huge and largely empty Highland area of Scotland was allocated something like three weeks. I reduced the quieter places and shared the days out amongst the rest in an entirely inconsistent manner. Still, Merseyside, in the bottom one-third of counties by size, only earned itself a single day. However, before I could even pretend to say I'd seen the place there were two important checkpoints I'd been told to visit.

I decided to ride out of Liverpool via the docks. This was Merseyside after all, and the first leg of my journey would be to ride along the side of the Mersey. Did you know that, like the Ganges, the River Mersey is considered sacred by British Hindus? Maybe that explains all the bodies floating in it.

But what else do we know about this area? There's a lazy journalistic device that, because I'm equally lazy, we'll return

20

to time and time again in this book. A reporter will see a recently released set of figures and, based on the numbers, declare a town to be Britain's capital of something or other. It's a con really. They don't give you the data. They just see that one town is more of this or that, even if it's only 0.01% more, and they have a story.

As a result, according to the tabloids, Liverpool is Britain's food bank capital. It is also its benefits capital, its whiplash claim capital and its dog attack capital. Merseyside as a whole is Britain's stalking capital. Do you fancy moving here yet? Maybe this one will swing it: Since Britain is the boob job capital of the entire world and Liverpool is Britain's breast augmentation capital, this means Liverpool has more silicone boobies than anywhere else on the planet. They've got more fraudulent tits than the House of Commons.

Looking at a map, Merseyside is an interesting shape, rather like a painful-looking sex toy or a weird blob giving the finger to America. While it's the fifth smallest county in England it's the sixth most densely populated. It's a bit of a squeeze, and that's without even considering all those fake breasts.

I would have liked to provide you with more tasty nuggets of information about Liverpool but they're impossible to find. If you type the word 'Liverpool' into Google you just get millions of pages about The Beatles. If you try to limit the search by looking for "Liverpool –Beatles" you break the internet.

Like most ailing industrial cities around the world, things weren't looking too good in Liverpool, especially here by the Mersey. Giant warehouses and old, ten storey mills stood empty, holding nothing these days but dust and dreams and broken glass from the windows skilfully shattered by local dipshits. How the hell did they manage to break the panes on the top floor? Maybe the vandals around here have sniper rifles.

As I escaped the clutches of Liverpool my stomach started to gurgle. Since all I'd had to eat was the scouse, it had to be the culprit. Why was my stomach bothering to process it? When it arrived on my table it already looked like it had been digested a couple of times.

My first checkpoint was on Crosby Beach and the site of Antony Gormley's impressive art installation, Another Place, one hundred cast-iron men stretching for two miles along the sand and staring steadfastly out to sea. I arrived at its southern edge and watched. The tide was coming in. The men were slowly sinking beneath the waves.

Still high on the dramatic improvement I'd made to that horse painting last night, I figured that perhaps one of Gormley's fellas would benefit from a little googly action. No one was about. I strolled purposefully across the sand to the nearest rusting man, supposedly modelled on Gormley himself, and attached two plastic eyes, a definite improvement. And then I retreated and sat to watch the tide claim the rest of the men.

Time passed. A red container ship slipped by lazily in the distance. As an Iron Man event it was a little disappointing but as art it was genuinely moving, watching the approaching tide drown the statues one by one. It's a little less moving when you know one of them is wearing googly eyes.

It was at this point I realised I was a prat. The sea would wash off the eyes, probably in seconds, and then, a day or two from now, some poor herring gull would end up choking to death on one of them. I felt bad. I vowed not to stick googly eyes in stupid places again and I apologise profusely to any seagull chicks I may have inadvertently orphaned.

With my loaded bike leaning against the beach's metal railing, an old couple walked by.

"Was it worth it?" the man asked.

Seeing my luggage he probably thought I'd cycled for days or weeks to reach this place and not just six miles on my first day.

"Yes, it is," I replied.

To be honest, if this had been the last thing I saw at the end of my estimated five thousand miles it would still have been worth it. It is inexplicably magnificent. The feeling of being baffled was wonderful. Why did it make me feel sad to see an iron man up to his waist in freezing cold sea water? I've no idea but it did.

The coastal path, the Sefton Way, continued on smooth tarmac by the sea. A sign told me a mere fifteen miles away was Southport. Was I really going to be able to cycle the whole distance on a lovely seaside path? Well, no, obviously I wasn't. Britain's cycle paths may be improving but there's still a hell of a long way to go. The path quickly fired me into a housing estate and, with no further signs to give me a clue, I had to find my own way out and ended up on a dual carriageway.

The air temperature wasn't particularly cold for this time of year, but the wind was – remember, we're trying to be positive – invigoratingly powerful and refreshingly in my face. I put my head down and pedalled into it. Southport and its funfair eventually appeared.

The tabloids may not have dubbed Southport the capital of anything, but thanks to local Barbara Pratt it was the first British resort to launch its own perfume. Apparently, it captures "the essence of Southport". I'm not sure there's such a large market for smelling like fish 'n' chips with a hint of sewage outfall. But then Mrs Pratt went one better and created a fragrance for the town's non-league Southport FC, described as "woody with aquatic notes". Let's hope "woody" here refers to something floral rather than the Urban Dictionary's definition. On launch day, the players covered themselves in it and won five nil, either a reflection of the perfume's luck or how effectively it repelled the opposing team.

As I entered the town along the coast road I saw an ice cream van parked up on the seafront. What could be more British, I thought, than attempting to eat a frozen dessert while an icy wind tries to remove it from its supporting cone? Bloody nothing, that's what. I scored me a 99 and sat on the sea wall thinking that perhaps a Cup-a-Soup would have been a better option.

The reason I'd headed to Southport was to visit a museum the likes of which exists nowhere else in the world. The British love their gardens and what is a garden without a lawn mower? Quirky eccentricities are also very British. Enter Southport's own British Lawnmower Museum, a venue that brings both of these things together and a mere three pounds allows you to see the magic.

The place is only small – three or four rooms – but it's rammed with gardening machinery, so rammed in fact that it's hard to concentrate on any one thing. While examining one piece of machinery your eyes are distracted by the next piece seemingly entangled within it. Unless of course, like me, you're not *that* interested in lawnmowers and then it just looks like some mad bloke's garden shed.

As well as a history of grass cutters they have a room entitled Lawnmowers of the Rich and Famous, full of celebrity pieces. Coronation Street's Hilda Ogden donated a mower as did Paul O'Grady. Was his mower adorned with a pink, fluffy handle and a leopard-skin grass collector when he used it in his own garden or was this just an addition for the museum's benefit? We'll never know.

One interesting sort of celebrity piece comes from Britain's last hangman, Albert Pierrepoint, who had personally stretched the necks of four hundred ne'er-do-wells and, presumably, a handful of unfortunate innocents, such is the nature of capital punishment. He was paid £15 per execution, which incidentally, according to a sign in the museum, was the cost of the mower he had donated, as if perhaps his grass cutter had the same value as a human life. Regardless, in the museum's only attempt at drama, albeit slightly tasteless, his mower hangs from the ceiling by a noose.

A glass cabinet includes a collection of smaller items from celebrities lower down the food chain. Trowels and gardening forks have been donated by the likes of Vanessa Feltz, Timmy Mallett and Alan Titchmarsh, although surely he still needs his gardening gear.

In the same cabinet was a dibber from comedian Lee Mack. He had a couple of reasons to be annoyed, aside from any association with the aforementioned Z-listers. The museum managed to spell his name incorrectly, an impressive feat for a moniker consisting of just seven letters. Not only that but his tool lay dangerously close to that of Fred Talbot, a man who, given his sexually deviant past, you probably want to keep your tool well clear of.

I have less than zero interest in lawnmowers but there was something utterly charming about the museum and it seemed like the ideal place to visit on the first day of this very British adventure. I said goodbye and turned the bike inland. Three miles later I arrived at a campsite, or the muddy field of a farm as it would be more accurately described if I wasn't being positive. I was the only customer. After all, early April is a bloody stupid time of year to go camping in Britain.

For my first night on the road I pitched my tent in the windbreak shadow of a huge barn and, despite the early time of day, fell asleep for an hour. What was wrong with me? I'd only cycled about thirty miles. After shaking myself back to consciousness I decided to stretch my legs. A one-mile walk brought me to The Richmond. The sign outside advertised a special offer: "Carvery and ice cream for £6.25". I don't know about you, but I prefer my carvery with gravy. Inside it looked uninspiringly like a Brewers Fayre, and it *is* one of Joseph Holt's 120 pubs, but if I was going to avoid pub chains, especially given there was absolutely nowhere else around here, I was going to be very thirsty.

After a couple of pints I returned to my tent as the first spits and spots of deliciously cool rain tumbled from the sky. Once safely inside, this turned into a pitter-patter, then a light drumming and it wasn't long before it sounded like a team of builders were pouring buckets of water over my tent.

I'd enjoyed my day in Merseyside but already I realised that, despite this being a multi-month tour of one tiny island, there was still so much I'd never see. I could have, for example, visited St Helens, Britain's teenage pregnancy capital. Or maybe Widnes, once Britain's chemical capital but now perhaps on a downer. Back in 1888 it was described as the "dirtiest, ugliest and most depressing town in England". When I typed the phrase "something positive about Widnes" into Google it returned a blank page. If I wanted to keep this ride upbeat it was probably best to avoid such places. But one day for Merseyside wasn't enough, but that's all it was allowed to have. And it would be the same story for Greater Manchester tomorrow.

*

I woke up to a delightfully grey morning of light drizzle. It's never nice to pack your tent away wet, especially my tent. Its outer and inner are permanently fastened together and so there's a good chance that when you unpack it again both are soaked through. That's not such an issue if you're erecting your tent in tropical heat – it dries out immediately – but today there didn't seem to be any heat on offer, tropical or otherwise. It was unseasonably Arctic.

An hour or so after setting off I found myself on the

outskirts of Wigan. As the pie capital of Britain you get the impression that meat-stuffed pastries are a big deal around here. And if a pie won't provide you with enough carbs, you can pop along to Galloways in the town centre and they'll do you "a pie on a barm cake". I think that's the most northern phrase I've ever written.

The town also hosts the World Pie Eating Championships. Originally the aim was to eat as many pies as possible in a set time. Anthony "The Anaconda" Danson scoffed a record-beating seven in three minutes. But to meet government healthy eating guidelines – as if pie-eaters ever cared about those – the competition was changed a few years back to the fastest time to eat a single pie. The record is 22.53 seconds.

Over the years the competition has been beset with more controversy than FIFA. First off, a vegetarian option was added a few years back but the meat-free pie was only 60% the volume of the standard. In 2007 a competitor's dog went all Scooby Doo and ran riot at the pie stand, eating twenty and damaging ten others. The contest nearly had to be cancelled. In 2007, the organisers ran out of pies before the competitors were finished and in 2005 there was a four-man protest when it turned out the pies had come from nearby Farnworth instead of Wigan. But the most serious gaffe occurred in 2014 when the results had to be voided after the competition ended up with the wrong size of pie. Apparently the batch of pastries intended for the event was mistakenly routed to a local divorce party. It's my hope that, whenever the name of Wigan is mentioned on the news in future, you'll forever conjure up the unbearably sad image of a group of middle-aged women sitting in a working men's club celebrating the end of a love-less marriage with a massive pile of over-sized pies.

I was approaching Parbold, unfortunately famous around here for its inclusion in the expression "Parbold Hill". I struggled up the steep slope with untested legs, the sweat on my forehead mixing with the rain. The bike was heavy. I'd packed too much stuff. You'd think I'd know by now.

Under the workload I was taking heavy slurps of water and had emptied my two bottles. I'd need to find some more and soon. And then it appeared: A church with a version of the now-hackneyed Stay Calm government poster. This one said Stay Calm and Trust God. I leant the bike against its railings and hunted around the building for a tap and – lo and behold! – God provided or, in reality, a long-dead plumber had provided. God can't take the credit for the water unless he's equally willing to own up to AIDS, ISIS and Donald Trump.

I was now in my second county, Greater Manchester. I'd decided very early that I wouldn't attempt to cycle through the centre of the city of Manchester. I'd once worked in Salford and I didn't need to be reminded of that miserable commute. There's a reason Manchester is, according to the BBC, the suicide capital of England.

Towns don't really end around here. The terraced houses of one place merge into the next in one huge conurbation. It's not great cycling, to be honest. I suddenly found myself, arbitrarily it seemed, in Bolton. I couldn't find a newspaper story naming it the capital of anything in particular but it does have a grim statistic attached. The saying that "you can't go wrong with bricks and mortar" doesn't apply here. Since the year 2000, average British house prices have increased 172%. That is, a home worth £100,000 in 2000 would be worth £272,000 in 2016. In Bolton, its value would be £91,000. Prices have actually *dropped* 9% over a decade and a half!

As if to underscore these numbers, the rain came down harder. My stomach was telling me it was time for lunch and so I ducked from the shower into a fish and chip shop. For £3.20 the portion was massive, a fish the size of a killer whale.

I could barely walk afterwards. It was just as well I didn't need to.

I cycled through the damp, grey town, passing a pub with a sign offering "Great Food Daily!" I could imagine the conversation inside.

"Pah! This steak is awful. I thought you said you did great food daily."

"We do. It's usually around six o'clock, before the kitchen gets busy. The rest of the time it's mostly crap."

I had a couple of places to look out for in town. One was Smithills Farm. I had my list of recommendations people had given me but without any explanation as to why I should go there. I parked up outside and looked at their sign. They advertised a special rate for Brownies and Beavers and I suspected this petting zoo wasn't really aimed at me. To be honest, the idea of patting sheep and stroking goats in the drizzle didn't hold much appeal.

As you might expect within an enormous conurbation, campsites are in short supply around these parts. While I slowly tackled Moby Dick in that chippy I'd found one on the outskirts of Bolton near Edgworth and phoned the owner to see if it was open at this time of year, and it was.

I climbed another long hill to reach the site – another farm – and rang the bell to a house. A woman appeared from behind me and her expression wasn't a happy one.

"Sorry, I assumed you were in a camper van," she said. "I tried to call you back to check but there was no response."

I told her how I had to keep my phone switched off when I wasn't using it otherwise the battery would be dead in 24 hours.

"Do I need a camper van? You've got fields," I said.

"I have, but look at them."

We opened a gate and squelched around in mud. It was like a paddy field. It had been a wet day in a wet spell of a wet winter in a region of Britain that is generally wet and the local clay soil doesn't drain well. Then more bad news came.

"Are you a member?"

"What of?"

"The Caravanning Club."

I had a tent. Why would I be a member of The Caravanning Club?

"No."

"Ah, then you couldn't have stayed anyway."

That might have been useful information on the phone.

"Could I become a member?"

"Not here."

Great.

"Right then, is there another site somewhere around here?"

"Yes."

"Good."

"It's just up the road."

"Great!"

"But it closed down." Not great. "But you could always go there and see if they'll put you up."

She gave me vague directions but I couldn't find the place and it seemed like a lost cause, hunting for a closed site amongst swampland in murky weather. I checked on my phone for the next nearest alternative and – joy of joys! – it was a mere fifteen drizzly miles away, the other side of Rochdale. Can you feel my positivity being tested already?

The route took me on busy roads through the centre of rush-hour Bury. I wasn't supposed to be here at this time of day. I'd planned a leisurely jaunt through the place tomorrow to sample their famous puddings, black ones and steak ones, but now, early evening, its famous market was closed. In the gathering gloom, Bury wasn't impressive, a place whose drabness on this grey afternoon was so similar to my home town of Blackburn, Britain's shisha capital apparently, that I thought I must have made a wrong turn.

The evening was drawing in by the time I passed through Rochdale and arrived at the campsite in Newhey. According to the ever-uplifting Daily Mail, Rochdale, or at least one area of it, is the sickest place in Britain. That's "sickest" as in "most ill", not some modern street way of calling it fab and groovy. The ward of Falinge, which itself sounds like a medical complaint, has 4,500 residents of which 1,100 are of working age although only 300 have jobs. The rest are unemployed or "on the sick". I've no idea if this is true. Most of what the Daily Mail writes isn't. So let's ignore it and find something nice to say about Rochdale.

If you want to invoke positivity there's no person better to recall than Hitler. He, so the story goes, absolutely loved Rochdale's Victorian Gothic town hall so much that he planned to take it brick-by-brick after WW2 and rebuild it in the Fatherland. This is one explanation for Rochdale's bomb-free war. Unfortunately, this story has the air of an urban myth – there's no documented evidence to back it up – and so maybe it's no better than the earlier one from the Daily Mail.

The campsite sits on the road leading up to moody and desolate Saddleworth Moor. The ghosts of past terrors lie amongst those sad hills. The bodies of at least four of Ian Brady and Myra Hindley's victims were buried in this peat bog. A further body, unconnected to the Moors murderers, was also found there in 2015. The poor sod had been poisoned with strychnine but his identity has never been discovered. By the time I arrived it was seven o'clock. I was freezing cold and soaked to the skin. I turned my back to the horror of the hills and set up my tent in the icy rain.

This site had survived the recent deluge better than the one in Bolton. It was still damp but not unusably so, and my tent was remarkably dry inside despite being packed away wet. The site only cost £6, half the price of the previous evening and with better facilities. I'd soon learn that there's absolutely no rhyme or reason to British campsite prices.

I needed to get warm and there was no way my clothes would have dried in my tent at this temperature. I had to find central heating and if a beer had to be supplied at the same time then, hell, I'd just have to take that chance.

"Is there a pub near here?" I asked the site owner.

"There are two of 'em," he replied. "Just around the corner is Bird In The Hand. A little farther is The Bird In Hand."

Eh? But that was how it was, two pubs with near identical names within about a hundred metres of each other. I wondered if, back in the days before mobile phones, it was a device to enable Yorkshire-accented philanderers to find an easy excuse to be somewhere they shouldn't without being caught.

"You said you were out at t' Bird In Hand last night! I phoned. You weren't there. Where were you?"

"T' Bird In Hand? Nah, that's Wednesday. Last night I was in Bird Int Hand, you daft ha'porth."

There may have been some truth in this. I would later meet a Rochdale man in a distant corner of Britain who told me that these pubs are famously used by cheating lovers because "they're up on the moors and no one knows who you are."

But back at the campsite, the owner explained the difference between the two establishments.

"The farther one is cheaper but it's rougher," he said.

For the pragmatic reason of not wanting to get any wetter than I already was, I decided on the nearer one and walked into what felt like someone's living room. About six blokes sat around and the conversation instantly halted when they saw me enter. Wasn't it around here that an unfortunate Yank wandered into that moorland pub in American Werewolf in

London? I got myself a pint. It was hard to believe the other pub was the cheaper one; a pint of bitter here cost just £1.80. It was like being back in the eighties. I sat myself down near a roaring fire and tried to warm my bones. Their chatter restarted a little self-consciously. They occasionally looked over towards me and then turned away again quickly if I caught their eye.

There was an excruciating conversation happening to my left. A bloke in his forties, Quinny, was sitting at the bar and was clearly coming on to Brodie, the pretty, ever-patient, 21-year-old barmaid, her long brown hair in plaits. He was explaining to her how he'd recently got divorced and was living in a van on the campsite for the next six months. This truth didn't exactly make him more attractive to the poor girl. He temporarily gave up and turned his attention to me.

"So what's your story?" he asked.

"I'm staying at your place," I replied.

"Yeah, I saw you come in on a bike earlier. Are you travelling?"

I nodded.

"Where you going?"

"I set off yesterday and I'm cycling through every county in Britain."

It took a second for this to sink in.

"Why are you doing it? Are you doing it because you want to?"

I already had a pint in me at this stage and so my bollocks filter had been removed.

"No, I don't want to do it," I lied. "I'm being forced to. Please help me!"

That got a laugh from the room. Everyone else's attention now turned towards me. Fresh meat, y'see.

"Where are you going to tomorrow?" asked another fella.

That depended. I wasn't exactly sure where I was. I may

have strayed over a county border and inadvertently found myself somewhere I shouldn't be until later.

"We're still in Greater Manchester, right?" I asked.

"Yeah," replied one bloke.

"Well, you're not," said another, laughing. "You're actually in Yorkshire."

"Nay, this is Lancashire," added a third.

Maybe county divisions are meaningless if you don't actually know in which one you live. A discussion broke out. Wherever we were it was close to several borders. The topic seemed to be resolved by barmaid Brodie.

"If you actually look at the border," she said, "we're in Greater Manchester."

The discussion got a little more heated.

"I'm sorry," I said. "I didn't mean to start a fight."

"Where are you from?" asked one of the guys.

"Lancashire."

"That's alright," he smiled. "People from Lancashire don't know where they are."

The evening continued with merry chat in a warm room with my clothes slowly drying and the cheap beer flowing. I stood up to get closer to the fire. Quinny was still working his magic on Brodie despite getting steadily more drunk. Occasionally, to convince her to take him on, I'd hear him say something hopeless like, "I'm good looking, me." She wasn't persuaded.

Another bloke, Tom, younger than the rest, entered the pub and took a seat at the bar.

"Hey, I know your brother," Quinny said to him with a slur.

"Yeah," replied Tom, not seeming to want to get involved.

Quinny got up and went to the toilet. It was clear from the reaction of absolutely everyone else in the pub that Quinny was a new face around here and wasn't very popular with the locals.

"He's always pissed," said Tom. "He's told me he knows my brother three times now."

"He just asked me out," Brodie said to him. "He invited me to McDonald's."

Quinny was clearly a smooth operator.

I got up to go to the bar for a final beer and talked to Tom. His surname was Power and his brother, the one that Quinny knew, was, brilliantly, called Max.

"Homer Simpson changed his name to Max Power in one episode," Tom said.

I decided to test the one fact I knew about Rochdale.

"Do you know Lizzie Bardsley?" I asked.

"Oh God!" he replied, shaking his head.

Even if the name doesn't ring a bell you might well remember her. She was on the very first episode of Wife Swap, back in 2003. She and her fella were both on the dole and claiming close to forty grand in benefits. She had so many kids she'd had to move out of that shoe into a massive pair of wellies. On the programme she was swapped into an extremely middle-class family and, just as the programme makers had hoped, sparks flew. She became a celebrity of sorts for about an hour and, despite being a larger lady of disputable physical attraction, posed topless for the Sunday Sport newspaper in what wasn't their finest hour amongst of lifetime of terrible hours. Unfortunately for her, despite earning money for her media work, she didn't stop claiming benefits and was subsequently busted.

"I can't believe we're talking about Lizzie Bardsley," he said. Tom spoke with a laid-back voice and an accent more Peter Kay than Peter Kay. "She's a scratter."

"A scratter?" I asked.

"Rough as toast."

I laughed. That's a great expression.

"So you know her?"

"Not really. But she lives just down the road in Milnrow. She chatted me up once."

This had been in a pub or a nightclub and I don't know if it was before or after Wife Swap but it clearly hadn't been an avenue Tom wanted to pursue.

It was the end of a long and lovely evening.

"I've got to go now," I said.

"You want to come back to my van?" asked Quinny. Perhaps he was just desperately lonely. "I've got beer," he added. But I'd had enough.

"Will you come back here?" asked Tom. "You're a nice man."

I smiled at his openness.

"Yeah," I said. "You call up Lizzie and then the three of us can have a party."

*

It was Day Three and I had an appointment with my third county, the first one to allow me more than a single day's visit. But I had to get there first. The rain had cleared, leaving a crisp morning under a blue sky. Temperatures, however, suggested it was still very much winter, and a Russian winter at that.

As I skirted its eastern edge, the gravitational pull of Manchester was strong with all roads leading to it. On my right I could see its distant towers as I passed by Ashton-under-Lyne and later the dark hills of the Peak District to my left. With all its traffic this part of the world isn't exactly beautiful, but it's far less ugly than it had been in my imagination. And the people were friendly. I received many a thumbs-up from drivers and no car came too close for comfort. If anything, they hung back when they probably had enough room to get around. Three or four times I pulled in and stopped to let buses or lorries squeeze past. There was no need to make drivers hate cyclists any more than they already did.

It was nice to leave the urban chaos of Greater Manchester behind and the instant that Cheshire's welcome sign appeared everything went wonderfully rural.

Driving habits changed too. Two cars – expensive ones – pulled out sharply in front of me and nodded curtly as if to say thanks for letting them out when, in reality, I hadn't intended anything of the sort. I had to brake quickly or otherwise crash into their doors. In both cases the driver was in his forties and wearing sunglasses in April despite the weak winter rays. But it's not unusual for money to turn people into arseholes. And this was definitely a well-moneyed area. I had a map depicting the regions of Britain and their associated stereotypes. I'd now apparently strayed into the land of the WAG, a useful term since it meant Abbey Clancy could update her CV without recourse to a spellchecker.

This is the so-called Golden Triangle, formed by Wilmslow, Alderley Edge and Prestbury, and contains the most expensive streets in northern England, which, since you've already heard about Bolton, might not sound so impressive. It's been home to most of the recent squads of Manchester's United and City. The houses of Prestbury's Withinlee Road average over £1.5 million, making it the most prestigious street in the north although, overall in the UK, about 4,527th.

Today had been about escaping traffic rather than visiting the interesting bits of Britain and I opted for a slightly shorter day that put me within easy reach of a genuine highlight tomorrow. Once again, campsites were thin on the ground and so options were minimal in the flat farmland of Cheshire. In charge at The Royal Vale Caravan Site were two lads, who both looked in their late teens and seemed to be running the place for a dare.

Eventually, after telling me everything I needed to know about the site, I asked what the damage was. The expression on his face suggested I was the first camper he'd ever had to deal with and so pricing was fluid.

"Er, let's call it twenty quid, shall we?" he said like he was doing me a favour.

Jesus! I nearly choked. That's the most I'd ever paid on a site anywhere in the world, even when I accidentally camped near Euro Disney. I suppose that's what you can charge if you stick 'Royal' in your name. But I didn't complain – I still had to get my breath back – because I didn't want to cycle miles and miles to another site. I didn't care if Wayne Rooney lived just around the corner, twenty quid was a lot of money to sleep in someone's field.

In the evening sunshine I set up my tent, enjoying the slightly more sophisticated, albeit expensive, air of Cheshire. The young robber at reception had given me a hand-drawn map of the surrounding villages with the local pub highlighted on it. It was a couple of miles away. I set off on my bag-free bike and very quickly the roads didn't match the map. I came to a junction, saw another cyclist and asked for directions to Lower Peover. He pointed me towards a pub although, as it turned out, not the one on my map.

The Crown felt a lot more upmarket than last night's living room affair and it had prices to match. Four quid for a lager is surely London prices, not northern England's, but this part of Cheshire wasn't a true reflection of northern England. If you receive fifty grand a week for playing two 90 minute games you'd earn more than the cost of that pint every second you're on the pitch.

Two well-groomed twenty-something blondes, who might have been in Hollyoaks but weren't, sat at a table sipping prosecco and probably talking about Botox. The cultivated air disappeared rapidly when a young bloke with Tourette's came in with his family. They kept shushing him, which only made him worse.

Everyone sat at their tables. The bar was just a place to buy drinks. This wasn't a pub for casual conversation with strangers, especially ones that once had the opportunity for intimacy with partially famous scratters.

Cycling home later I got lost again. After ten minutes of hopeless pedalling I was getting worried. I didn't have any pockets and so, pannier-free, I'd left my phone back at the tent. I asked a bloke waiting at a junction if he knew where the campsite was. He'd never heard of Royal Vale and, worryingly, his own phone wouldn't find it. Wonderful. Eventually, with the light failing, I mentioned another business I'd seen near the campsite and he assured me it was down the road I was on. What I also learnt was that the map the site had given me was printed upside down, with south at the top. That's quite a useful-to-know little detail. I'd set off in entirely the wrong direction.

*

It rained all night and was still drizzling in the morning. Fortunately I didn't have far to go today. I waited for the rain to stop around ten and then packed up and set off to Jodrell Bank, British engineering at its finest.

Google Maps told me it was easy: Just a straight three mile trip – no deviations – up the same lane as I'd accidentally stumbled upon the day before. But after four miles I was getting concerned. Two women on horseback sent me back the way I'd come, then right, then left at the church and then another mile and a half. Even Google was getting lost around here.

Eventually I stumbled into the Jodrell Bank Discovery Centre and what educational fun it was. There were loads of interactive toys demonstrating stuff like the effects of black holes as well as heat-sensitive imaging devices in which my head seemed to glow a brighter white than anyone else's. I hoped this was down to having cycled in rather than a sign I need to increase my blood pressure medication.

There were also videos to show how its massive dish had been involved in the Space Race, sometimes helping the Russians as well as the Americans, demonstrating how wonderfully cross-border science can be. They'd probably even work with ISIS if they were asked. Maybe they could build a big ship and send them all into space, maybe in the direction of the sun.

There was a half-hour lecture about star formation. I'd studied some of this stuff before with the Open University but I suspected it was a bit technical for some of the people there when the first man to raise his hand in the Q & A session asked, "Yes, but how are stars actually made?", something the lecturer had been banging on about for the previous thirty minutes.

I walked outside to go and stand in the shadow of the huge, 76-metre dish. At the time it was constructed it was the largest radio telescope in the world, although now it's only the third largest moveable one, which still isn't bad. Most interesting from a British engineering point of view was that, in the fifties, it had been budgeted at £120,000, equivalent to £3.25M nowadays, but eventually cost £700,000. That's quite a miscalculation. Did someone mention HS2?

From the dish I headed out east to Gawsworth to find another suggestion I'd been given for Cheshire, the odd story that is the grave of Maggoty Johnson. In life, during the 18th century, Maggoty had been known as Samuel and was a musician, actor, playwright and one of Britain's last jesters. He designed a tomb in the woods on Maggoty Lane for his faithful servant, but, being around in superstitious times, her brother refused her burial on unconsecrated ground and so

Sammy took the spot himself. So there he lies, in Maggoty Woods, buried without religious fuss, like someone's pet gerbil, but in a slightly grander enclosure.

I cycled back to a sign I'd seen earlier in the village: "Local Shop". Obviously no one around here watches The League of Gentlemen or, if they do, they clearly weren't worried about inviting comparisons to Royston Vasey's piglet-suckling shop owner, Tubbs, and her demonic husband, Edward.

On the door of the shop was a sign that said: "As seen on the BBC". I had to ask.

"It's a community shop, not run for profit," said the lady behind the counter. "We have around forty volunteers, and the Beeb were interested in the story."

That's one hell of an effort just to keep a shop in the village alive, but an important one. A village without a pub, shop or post office is a dead one. I'd already seen lots of these on my ride and I would see many, hopelessly many, more in the coming weeks. This is what happens when we all use supermarkets.

When the shop lost its licence to be a sub-post office in 2009 and the revenue that brought in, the locals decided to change the system. And running it for love certainly affected the enthusiasm of the staff. Rather than a typically sullen nineteen-year-old depressed that she couldn't find a better job elsewhere, the two volunteers today were bouncily happy to be there.

"It's my first day today," said a second lady behind the counter. "This is the first pie I've had to heat," she added proudly, handing me my steaming local meat and potato pastry. It was wonderful.

It was time to locate my first mud-free bed of the tour. Maggoty Johnson might have been a jester but so was Dave, my host for the evening. Visiting the grave had been his suggestion.

Back in 2005 I produced a comedy sketch show in Nerja, a small tourist town on the south coast of Spain where I lived. It was a reckless venture. I'd never done anything like that before and was just making it up as I was going along, a lot like this bike ride. Between us we wrote the entire thing but once per show Dave had his own segment. He would appear as José Maria, the Jazz Poet, a Spanish, painfully drug-addled verse-meister with a huge, two foot-long doobie. He would recite his own incoherent, narcotic-related poems over an awkwardly spiky, electro-jazz backing track. It was surreal stuff. Half the audience would laugh at him without really knowing why, while the rest would stare at him in open-mouthed silence. Yes, that was the sort of show we were putting on. If 50% of the audience laughed we considered it a victory.

"I still can't believe to this day that you said, yes, let's put José Maria in it," he said. I smiled at the memory. "And I still remember looking through those sunglasses, at the crowd, while performing it and thinking to myself, 'What the *fuck* is going on?'"

"Yeah," I replied. "I had a few moments like that too."

They'd been fun times, although not always for the audience.

Dave's home was now in Congleton, also known as Beartown. Back in the 1600s, in the days before Amazon's powerful discounting, the town had been saving up to buy a big ol' expensive Bible. Unfortunately, the town's main draw, bear-baiting, was suffering for want of a decent fighter and so, when it came time to make the purchase, the bloke in charge of the purse strings decided to spend the money on a large, aggressive bear instead. This might have done little for the religious education of the local community but surely made church services a lot less dull.

For a town with painful traffic problems, the centre of

Congleton is a quaint, little place. Dave took me to the Olde Kings Arms, a pub with a unique history. Tunnels beneath the pub supposedly once led to the town jail so that prisoners could get one last drink before taking another tunnel to the churchyard where they would be hanged. I asked the barmaid if we could have a look at them. She went away to find out but came back with bad news.

"Sorry, guys, it's just not safe."

The landlord appeared.

"Do the tunnels really exist?" I asked him.

"Oh yes. We use one as a cellar. But they're bricked up."

"And no one's ever unblocked them?"

"Not as far as I know."

"You could open them up and make a tourist attraction of them."

"Hmm."

He didn't seem convinced.

*

After a great meal made by Jacquie, Dave's missus, and a comfortable night's sleep I was back in the centre of Congleton, this time alone.

I'd been told to try a regional delicacy, the oatcakes from a shop on the high street. To my mind, oatcakes are Scottish biscuits that require more saliva than I can usually muster, but not here. These ones are plate-sized oatmeal pancakes. There was a choice of fillings and I opted for sausage and cheese, a lovely if gooey and difficult to eat breakfast.

"Are these a Cheshire speciality?" I asked.

"No, actually they're from Staffordshire," replied the owner. "That's where we're from."

"So why are you here?"

"The Cheshire water is better."

"Traitor," I said.

"Yes, we are," he smiled.

My plan had been to visit the town's museum to find out more about the tunnels but it wasn't open until midday – two hours away – and I didn't know how long today's hilly escapades were going to take. Instead I asked the women in the tourist office about them.

"Do they really exist?"

"There are catacombs beneath the town hall."

"But tunnels linking the prison to the pub and to the church?"

"I don't know. You can only go down so far and then they're bricked off."

I couldn't help thinking it would pull in the punters if you could get down there and walk the walk of the recently condemned. But no one seemed too bothered to see if the story was true. Maybe they were worried it wasn't and, with the death of their legend, all they'd have to fall back on was that killer bear.

I headed eastwards into the soggy hills of Staffordshire. The temperatures were low under a grey sky but the air was perfectly still.

Staffordshire has a number of claims to fame. Apparently, according to the Stafford Post, its Cannock Chase is the place in Britain you're most likely to see a werewolf. And from that we can deduce the Stafford Post is the newspaper in which you're most likely to see a load of bollocks. And then there's Tamworth, Staffordshire's second most populous town, which is both Britain's obesity capital and its teenage pregnancy capital. Maybe the chubby girls can't run away from the horny lads fast enough.

Staffordshire also has two records. One is that the munitions storage depot at RAF Fauld near Hanbury was the location of Britain's largest ever explosion. Its 1944 blast left a crater 250 yards wide and 100 feet deep and killed seventy. The other record is the place I was visiting next, Flash,

Britain's highest village.

Once off the hilly A54 there was a steady gradient on the most peaceful road you're likely to find in the southern half of Britain. Over a period of fifty minutes only two cars passed me. A rabbit hopped along the road without a care in the world. A pheasant marched across the tarmac free of any fear of being squashed flat. The only sound was the occasional metallic squeak from my bike and my own heavy breathing. The colours were muted greens and browns, and dampness was everywhere, with dry stone walls so moss-covered they looked like they'd been upholstered.

I suddenly had a feeling of utter contentment. I was cycling around Britain and actually enjoying it. The scenery was great and the traffic was elsewhere. These weren't the temperatures I preferred, just a few degrees above zero, but I was overcome by an inner peacefulness. I was Buddha on a bike.

Eventually I reached Flash, sitting at 1518 feet in the Peak District National Park. It's a small collection of stone houses, a church, a pub that was unfortunately closed today and a primary school.

I loved its name. In fact, I like any adjectival town name. When it's placed before a typical shop or service it takes on a new meaning. Flash Primary sounds like a feeder school for Eton, except that, due to the village's tiny population, it's now closed down. Of course, adding a descriptive town name to a service works the other way too. There's a village in Scotland called Dull.

Coming down the other side of the hill towards Leek, the wind chill of the steady descent dropped the temperatures farther still. It was nipple-stiffeningly cold. Fortunately, after a mile or so, and still out in the wastes of the moorland, The Winking Man appeared to offer some restoring warmth and a pint of really quite nice Burton's Ale. I found a snug corner and defrosted my extremities.

Resuming the ride, the temperatures hadn't become any warmer but it had now started to spit too. I passed a welcoming caravan site but saw its unwelcoming sign: "Sorry, no tents!" It was the sort of place that demanded a better class of customer. No canvas-dwellers here, just a resort exclusively for those who preferred holidaying inside tin cans.

The rain came down harder. It was another eight miles at least to the site I'd found on my phone and I suspected it might be back up another, even colder hill. And then, like a mirage, another sign appeared, one of those brown tourist ones that depicts a little tent next to a caravan. It was still early but with the clouds so low it didn't look like this rain was going anywhere soon. I ducked into their office and confirmed the lack of pattern to the amount I was paying each night. This one was just over a fiver, the cheapest yet and today, in the gradually thickening rain, my saviour.

As soon as I could, I threw the tent up and shoved myself and all the bags inside and waited for it to stop. But it didn't. I fell asleep for a couple of hours but the cold rain just came down harder and harder. The drumming on the tent's outside made it sound like I'd pitched my tent at a Stomp gig.

I've got two tents, a larger, heavier one that has a decent porch to allow cooking even in the roughest of conditions, and a smaller, lighter one without a porch at all. Have a guess which I'd brought with me? This was a dumb choice given the probability of moist weather in Britain. I remembered seeing a few groceries back in the office and so splashed back through the rain to see what stove-free meal I could cobble together.

"Oh sorry, is this a board meeting?" I asked as four people huddled over their desk.

"Yes, it is," replied the lady who'd served me originally.

"Do you want a job?" she said with a smile. "You can be managing director if you like."

Seeing my dampened state she picked up the office kettle.

"Fancy a coffee?"

"That'd be great."

I gathered from their shelves a motley collection of dinner ingredients: two Snickers bars, two packets of crisps and a packet of Jammy Dodgers. I put them on the counter.

"There you go," I said. "That's my five a day."

"I think it's supposed to be five fruits or vegs."

I looked down at my E-number collection.

"S'alright," I said. "Peanuts, potatoes and strawberries in the jam."

I didn't possess a tin opener – all the food I was carrying was dried – but they also had a can of hot dog sausages. With the kind lend of an opener I scuttled back to my tent with my mug of hot coffee and hid from the rain for the rest of the evening, eating cold wieners from a tin, just like the Sultan of Brunei does when he's on holiday.

Even when the weather was as awful as it was today, it wasn't hard to be positive with such nice, kind people about. Well, it was a little bit hard, but freezing rain wasn't going to bring me down. Not yet at least.

The temperature dropped further and the rain got harder. To soak up more Britishness I put on my radio and tuned in to Radio Four. There was something about the station's gentle tones accompanied by the wind and rain outside that made it almost too homely to bear, like listening to a distant message from home while on a wave-tossed boat in the middle of the Atlantic. Eventually the tiring batteries of my little wireless couldn't compete with the heavy drumming of the leaking sky and so I had to give up.

The night was freezing. I realised that, as a result of my lack of preparations, I'd packed my older, more knackered ground mat – one I'd had since the Boer War – which, over time, had compressed to the approximate thickness of a sheet of paper. It really wasn't up to the job of a cold, damp floor. I put on a warmer t-shirt and a second fleece but it still wasn't enough. I barely slept, shivering through the night. Tomorrow I'd have to stock up on some British spring-proof evening wear, or buy a three-bar electric heater and a generator.

*

After a night that lasted at least thirty-six hours the morning sun rose and gently heated the tent's insides. I lay there, recharging my body, like a lizard on a rock, until half past nine when I decided to venture out. The sun might have been warm through the skin of my tent but out in the open air it was still bitterly cold.

I popped back to reception to return the coffee mug and tin opener.

"Did you sleep well?" the lady asked.

I told her the truth.

"Is there no room in your budget for a bit of luxury?"

Sadly, there wasn't. This trip wasn't the £1-a-day of last year's adventure but British hotels are vastly overpriced. It wasn't unusual to pay £15 for a clean and comfortable room in Spain. Even this seemed expensive after the £6 I paid in Ukraine. Britain's hotels, even Premier Inns, are typically ten times this at least. And you sometimes have to share a room with Lenny Henry.

The lady's husband told me they used to run a campsite on Loch Lomond. He said the Scots took some getting used to.

"They were great people but you couldn't tell them what to do or else they'd just call you 'an English bastard'. You had to treat them carefully. Since we left the camp it's changed hands three times. The new owners couldn't hack it."

She was more disparaging about some of the English tourists who visited.

"The Scottish don't mind the rain. They're used to it. But you'd get people from Kent coming there, looking up at the sky and saying, 'How long's it been like this?' They thought it was our fault."

I returned to my tent and started to pack away. A smiling Mrs Campsite came out again with another cup of coffee for me.

"We were making it anyway and thought you'd like one. It'll warm your hands."

Did I have to leave this place? Well, yes, because I had an appointment down the road that evening in Stone.

On the way there I stopped in Leek, a pretty market town that seemed to have done its best to resist the cancer of chain shops and restaurants. Most of the cafés and snack bars were local as were many of the other businesses. The town's only camping store provided a second, hopefully warmer mat, some thermals and a pair of thick bedtime socks. As the Scandinavians say, "There's no such thing as bad weather, only the wrong clothes." But tell that to the residents of Cockermouth, chest deep in flood water.

The route continued along quieter roads. The sun had tried to remain out but it was mostly a losing battle. Hills came and went, including some silly ones with gradients of 17%. People at the side of the road smiled and waved. And then, ten miles earlier than I was expecting, I popped out in Stone just as I felt the first flecks of rain.

Under such conditions and with time to kill, a visit for a local pint was required and I descended upon the warm lounge of Langtry's for a mug of Joule's – pronounced 'jowls' – Slumbering Monk brewed not far away in Market Drayton. I'd forgotten it was Saturday and was greeted with more Britishness in the form of Premier League football, Norwich against Sunderland, two places I'd never visited but maybe would before this ride was out. I hoped they'd be more interesting than the match.

I asked the landlord if he knew anything odd nearby and he recommended The Star Inn, a pub he'd once run and that's in the Guinness Book of Records for having the most number of levels.

"Is it a tall building?" I asked.

"No, it's only single storey but it's subsided."

"Oh."

I rode the few metres to The Star and had a pint of refreshing Sunbeam. I asked the landlady how old the pub was. She didn't know. She asked one of her staff.

"It's..." the barmaid thought for a minute, "...old. Very old."

Thanks.

"But if you like this one," she continued, "you should see The Crooked House in Dudley."

I took my pint to the beer garden, sitting there with a few others, pretending it wasn't freezing.

My reason for visiting Stone was Pru. I arrived at her house and felt immediately at home. I'd never met her before but she's the sister of Nem, a pal of mine from Austria. They looked so alike, and with the same bubbly mannerisms, it was like talking to my old friend.

Pru cooked up a Thai green curry and mentioned she'd a tendency to make things too spicy. She dished up the meal. After taking her first spoonful of curry, that thing happened you sometimes see in cartoons, her eyes bulged and steam spurted from her ears.

My arrival date had clashed with a cultural event Pru was attending and so she got me an extra ticket. We drove up the motorway to a theatre in Crewe – almost all the way back to Congleton – and met her daughter Bella, Bella's boyfriend and his family. The play *The 39 Steps* was a comedy version of the Hitchcock film and was a lot of fun with a cast of four hard-working actors playing all the roles. The evening felt surreal, a million miles from the previous tent-based evenings I'd enjoyed, and sometimes suffered, on the ride, like I'd fallen into another world, one in which people didn't spend all day every day sweating their tits off while simultaneously being drenched by rain.

With Bella now on the back seat we headed for home and Pru seemed unsure where to go. We came to a roundabout and she looked to be heading off in entirely the wrong direction.

"I think you need to go down that one," I said, pointing to a huge M6 sign.

"Is it?" she giggled. "Oh yes, alright."

Bella piped up from the back with teenage directness.

"Why are you pretending that you aren't like this every single time you drive?"

*

Oh look, what was this? Through the curtains of my room I could see a beautiful, blue sky. It was time to get up. I knew this because I could smell bacon.

After a delicious English breakfast (which I would later discover is exactly the same as a Cornish breakfast, a Welsh breakfast and only differs from a Scottish breakfast by the omission of haggis) I was in front of Pru's house about to leave.

"You're carrying a helmet," Pru said, spying it hanging from the back of my bike.

"Yup."

"Why don't you wear it?"

"I don't like to. I only bring it in case I get stuck on an extremely dodgy road."

"You should wear it," she said, looking serious.

51

I could have quoted the usual statistics but, to be honest, I don't even know if they're true. I just hate wearing it.

"Put it on," she said. "Please."

She'd been kind, and great company, and it seemed to upset her that I was being so cavalier with my skull and so I slipped it on my head, thanked her for everything and cycled off. Two hundred metres down the road it was digging into my head and so I took it off again. Sorry, Pru.

Chapter 3: A nurse with a verse

West Midlands, Warwickshire, Worcestershire, Herefordshire and Shrophire

I arrived in Stafford, one of Britain's many soulless Anytowns, with centres so given over to cut-n-paste chains they're entirely and boringly interchangeable. There's nothing particularly unpleasant about the place. It's just that it's about as memorable as Police Academy 7.

It's impossible to be positive about this aspect of Britain. The chains leach money from the local community and send it back to the already over-stuffed pockets of their shareholders, slowly bleeding each town dry, the employees on minimum wage and/or zero hour contracts. And whereas a local shopkeeper might take pride in her products this isn't true of chains because there's no relation between the product and the person who sells it. The sole reason for the enterprise is profit. There's no attempt to make something great. The question in the boardroom isn't "How good can we make this for £1.99?"; it's "How crap can we make this and still get away with £1.99?" Fewer coffee beans or less meat or dodgier meat. I've yet to eat a cheap burger from a roadside van that hasn't been orders of magnitude better than a McDonald's. A one euro coffee in any bar in Spain embarrasses the weak, overpriced pap produced by Starbucks. But we rolled over and let them do it and without a concerted effort from the entire population it's too late to go back. And besides, most people probably don't even want to go back. If you're at least guaranteed mediocrity, why risk it for something else?

Just the other side of Stafford I bumped into a cyclist, Pete. He was retired and aiming to cycle a hundred centuries – one hundred mile bike rides – this year. He warned me against the main road I was planning to use and so we cycled together down a lovely network of leafy lanes in perfect cycling conditions. The route took us through delightful Brewood and past the site of the original Royal Oak near Boscobel House, where Charles II hid as he attempted to scarper to Wales.

After two hours of pleasant pootling, during which time my brand new cycle computer decided to expire, Pete said goodbye and pointed me on my way. I entered my fifth county, West Midlands, Britain's most densely populated, with over 16,000 tightly-squeezed people per square mile.

The idea of cycling somewhere so crowded didn't appeal much but the outskirts were more rural and, on the edge of Dudley, I found a lane that felt like I shouldn't have been on it and arrived at The Crooked House.

The pub is impressively knackered, leaning heavily to its right, looking like it's about to topple over any minute now. Rather than being condemned, its owners decided to make a feature of this health and safety nightmare.

I left my bike outside and went in. You immediately feel like you've had one too many. The wooden floors all slope in different directions and doors either require more effort than normal to budge or fall open unexpectedly, hanging loosely on their hinges. This is what a house would look like if I'd built it.

I waited for a pint as a chubby fella negotiated the angles. He shuffled unsteadily across the floor and then lunged, arms outstretched, towards the bar, grabbing it with obvious relief. He looked up, shaking his head.

"This place always fucks me up," he said.

I took my pint of The Tilted Tipple, brewed especially for the pub, and sat outside on a bench in the weak but heartening sunshine. A woman came out of the wobbly pub and tripped over the crooked doorstep. She was followed by a bloke on crutches. I'm not sure he had them when he went inside.

I considered staying for more but feared it wouldn't take many in a bar like this to have me in a heap in the middle of the floor. Reluctantly, I climbed back on my bike and headed citywards.

The West Midlands obviously includes Britain's second city, Birmingham, but despite its collection of capital awards – the cycle-to-work capital and tattoo capital of Britain as well as the less appealing "boy racer" capital, divorce capital and rat capital – I had no intention of going anywhere near it.

My plan was to follow the A459 through Dudley but then the signs gave up and I found myself lost. I was in a town centre, busy with traffic but light on people, just groups of feral-looking, late-teenage kids, gaunt and baseball-capped, jeans hanging low on their meatless backsides.

The road took me beside a gang of white lads. One of them, using that pretend black accent like a bad impression of Ali G, called out to me. He'd seen the logo on my bike.

"Oi, KTM boy!" he shouted.

It wasn't a greeting, but a command to stop. I didn't fancy a chat. He sounded threatening. As a positive it was nice to give him some practice with his alphabet. I reckon if I'd been riding a Dawes Galaxy he'd have been stumped.

"Oi, KTM boy. Like how much iz dat bike, bruv?"

I kept cycling.

"Oi, how much?"

"Free!" I shouted back.

I figured if it had no value he probably wouldn't stab me in the throat to get it.

"Free quid? Free quid?" I heard him ask his mates, confused.

He'd have been disappointed if he'd taken it. It was

probably older than he was and its brittle aluminium welds were now well past their use-by date. It could fall apart at any minute. Which would have been apt around here. This part of Britain was clearly on its arse. I'd really enjoyed my first week of cycling in England's north-west but this wasn't pleasant. Closed down pubs stood between pound shops and bookies. There was no reason to ride here except to tick the West Midlands box. I'd ticked it and wanted to get out of there as quickly as I could, hopefully with my bike and as many limbs attached as possible.

I eventually made it through Halesowen and found the road to the green village of Romsley, in the Clent Hills, seemingly a thousand miles from the urban sprawl of that afternoon although, in reality, only ten. I cycled up an endless ascent looking for the campsite. I couldn't see it and so I cycled down the other side of the hill and then checked my phone. I'd gone past it, silly sod. I turned around and cycled back up the hill.

Like the site near Leek, this one was a member of the Camping and Caravanning Club and so offered its cheap Backpacker rate to motor-less visitors like myself. Almost all the best value sites in Britain were members of this club. Don't confuse it with the Caravan Club. They'll charge you the same rate whether you turn up in a £80,000 motor home or a £25 tent from Argos.

I popped to the supermarket to buy something for dinner. At the till, with only two minutes to closing, the Asian owner tried to give me the remaining items in the shop's About-To-Go-Out-Of-Date basket that stood on his counter, including a pack of stewing steak. I really didn't have the fuel to boil the meat for hours on end and so I declined the offer. Hopefully his next customer, probably the last of the day, would appreciate it more. He tried a second time, confused that I could turn down free stuff.

Back at the tent I cooked up a quick sausagey stew and switched on Radio Four again. I'd never really listened to it before this trip. I'd once tuned in for a comedy starring Prunella Scales years ago and not only was it as funny as anthrax but I couldn't even see where the jokes were supposed to be. I gave it up thinking it wasn't for me, but now, during this Britainfest of a bike ride, I was slowly getting hooked. But not on The Archers. I hated that middle-class soap with a passion, from its twee theme tune to its tedious characters. Even having one of its stars knife her husband couldn't make it worth listening to. Every day at seven o'clock I'd have to turn the radio off or risk smashing it to pieces. At least the schedulers knew the limits of human endurance and limited it to fifteen minutes. It's the world's longest running soap and, Christ, does it feel like it.

*

Yesterday's blue skies had clearly been an anomaly. Today we were back to uniform greyness and the sort of blustery wind that made pigeons long for a bus pass.

On the way out of Romsley I stopped at the supermarket again. At least the stewing steak had disappeared by now. Maybe he'd just put it back on the shelf with a different date label. I bought myself a Gingsters Cornish pasty and immediately regretted it. I resolved to stick to local pie shops from now on. It had a crust like soggy cardboard and less filling than an After Eight mint.

It was Monday morning and I was on my way to Warwickshire. It should be one of those counties in the middle of England that's difficult to identify in a pub quiz except that its odd shape makes it stand out. It looks like a cartoon whale that's been rotated ninety degrees and badly beaten.

This part of Britain, where the West Midlands merges with Shakespeare's home county, has a reputation for achieving world records, particularly utterly pointless ones. Take, for example, the recent world's largest gathering of people dressed in Disney costumes – 361 to be exact – or the 428 folk who turned up for the world's largest Taekwondo display in 2013. And then there's Stratford-upon-Avon College, which baked the world's largest meat pie in 1998. It weighed a whopping ten and a half tonnes. Wiganners, dry your eyes!

But my favourite pointless record was achieved in Coventry in 2014 by students of Warwickshire University when 314 students crammed themselves into a single pair of underpants. The event was to launch that year's Jailbreak, when students try to get as far from home as possible in 36 hours without money. If the idea of being forced to share your pants with 313 others fills you with horror and you can empathise with anyone whose personal space has been occupied by an army of people with no legitimate claim then you'll see it was entirely fitting that the Jailbreak winner made it all the way to Israel.

I hung a left towards Stratford-upon-Avon and passed the splendid Wootton Hall with its grand house and little waterfalls in the garden. And then I tumbled into Stratford itself and followed the signs for the racecourse, which also has a campsite. I'd only cycled thirty miles today but I felt sluggish. A week of daily peddling was catching up with me.

After setting up the tent I walked to the centre of town. Looking at the names of businesses around here it makes you wonder what they would've been called if it wasn't the birthplace of the Bard. There were B&Bs called Shakespeare's View, Hamlet House and Cymbeline House, and Iago Jewellers. That last one was odd, because Iago was a dodgy bugger, but maybe that was true of the jewellers too. It could have been worse. There could have been Othello Marriage Guidance Counsellors or the Richard III Child Care Agency.

I headed for the HQ of the Royal Shakespeare Company.

After Saturday's cultural interlude with Pru I fancied myself a bit more theatre but despite this being the 400th anniversary of the playwright's death there was unfortunately nothing Shakespearean on tonight. But all's well that ends well. I saw the house in which he was supposedly born. In a brick-by-brick relocation that pre-empted Hitler's plan for Rochdale Town Hall, circus impresario P.T. Barnum once planned to take the entire building back with him to the States. It took a committee that included Dickens to gather the necessary funds to prevent this from happening. Barnum's money wasn't wasted though. He spent it instead on circus freaks and a "man-monkey" called Bill.

I fancied a pint but a sign outside the supposedly oldest pub in town, The Garrick Inn, admits that it wasn't even a pub until the 1800s and so there was no chance of sharing the same space as Shakey himself. Instead, I headed to The Golden Bee on Sheep Street, a Wetherspoon's, the one chain I was allowing myself on this trip since they sell good beers more cheaply than anywhere else and I'm a skinflint. Like Wetherspoon's everywhere, an old bloke in a long mac leant against the bar, running boney fingers through his greasy grey hair and apologising slurringly. The Eastern European bar manager assured him it was something that had happened loads of times in the past. I never found out what it was. Such is life in Wetherspoon's.

I was in a good mood. I'd checked the weather forecast for the next three days and it was supposed to be sunshine all the way, and that would certainly help in the pretty counties up next, like Worcestershire, Herefordshire and Shropshire. But, as it turned out, perhaps I hadn't checked far enough ahead.

An old fella in a long lumberjack shirt with pink-streaked hair came in through the back door. He looked like he'd been sleeping rough. As I waited for my nachos to arrive – I fancied a break from my week-long, British diet of pies, pasties and cooked breakfasts – I overheard the middle-aged glass collector talking to him.

"You need to get yourself sorted, lad. There's snow due on Friday."

No! I asked him if it was true. I thought perhaps he got some sort of perverse pleasure out of tormenting the homeless. But he said, yes, an Arctic wind was on its way. The timing was great. It would arrive just at the moment I turned back north. The Wind God still hates me.

*

I was woken early by raucous squawking in the branches above my tent. A starling had accused a rook of looking at his bird. The rook told him to keep his beak out, and then feathers went flying.

After my first eight days of moving generally southwards and eastwards it was time to turn around and head west. I cycled into Alcester. English towns that end in "ester" tend to have unpredictable pronunciations. I found a café and ordered what was billed as a "proper" bacon sandwich.

"Is it pronounced Alchester, or Alsester?" I asked him.

"No."

I tried again.

"Alster?"

He shook his head. What else could it be? Maybe it was *really* unusual.

"Or Als? Al?"

It wasn't any of those.

"It's Olster," he replied. "Whatever you do, don't call it Alsester to anyone around here or else the church bells will ring and monks will come out with flaming torches."

I munched through the food and went to pay. The owner was talking to a woman.

"Great bacon sandwich," I said.

"Best bacon sandwich in Olster!" said the woman.

"See," he said. "It's Olster. She's local. Count her fingers."

I opened the door of the café to bright sunshine. The forecast had been right. I cycled along lanes under a perfect blue sky with the occasional fluffy white cloud. Lambs frolicked in the lush, verdant fields that surrounded me. Every now and again the green would be replaced by the vivid yellow of rapeseed. The route took me past Feckenham, a name that sounds like the sort of thing Father Jack would shout at bacon.

Approaching Redditch, county number seven was soon upon me. I'd reached Worcestershire. When it comes to certain details, Worcestershire is very average. Of my 97 counties, it's the 48th largest and the 49th most densely populated, right in the middle of both lists. But, on the plus side, it's the only county with a sauce named after it.

Worcestershire sauce is one of those food products that should never have been, like Pop Tarts. Its makers produced a barrel of the molasses, tamarind and anchovy condiment and, as it sounds really, decided it was too disgusting to use. Eighteen months later, having forgotten about the barrel, they tasted it again. In the meantime it had fermented and become the worldwide ambassador for Britain that it is today. In many countries it's known as "English sauce", although in France "English sauce" probably means any gravy that's burnt or has bits of broken glass in it.

Just short of Bromsgrove I arrived at another of Britain's odd museums, Avoncroft. It's mostly a bunch of old buildings that have been collected from around Britain and painstakingly rebuilt here brick by brick. Hitler would have been proud. They have a windmill, a threshing barn, a perry press, an old jail house, a church and loads of others. But it also has a telephone box museum, a collection of kiosks from throughout the ages. They even had a Doctor Who-style police box but, unfortunately, it wasn't bigger on the inside.

There was also a rebuilt automatic telephone exchange originally from Essex. A guy showed me how it worked.

"It seems like a lot of effort to look after," I said.

"Yes, we have an old fella come in to maintain it," he said. "He's eighty. We need to get him to train us."

"And soon."

"Yeah," he replied sadly.

Apparently, the first automatic exchange was invented by an undertaker. He'd split from his wife, also an undertaker – their pillow talk must have been grisly – and he came up with an automatic exchange because he suspected the manual one was favouring his ex-wife's business, presumably patching through to her anyone with a bit of a cough. As they always say, mean-spirited rivalry is the mother of invention.

I wandered around the buildings. It was a great and eclectic collection. A Tudor house had just been finished. Outside, the garden was being replanted with Elizabethan vegetables. In its original location it had been about to be demolished to clear room for a new road. Instead it was teleported to the museum. Inside, they'd tried to make it as authentic as possible, with a large fire burning on the floor and smoke throughout the house. A couple in period costume poked at the embers and answered questions. They worked here as volunteers.

"This was a very comfortable house," said the fella. "The home of a rich man. Go upstairs and have a look."

At the top of a large wooden staircase was the bedroom complete with straw mattresses. This was the origin of the expression "to hit the hay". They were a haven for bugs and fleas. For this reason, Henry VIII changed his straw mattress every day, almost as often as his wife.

We talked about the perry press. It had been a local one. I wasn't aware that Worcestershire made perry and cider but, as it turns out, even Worcestershire's county flag contains pears.

"Oh yes. And if you want a good one, try the Wildmoor Oak."

I wasn't about to ignore such a suggestion, especially when I learned it was near a village called Bell End. Even better, the ride there took me through Lickey End too. British place names are wonderful.

I sat in the sunshine and tried both a perry called Pickled Parrot and a local cider, both over 6%. I felt decidedly tiddly. Another couple sat in the beer garden outside. They asked where I was going.

"And it's all been great so far," I said. "Though Dudley was a bit ropey."

They nodded their heads.

"Good people though," said the man.

"Yeah," I replied. "There are good people everywhere."

I hadn't come across any real trouble in any of the 53 countries I'd cycled in Europe. But the couple didn't look convinced.

"Not everywhere," said the woman.

"Really?" I replied. "Where aren't they good?"

"London. They're not good in London."

Over these last two days I'd cycled in a huge circle and was now back at the cheap campsite in the Clent Hills. That evening's meal didn't go according to plan. While kneeling on the ground trying to light the methylated spirits in my stove I dropped the fiddly lighter into the purple liquid and the whole lot went up in flames. With my foot I quickly kicked the stove away from my highly flammable tent and then the lighter exploded with a dull thud, fortunately at a safe enough distance not to blow off a limb or set fire to my tent. I decided to go with sandwiches instead.

*

I woke up to more beautiful blue skies, not a cloud in

sight. I decided to enjoy my breakfast – some blueberry muffins I'd bought the night before – with some coffee on the site's only flattish picnic table. I treated the stove with a little more respect than last night.

As I sat there, a woman in her late sixties came up for a chat. She'd once backpacked all over the place but her body wouldn't let her any longer. Regardless, she toured around Britain in her camper van.

"Do you ever go abroad?" I asked.

"No need," she replied. "There are enough beautiful places here."

Not everyone was down on Britain.

I left the site. A few miles past Hagley, I fell upon something glorious that I remembered from previous rides through Britain, the roadside snack van. Operating from this one was a woman from Thailand and her signs offered Hot Pork Sandwiches. Although I'd only had my breakfast an hour earlier I had to take advantage of this.

"Do you want everything, sweetheart?" she asked in a sing-song Thai-Cockney mix.

Of course I did. She loaded a large split bun with a mountain of pulled pork and stuffing, and then added a few strips of crackling and a large dollop of apple sauce.

"There you go, sweetheart."

The whole thing was impossible to eat as it was. It had to be picked at until it resembled a sandwich rather than a porkberg but it was amazing. If you're a keen cyclist on Britain's roads, don't expect to find vans like these on the continent.

I made it to Kinver, the location of a suggestion from Pete, the guy who I'd cycled with a few days earlier. Before I headed to this recommendation I rolled over a lock. A barge was approaching. I'd never seen the process that gets someone through the watery gateway.

Watching with me was a group of three, an older couple and a younger bloke in an electric wheelchair, who were having an argument. The baddie seemed to be the disabled fella.

"Why do you have to shout all the time?" the older man asked the younger.

"I don't shout," he replied.

The bargee – that's the barge's driver, not an Indian starter – opened the valve to empty the lock chamber.

"Yes, you do," shouted the woman in the team. "You go all shrill."

The bargee opened the lock gate and his boat slowly motored into the chamber.

"I don't shout," said the man defending himself and raising his voice.

"Yes, you do!" they both said at the same time.

"No, I don't!"

"You're doing it now!" yelled the woman.

"Only because you're making me."

The older guy shook his head.

"You need to calm down," added the other man.

The guy in the chair stared coldly at him.

"Oh fuck off!" he screamed and wheeled himself away. I thought they were going to run after him and tip him into the water.

I walked away to talk to the bargee, who was grappling with the second gate.

"How many locks do you have to go through a day?"

"That's like asking how long's a piece of string. Some days it can be hardly any and then you come to a series of twenty-odd locks in a row."

"And how long does that take?"

"It can take three or four hours. But of course, there could be a queue."

"At least it's peaceful," I said, looking towards the trio who were still bawling at each other.

I cycled on to Kinver's Rock Houses, a sandstone outcrop that had been carved into troglodyte dwellings and are believed by some to be the inspiration for Tolkien's "hobbit holes". They were lived in until as recently as the 1960s. Unfortunately they were closed to the public on a Wednesday and so I had to view them from afar, but they looked impressive and marginally more homely than a Travelodge.

I turned the bike round and headed thirty miles south, over loads of those little, round, steep-sided hills that appear on the opening sequence of *Postman Pat*. They're easy in a van with a black and white cat but not on a heavily loaded bike. I had to get off and push.

Despite the beautiful weather, a quick glance at the trees told me this mini-heatwave was out of time. They stood in silhouette, black against the bright blue sky, mostly naked, the occasional one just in blossom but most not even beginning to contemplate growing a new outfit.

At the top of one of the longer hills I looked down at the beautiful rural scene before me, the smoke from a steam train rising from the valley floor. This was the England of old paintings. I'd arrived in Herefordshire.

Herefordshire is the least densely populated county in the southern half of England with only 219 people per square mile and half of the 183,600 population lives in its five largest towns. It was nice to cycle in the gaps between them. The county is mostly agricultural and famous for its fruit and cider – babies were baptised in the stuff in the 14th century – as well as its Hereford cattle. Taken at face value, its traditional county motto does a good job of describing it: "This fair land is a gift of God." But then again, so is smallpox.

I turned a corner and took a step back to a previous

century. Two travellers were sitting on the grass outside their colourfully-painted wooden caravans, parked up on the verge, their horses grazing a little farther up the road.

"Seems like a nice life," I said to them.

One of the travellers tilted his head sideways, non-committally.

"S'alright," he replied. "It has its moments."

"Do you get any grief?" I asked, remembering Romany caravans being hassled by police in Romania.

The guy was shaving a stick with a large knife, which he raised with a smile.

"No. No hassle." He put the knife down. "We just move on."

"But how do you manage to support yourself?" I asked, before realising how intrusive a question it was.

He smiled and then his look turned cold.

"We have a YouTube channel," he replied.

"Really?"

"Piss off," he said, exploding with sarcastic laughter.

Whether he meant it as a command or not I decided to act as though it were.

I couldn't find any tabloid stories to place any of Britain's capitals in Herefordshire although given that Bulmer's is the largest factory of its kind in the world perhaps Hereford should be the cider capital of Britain, maybe even the cider capital of planet Earth.

But this lack of capitals amongst its fields and orchards doesn't mean the place is a backwater. After all, in an attempt to be modern and tediously 21st century, the council recently spent a small fortune to rebrand itself. It came up with the utterly empty slogan: "Herefordshire – Here you can!" Indeed, that motto had greeted me on the county's Welcome sign as I cycled into the place. But what is it that you "can" here? The readers of the Hereford Times were scathing about the project, suggesting the only thing you can do around these parts is "put fruit into tins".

If local companies want to use the branding on their own promotional bumpf they have to get past the county's Brand Guardian, the end-of-level boss whose job it is to protect those three precious, meaningless words. To find out what it was all about I visited the brand website – *hereyoucan.co.uk* – and clicked an area labelled "Understand our brand" but unfortunately the link didn't work. Well done, Brand Guardian!

With some research I found one thing that you "can" do here that you definitely can't anywhere else. Due to an ancient, unrepealed law, you can shoot a Welshman with a longbow on a Sunday on Hereford's Cathedral Close. So that's probably what the council are on about.

What the area lacks in marketing skills it makes up for in naming ability. You can visit the delightful villages of Trumpet, Cockyard and Booby Dingle before popping on your walking boots and ascending Lord Hereford's Knob. At 690 metres it's quite a big one.

I rolled into Leominster – pronounced Lemster for no good reason – and found a town with character. I discovered a great, little backstreet that shared many of the properties of Diagon Alley. Despite being the largest place for miles, it seemed almost entirely devoid of chains. Nearly every shop was local. That said, most of them sold antiques. Over the years Leominster has been a popular venue for Bargain Hunt, a TV favourite of the housebound. It's also got a food colouring manufacturers in town. Perhaps that explains why David Dickinson ended up looking like a Cheesy Wotsit.

I needed to find a campsite and one mile from the centre of town was a pub called Baron's Cross with a field and, for a fiver, that's where I stayed. The sun was still shining. I sat outside with a pint but realised I was at a disadvantage because this was where the locals came out to smoke and some of them wanted to talk. I mean, *really* wanted to talk.

"You on a bike?"

"Yep."

"I like all that racing. You know, Bradley Wiggins an' all that."

"Yeah, I don't really follow racing."

Then followed a fifteen minute monologue about the Tour de France. I'm too polite.

But the bar staff were lovely and they all came outside too. I don't know who was running the bar. Maybe it was a free-for-all. They constantly took the piss out of the landlady, mainly because she wasn't local, but she took it in good part. Maybe that sort of thing matters around here.

"So you're going to see every county?" one of the locals asked.

"That's the plan."

"What are you looking forward to the most?"

"The fleas," I replied.

"What?"

"There are some famous fleas in Hertfordshire."

I gave her the rest of the tale.

"You know which is the most beautiful county?" she asked.

"Not yet."

I was expecting her to say it was Herefordshire.

"It's Shropshire."

"Good, that's my next one."

"And then it's Herefordshire."

I'd had an identical conversation with someone else earlier in the day. I wasn't sure what measure they'd used to judge each county's beauty. It would be interesting to see if they were right. But it was certainly beautifully rural around here. Just one mile from the centre of the largest population for miles and the phone signal was rubbish.

I popped into the pub's lounge where the TV told me today had been the warmest day of the year but since it was only the 20th April that wasn't so impressive.

"But don't get used to it," said the weather woman.

She then undid her good work by using phrases like "not going to last" and "wintry showers".

"Here you go," said the barmaid, delivering a steak pie, cheesy mash, peas and an ocean of gravy. I'd decided to give the stove a night off.

An old woman, easily into her eighties, was also sitting in the lounge, a large Labrador at her feet. She was complaining about her children to a man leaning against the bar.

"They only want me for my money," she said. "My son even forged a cheque to get it." She shook her little, grey head. "An' our Tracy lives in Birmingham. I never see her."

The man seemed to be tiring of her, remembered he'd promised to get something for her from the shops and disappeared for ten minutes. She spent the entire time complaining about her kids to her dog. The man returned and handed her a package.

"Thank the nice man, Boney" she said to her pet.

The Labrador looked up at her.

"Go on, Boney, thank him."

The Labrador tilted his head wordlessly towards the man.

"Thank him for Christ's sakes!"

*

In the same field as my tent was a camper van. In it was a bloke of about sixty. He invited me in for a morning cup of tea. Unlike the woman the morning before who was exploring the whole of beautiful Britain, this poor fella was lost. His wife had died a year ago and he drifted, here for one week, another site for the next, but rather than travelling purposefully he seemed to be killing time.

"It's difficult without her, y'know," he said, sipping his tea. "We used to do this together, but, well, now..."

He trailed off, looking out of the window, close to tears. Maybe keeping on the move fills the time, but sometimes it's better to stay in one place and get yourself grounded, make some new friends.

The bananas I'd had for breakfast hadn't done the trick and so, en route northwards to Ludlow, Britain's foodie capital, a smile crept across my face as I spied in a layby a big, red double decker bus that had been converted into a café.

Inside was a large bloke, also around sixty. He struggled to move around behind his counter. Keeping to the theme of British health food I ordered a bacon and sausage sandwich.

"You're doing what?" he asked.

I repeated what I'd said.

"Then this is on me."

"No, c'mon," I replied. "That's kind but you're a business."

"Nah, four lads came through the other day doing Land's End to John o'Groats an' I gave 'em theirs free too."

"Well, thank you."

"My son's into all that. He's forty. A while back he did a marathon and then rode five hundred miles home. It's his birthday today. He's gone skiing."

"Somewhere nice?"

Austria? Switzerland? The Pyrenees?

"Tamworth."

"Oh."

"It's indoor."

"Britain's obesity capital," I said.

"Eh?"

"Never mind."

We started talking about charity rides, and then he mentioned how charities are corrupt, paying their staff rather

71

than funding their cause, and we crawled down a political cul-de-sac.

"It'll all be fine once I'm Prime Minister," he said. He knew how to solve Britain's problems. "I'd have all the unemployed sweeping the streets."

"They do something like that in Spain."

"Yeah? And the disabled." He raised his eyes and tutted. "They wouldn't get any money off me. Fuckin' shirkers."

That was a bit harsh. I think I'd stumbled into Alf Garnett's van.

"C'mon, lots of them *can't* work."

"Bollocks. Fuck 'em."

"You can't speak like that when you're Prime Minister."

He looked directly at me.

"I can and I will." Bloody hell, he was serious. "Enoch Powell did. He had it right."

"What, rivers of blood and all that?"

"Yeah, all these coons comin' over!" he sneered.

Oh dear.

"Y'know," he continued, "there was a young lad an' girl round here who killed someone recently. You know what I'd do to 'em?"

I could hazard a guess.

"I'd put 'em in a secure prison until they were eighteen..."

Well, that was a surprise.

"...and then I'd hang 'em."

"Well, thanks for the sandwich," I said, turning to leave.

He stopped ranting and smiled.

"Sorry to have lectured you."

"No, it's fine," I said. "It's just nice to meet the next Prime Minister."

I'd now crossed the border into Shropshire and it was, if it's possible, even more rural than Herefordshire. The first town of any size was Ludlow, one of the loveliest places I'd visited so far. Its 11th century, medieval walled town and five hundred listed buildings would suggest it's all about history but, nowadays, it's more about food. It has an annual food festival and at one time was the only town in England with three Michelin-starred restaurants.

I was a little peeved I'd opted for that damn tasty but racist bacon and sausage butty so recently. There was no room for the delicious-sounding hot roast beef and horseradish sandwich being peddled by a van in the main square.

Just before Craven Arms, which is a town as well as a pub, I saw a sign for Stokesay Castle. My budget didn't allow for many entry fees but I figured the money I would've spent on the bacon butty could be channelled in a more cultured direction.

Stokesay Castle isn't really a castle at all but the best-preserved medieval fortified manor house in England and I enjoyed looking around it so much that when the young woman at the ticket desk told me I'd get my money back if I joined English Heritage I signed up immediately. Rather than shun places with entry fees I'd have to seek them out to squeeze as much value as I could from my £52. With 400 historical buildings to see, that worked out at 13p each. Even I could afford that.

I now turned left and headed towards the little village of Clun, not far from the Welsh border. I had someone to meet. The road seemed to be disappearing into rural oblivion. Nothing but empty fields and hills lay ahead. Shropshire should drop the 'Shrop' and just call itself The Shire. Maybe they could give out fake hobbit feet to everyone.

I'd been told the local youth hostel allowed camping on its grounds. When I got there, the place was locked up but there was another tent already set up. Apart from mine, this was the first tent I'd seen on this trip. April didn't seem to be such a popular month for camping in Britain.

Very soon, the tent's owner, Robin, turned up. We stood around our two-tent town and chatted. He's a keen cyclist who I only knew virtually from cycling forums and Facebook. He lives somewhere near Milton Keynes but was here doing out-and-back rides around Shropshire for a few days. He's a vet and seemed a happy chap and so it was a surprise when he said what he said.

"Did you know that vets have the most depression and highest suicide rates of any jobs?"

"Really? Why's that?"

"The public," he replied, shaking his head. "The worst ones are usually those with Staffies."

Recently one such owner had phoned his surgery, yelled angrily at his assistant and called her just about the worst thing he probably could. When the bloke turned up with his dog, Robin refused to examine it until he'd apologised to his assistant. Robin wasn't a physically imposing man but the bloke backed down and said he was sorry. Don't mess with Supervet!

We swapped stories and then, being British, went for a pint. First up was the 15th century pub, The Sun Inn, selling beer from the Three Tuns brewery, the UK's oldest, making beer since 1642, and then we staggered to the White Horse Inn, a place that brews its own ales. Over too many pints and a great English meal of wild boar paté and toast followed by pork and apple sauce stew with mustard mash we continued talking.

"Do you do cosmetic surgery on animals?" I asked jokingly.

I was imagining face lifts for ageing beagles or poodles with fake breasts.

"Well, it can happen," he replied.

"Eh?"

"Some people want fake testicles for their dogs after they've been neutered."

How odd, but maybe not. I knew that in Spain a lot of men refuse to have their dogs neutered because they see their pets inability to procreate as some reflection upon their own masculinity. If your own identity is that closely tied to that of your pet maybe you're less in need of a plastic surgeon than a psychiatrist.

To begin with, Robin seemed a little reserved and so it was another surprise when he said he performed in pubs, singing and playing guitar.

"I've been in bands too. Doing covers, indie stuff. But I prefer doing it by myself," he said. Then he smiled. "You get to keep all the money."

"What were the bands called?"

"One was The Bandits, and then another one called Face to Face, which is a crap name."

I love bands with rubbish names because I've been in a few. I started off in the mid-eighties in a synth band called The Slaves of Circumstance but then the only member with any talent decided to leave. That left just me, playing one-fingered on keyboards, and Pat, a singer who aimed to emulate the limited vocal talents of Gary Numan and didn't quite manage it. We worked at the same place and another lad there kept doing impressions of Tuco, a character from The Good, The Bad and The Ugly. For reasons long since forgotten, we changed the name of the band to Tuco Talks. This flummoxed everyone. At a working men's club in Blackburn we were in their "changing room" (i.e., the toilet) about to go on stage before a roomful of eighty-year-olds – octogenarians love Depeche Mode! – and the M.C. announced us.

"Now, please welcome two young lads from Blackburn. It's the first time they've played here: *Two Coat Hooks*!"

Now *that's* a great band name!

*

The next morning I said goodbye to Robin and cycled back to Craven Arms passing Aston-on-Clun, where I saw "the world famous" Arbor Tree. No, me neither.

The weather suggested rain was imminent, a dull grey sky. The greens of the last few days were now washed out. The naked trees were covered in ivy climbing towards a sun that today was hidden from view.

I decided on a plan. Rather than lug all my gear around unnecessarily, I'd find a campsite in Much Wenlock, dump my bags and then run off to see the local sights. The A49 was reasonably flat but when the route to Much Wenlock turned right I had mini-mountains for the final ten miles. I was up and down like a manic depressive in a lift.

I found a campsite in town and just £7 would get me a pitch, along with a promise to use my stove on a wooden pallet because arseholes like me kept setting fire to their grass. I said I didn't really need the pallet because my stove was raised from the ground, but then again I'd forgotten mine had exploded only a couple of days earlier.

I jumped back on to the bike and popped into the Cistercian Buildwas Abbey, a ruin but a good one, founded in 1135. I had the place to myself. At first this made me think perhaps people didn't care much for these amazing places until I realised what time it was and concluded it was empty because it was a weekday afternoon in April and everyone was at work.

Cycling away from my second religious building of the day, Wenlock Priory, I passed the rugged-sounding Bastard Hall, a 15th century, oak-panelled country house. It belonged to Richard le Bastard – a French Bastard I'm assuming – in 1267. At the time of writing, the place is up for sale for half a million quid if you'd like an address with some real oomph.

Tomorrow was St George's Day and Much Wenlock had a George and Dragon pub. It felt only right to go there and have a pint. I'd finished my riding for the day and so I left the bike at the site and walked back into town, past a little wood full of rabbits. For five o'clock the place was rammed, mostly with men who I assumed from their clothes were painters and decorators. One of them looked like the arse of his jeans had just had a run-in with an angry shark, his blue and white-striped underpants on view to the world.

Much Wenlock's poetry festival kicked off today but only for official invitees or if you wanted to pay top dollar to hear a serious-looking bloke with an African name who I'd never heard of. Tomorrow, though, it would open to the public. There was someone there I wanted to meet, someone with a job like no other.

*

I got up lazily, made coffee and breakfasted on a packet of double toffee cupcakes. There was no point in rushing. Nurse Verse wouldn't get going until eleven.

Yesterday's grey skies had been replaced by a much more cheery shade of blue. It was bloody cold though and the wind was getting up. I cycled back to the priory, where an old ambulance was parked up, awaiting patients. Outside, a woman, the coordinator of this enterprise, was talking to a Sikh fella, a magnificent-looking chap with a turban and a huge waxed moustache. He looked like he should have been something big in Bollywood. I made an appointment with Nurse Verse, the Emergency Poet, and was then interrogated for a little while.

"Will you be going to Cumbria?" asked the man.

I was a bit mesmerized by him. His skin appeared to glow, like he was made of gold.

"Hopefully."

"I was there once, walking up Sca Fell," he continued.

"The weather was terrible. It was so windy it blew off my turban."

I probably shouldn't have laughed because I quickly realised from his expression that this was a source of real pain for him, but, well, I did.

Another woman climbed out of the ambulance.

"The Emergency Poet will see you now."

I entered the mobile clinic and what followed was a surreal experience. Nurse Verse instructed me to climb on to the couch and get myself comfortable.

"Now I want to ask you a few questions and then I'll prescribe a poem," she said.

"Alright."

This wasn't weird at all.

"First, can you remember the last time you stood by the sea?"

That was easy, watching iron men drown and seagulls choke to death at Crosby Beach twelve days ago.

"In your everyday life, what do you do to relax?"

"Maybe I'm weird but I'm always relaxed. Is that unusual?"

"I think it probably is. Do you read poetry?"

"Not much. In fact, hardly ever. But if I do I either love it or it annoys me intensely."

"Yes," she said, laughing. "A lot of it is terrible."

She asked me about my favourite books, music and places.

"Can you describe your ideal room when you're old and grey and can't be bothered to move."

"Just a comfortable chair and a room full of books."

"A dog or a cat?"

"Yeah, a little dog."

"And what would you have immediately to hand?"

"A pen, and a pad. And even though I've never smoked I always thought I'd fancy a pipe when I'm old."

"Now then, do you have any condition that I could give you a poem for?"

I thought for a second.

"Tired legs?" I offered. "Or motivation to get going in a morning when it's bad weather and I don't want to leave."

She searched through her folder of poems. It was my turn to ask the questions.

"Do you do this at the festival every year?"

"I do it all over the place," she replied.

"What? Is this your job?" I asked incredulously.

She laughed.

"It's one of my jobs. I teach poetry at Worcester University and do other writerly things too."

"Because this has got to be one of the strangest jobs in the world," I said. "And great too."

"Yes. It *is* great. I just completely made it up. There's no one else doing this. Next week we're at Stratford Literary Festival. The week after that we're in New Zealand."

Wow, an international verse nurse!

"And do you write poetry yourself?"

"Yes."

"I'll look you up online."

"They're a bit rude actually."

"Good. I like rude. Stuff like 'There once was a man from Nantucket'?"

"A lot ruder than that," she said, extracting two sheets from her folder. "Right, I've got two poems for you." She handed me The Table by Turkish poet Edip Cansever. "It's about a man piling things on a table. It's a metaphor for a life richly lived, which I think yours is."

That was nice.

"And there's this one for inspiration."

She gave me Variations on a Theme by Rilke written by Denise Levertov. It concluded with the words "I can", just like Herefordshire. I looked at the photocopied sheets. She'd written "Take poems with good local ale at lunchtime!"

This felt like something that could only happen in Britain, an intelligent person doing something bonkers for the hell of it. She's called Deborah Alma, by the way. Check her out. And she was right; her poetry is gloriously filthy.

I cycled out of town, down lovely car-free lanes, to see the remains of a Roman city, the Wrekin standing tall in the distance. Watling Street, the Anglo-Saxon road that was paved by the Romans and connected the south-east to the rest of Roman Britain, originally terminated here at Wroxeter. It was later extended to Hadrian's Wall, olive oil and wine moving northwards, shortbread and aggressive gingers coming south.

Wroxeter, originally called Viriconium, or the place of werewolves, was the fourth largest Roman town in Britain, almost the same size as Pompeii. It took some effort to imagine how the city would have looked but you could get into the part if you wanted to. A dressing up box was available. I pulled out a toga but it looked like it had been used to wipe the face of a plague victim and so I decided against it.

The Wrekin – pronounced Ree-kin – is a famous 407-metre hill, a landmark visible for miles on the Shropshire Plain. The phrase "all around the Wrekin" is used locally to mean "the long way around" and it can even be used to forecast the weather.

If you can see the Wrekin it's going to rain. If you can't see the Wrekin it's already raining.

Apparently, from the top on a good day, which doesn't sound very likely given that forecast, you can see fifteen counties.

A legend says the hill was created by a giant who wanted to kill everyone in Shrewsbury. He gathered a giant-sized spadeful of soil and set off towards the place, planning to dump the earth in the Severn to flood the town. A shoemaker was travelling in the opposite direction and carried a large sackload of footwear that needed to be repaired. When the giant asked him for directions, the shoemaker, wanting to save his countrymen, showed the giant his sack and told him he'd worn out all these shoes walking back from Shrewsbury. The giant couldn't be arsed to trudge that far and so dumped the soil, which became the Wrekin.

Even by the standard of legends this is complete bollocks. Using a back-of-a-fag-packet calculation, the Wrekin has a conservatively estimated volume of around 700 million cubic metres. The giant would have had to be around 6,000 metres tall, over two-thirds the size of Everest, to carry the Wrekin on a spade. Wherever he was in Shropshire he could've seen Shrewsbury and walked right across the county in thirty paces. Maybe I'm taking this too seriously.

The wind had become stronger, an icy knife in the face. As to be expected it was coming exactly from the direction I was cycling. A few miles farther and the quiet roads disappeared. I was in Shrewsbury, Shropshire's county town. I'd always thought the correct pronunciation was Shrose-bury, but the newspaper said 81% of people in and around the town prefer Shroos-bury, which makes it one of the few British towns to be pronounced as it's spelled.

It's a pretty town for a mid-afternoon food stop, full of spires and a stone bridge crossing a Severn that's already impressively wide even this far north. The town was heaving. In the main square people were fencing. I didn't know if this was a display for St George's Day or just the sort of thing people got up to in Shrewsbury.

Shrewsbury has a few unique features. It's got the world's

oldest skyscraper, the world's longest running flower show and the world's oldest building to host a McDonald's, although I'm not sure that last one is much to be proud of.

Tonight's campsite was a farm down a series of lanes designed to get you lost, and so I obliged. They only wanted a fiver, but it had a nice, fully featured kitchen for us campers including a kettle and tea bags. A pile of fishing magazines sat on a table. The top one was called Total Carp. Surely that's a joke title. I looked through the pile to see if I could find any similar ones – Massive Pile of Carp, What A Load of Carp – but they didn't.

I made a cup of tea and sat at the table trying to write a poem, inspired by this morning's appointment.

There once was a man on a bicycle,
On his nose he developed an icicle,
'Cos The Shire was cold,
And the wind strength too bold,
But the landscape was rather quite nice-icle.

Nurse Verse was right about one thing: Most poems *are* terrible.

This would be my last evening in England for a while. Tomorrow I would continue west into the wind, and into the wonderful wilds of Wales.

Chapter 4: Cannibals, Satanists and a piglet or three

Wrexham, Flintshire, Denbighshire, Conwy, Gwynedd and Powys

I set off towards Wales and, just up the road, stopped for breakfast in Chirk. In another celebration of Britishness I had my first ever mug of Horlicks. And probably my last too. It tastes a lot like hot chocolate but with no chocolate in it. It was invented in Chicago by the brothers Horlick from Gloucestershire. If you think Horlicks is a dodgy name, it was originally called Diastoid, a great name for a killer robot, and advertised under the slogan "Horlick's Infant and Invalids Food".

The wind was still cold and directly in my face. I passed a sign that welcomed me into Wales, into the county of Wrexham. I wasn't far from the Pontcysyllte Aqueduct, the 300-metre long, three-and-a-half-metre wide canal-in-the-sky. It's the longest and, at 38 metres tall, the highest aqueduct in Britain. It would have been nice to cycle across but if the wind was this strong down here, up there it would've blown me into the water or off the edge. I doubt even Invalids Food would have helped.

I took the quieter road beside a busy dual carriageway and went through little Johnstown. On the outskirts, the New Inn's blackboard advertised this evening's entertainment, Shagger. There were no other details. Maybe it was DJ Shagger, or a Shaggy tribute act, or maybe it was more literal and she was just a very popular local.

The town of Wrexham is, according to local councillor

Paul Pemberton, "the car arson capital of the UK" and didn't seem to offer much. Its roadworks prevented me from going to the centre or at least suggested it wasn't worth going there, especially if all I was going to see was a load of smouldering Subarus.

Wrexham is supposedly the baldest town in Britain but I looked out for shiny scalps and saw none. Maybe they were all wearing wigs. Some people had clearly over-compensated. On the edge of town I saw a bloke with such a fluffy mane he could have been in the Hair Bear Bunch.

I cycled on to my second new county of the day, Flintshire. It has the highest percentage of witches and Satanists in the country, but there are still not many. Their last census figures were interesting. There were just seven Satanists, nine Druids and 117 Pagans. Much more popular were the more realistic religions, such as 374 Jedi Knights and thirteen people who simply listed their faith as "heavy metal".

Not far over the invisible county border is the manky-sounding town of Mold. The reason for its name is unclear but it has nothing to do with curled up sandwiches. If Mold's name sounds unsavoury, so was the policing here in 1869 in an event that shaped how the force responded to future civil disturbances. The manager of the local colliery, already unpopular for banning the Welsh language, announced a pay cut. As a result, several miners attacked him, were arrested, found guilty and the ringleaders were sentenced to a month's hard labour, which, for a miner, must be a busman's holiday. A crowd of 2,000 gathered to listen to the verdict and, while the convicts were being transported away, they grew angry and started throwing missiles. Expecting trouble, the police had called in the 4th King's Own Regiment for backup. The soldiers opened fire on the crowd, killing four, including an entirely innocent 19-year-old woman. An inquest was held by Coroner Peter Parry, a half-blind old dodderer who required the use of an ear trumpet to hear the evidence. After five minutes of consideration, the jury returned a verdict of justifiable homicide. Many of those involved in the riot were sentenced to ten years. Later, the authorities rethought their gung-ho approach and vowed to employ less heavy-handed policing techniques in future. So you've got Mold to thank for that. Now the police will only shoot on sight if you look a bit foreign.

It was a quiet Sunday in Mold, certainly quieter than it was in 1869, and lacking entertainment I cycled on to Hendre, the location of this evening's muddy field. From my tent I looked out over the Clwydian Range, a lovely low bunch of nicely rounded hills dominated by 555-metre Moel Famau with its derelict Jubilee Tower on top. I sat there and admired the view for what felt like hours, a beautiful, tranquil space.

I wonder how Shagger was getting on.

*

It rained all night and from inside my tent it sounded like I was in the middle of a tornado. I knew I didn't have far to go today and so I waited it out. Yesterday's hills were shrouded in low cloud and a dark sky hung just inches over my head, like a big, wet hat doesn't.

The bike was a little lighter this morning. After our discovery of the Om, the super-omelette staple of our £1-a-day ride, I'd brought the ingredients to recreate it on this trip but I'd only made it once so far and decided to ditch the ingredients, including a big bag of flour, in an attempt to trim a few pounds from my load. As I rolled down the lane away from Hendre, I caught a whiff of roadside ramsons – wild garlic – a great green to add to an Om, but now I'd no reason to collect it.

Within seconds of setting off, the heavens opened and within five minutes I was drenched. This was the Wales I was familiar with. Through the seeping cloud, a burger van appeared. It was run by a smiling father and son team. The dad explained their mission statement.

"We do it for a laugh really," he said chuckling, then changed his mind, and became more serious. "Well, not a laugh. We just...do it."

It didn't bother me. I didn't need a jester, just a black pudding, mushroom and cheese sandwich and the rain-denying overhang of their van. I'm not sure this business was really a two-man operation. The son's job seemed just to be buttering the bread, but they seemed happy enough. I said I was heading for Rhyl, the unemployment capital of Wales, but dad warned me off.

"Don't go. It's a shithole," he said.

I sort of knew that already. On his coastal tour of Britain, Mike Carter described it in *One Man and His Bike* as "plug ugly". Plus, I'd been there before.

I decided to change my route. The rain eased and with pig grease on my face I continued on to Denbighshire, the bit of Wales with the most ancient inhabitants, like Catherine Zeta Jones's pants when Michael Douglas is in town.

I arrived in St Asaph. It's Britain's newest city, only attaining that status in 2012. With its population of 3,355 it's also Britain's second smallest. Its little cathedral is rather lovely except for a life-size crucifix containing what looks like the dried, decomposed body of Christ, a sculpture by Michele Coxon. I was surprised the Church allowed such heresy in a cathedral. After all, if Christ had rotted like that, it suggested He was never removed from the cross and was therefore never resurrected. Which of course He wasn't, but you'd think at least a cathedral would stick to the official fable.

Two minutes after entering the town, and having passed the sculptural tribute to local lad Henry Morton Stanley, the man who found Livingstone in central Africa, and which the local residents want removed for being "hideous and phallic", I was out the other side.

At the edges of my sky, blueness was appearing, accompanied by the odd white, fluffy cloud. With a howling, freezing wind in my face, better weather was coming in my direction. I opted not to go directly to the coast – surely it would be windier there – and found a nice, straight B-road on my map. Normally such straightness would imply a flat road, but not here. I wound my way up the hillside, in the process entering the county of Conwy, until I'd had enough. I got off and pushed and then spotted something very British, a soft-core porn mag in a hedge.

I turned my bike coastwards and rolled into Abergele, a townlet between the tourist centres of Rhyl and Colwyn Bay. I hadn't been sure where I was going to end up today and so I knew nothing about Abergele. I went online to see if there was anything interesting here, and there was.

I set up my tent on the town's campsite, fighting the gale. Inside, I put a pannier in each corner to prevent the whole thing from blowing away and walked into town. My first stop was the graveyard attached to St Michael's church that contained an undated gravestone for a fella who "had his dwelling three miles to the north". Elsewhere, this wouldn't be curious, but Abergele is on the north coast of Wales. Maybe he was originally going to be buried somewhere else and so the headstone was incorrectly inscribed, or perhaps he was just very good at treading water.

I walked down the high street and did a bit of window shopping. A sign outside a butcher's offered "home killed beef, lamb and pork". His living room must be a right mess.

My next job was to find a house called Linor on Gele Avenue, which, when I originally found the story, was called "the most haunted house in Britain". In the late 1800s two sisters kept their brother prisoner in their attic for several years. Eventually, the brother escaped and, seeking vengeance, killed his sisters and then, probably feeling a bit peckish after his prolonged incarceration, ate them. The ghosts of the women supposedly told a more recent owner of the house where their bones were buried.

The odd thing about this story is that, since I read it on Wikipedia at the end of April, it's been removed from the page and the only place I could find any mention of it when I looked later was in a cached copy. Today, even that cached copy has disappeared. The story doesn't appear anywhere else on the internet. And so maybe the ghosts have removed the story because it made them look bad. Or perhaps someone was dicking around on Wiki the day I arrived.

Whether true or not, I found the house. It was an unassuming place with a dark blue door on which hung a sign. I walked closer to read it. I assumed it was going to say, "Piss off and stop bothering us with your stupid ghost nonsense" but it didn't. It ordered visitors not to press the bell because their baby was sleeping. Probably Rosemary's baby.

Around the corner is the George and Dragon, a surprisingly English name for a pub in Wales. An old man sitting next to me had a question for the barmaid. He held up the menu.

"This fish dinner with hand-battered fish?"

"Yes?"

"Is it any cheaper if it's battered without the hand?"

He was joking, but maybe the escaped brother wasn't the only cannibal around these parts.

*

The night stayed dry and the freezing wind seemed to have eased but the hedge I'd camped behind gave a false impression. I quickly realised the gale was as strong and as cold as ever. Had conditions been better I would have popped along the coast to the town of Conwy itself but, this being a spontaneous trip, I decided to use the wind to my advantage and have it carry me up the hills towards Snowdonia National Park. Short of the brief flurry of hailstones, the forecast wintry showers didn't arrive but it never stopped being as cold as an Inuit's icebox. The fourteen-mile climb to Llanrwst, a village that looks like it's been mugged of some vowels, would have been enough to warm me but the route completed with three steep, frozen downhill miles. The temperatures though were a mere distraction. Bright green fields dusted with lambs were backed by brown forests and topped with snow-capped mountains. Wales is effortlessly beautiful.

Although it's only a dot of a place with a population of just over three thousand, in 1947 Llanrwst applied for a seat on the United Nations Security Council as an independent state within Wales. The town has a history of independence. In 1276 it was granted the title Free Borough of Llanrwst by the then Prince of Wales. Its motto was the divisive "Wales, England and Llanrwst". Unfortunately, the UN turned down their application, which was a shame because maybe England would have found a football team they might beat. But then again.

In Llanrwst I decided I needed heat and found a fish 'n' chip shop that had a single, small table for two by its window. The sun shone through the glass and warmed the wooden furniture. I gathered my chicken and mushroom pie and chips soaked in salt and vinegar and took my place. An old fella approached and asked if he could join me.

He was a nice, smiley bloke, lacking a particularly strong Welsh accent, but whose speech was made mostly incomprehensible by his muttering, although he started off fairly lucidly.

"The problem isn't the English," Glyn said. "It's the Welsh, the ones that leave and then come back again. They think they're Welsh but they can't speak the language."

"Is Welsh your first language?" I asked.

"Aye, lad."

"And you've lived here all your life?"

"Yes. It used to be something here. You could get whatever you wanted."

"But not anymore?"

"No."

He looked soulfully out of the window and then contradicted himself.

"See that electrician's. You can buy anything you want there."

I tried my best but lots of what followed seemed not to form a coherent whole.

"Took it to Cockermouth and left it there...found its way back home here."

I had no idea what he was talking about. He continued for a bit and finished one ramble particularly strongly.

"Oh yes," he said," and parsnips!"

"Parsnips?"

"What?"

"You said parsnips."

"No, I didn't."

I decided to sit back and just let him speak

"They were true Driscolls. How can you tell? Easy. Piggy eyes. They all have piggy eyes. Ha! Took some Sellotape and fastened one eye open and one eye shut."

What the hell was he on about? It didn't matter. He sat there chuckling to himself. It was time for me to move on. I said goodbye and he seemed to wave but the conversation continued without me.

I'd expected a four mile climb to Betws-y-Coed but it was delightfully flat with a trailing hurricane and a brightening sky. The town Betws-y-Coed is a lovely spot on the edge of the Snowdonia National Park, surrounded by hills and mountains and built from slate with a river trickling through it. Its shops are a bit samey though. It's serviced by about 25 outdoor stores, all selling jumpers and hats and walking paraphernalia. People walk about the place using poles, even if they're just popping to the little supermarket.

The centre of town has a small railway station, an attractive, solid-looking, slate building covered in ivy. It looks like the sort of station people recreate when building models. And model railways are what this place is all about. On the station platform is a model railway shop that also houses the Railway Museum and £1.50 bought me entrance to a world of miniature wonder.

The rooms were loaded with train memorabilia but the fun was in the model railway towns built and displayed in what looked like huge fish tanks. The devil was in the details. A quick look at a complex scene showed an industrious, functioning town with hundreds of tiny, five millimetre-tall figures captured in a frozen moment of time while milling about their daily business. But look more closely and you could see the chaos that lurked just beneath the surface. A woman, a nurse perhaps, had collapsed outside the entrance to the main shop and yet no one was rushing to help her. A horse pulling a large load was in the middle of a stroke and tumbling to its left, about to carry its cart with it. Even worse, a tiny dog had done such an unwieldy piss against a lamppost that its entire structure had collapsed, taking out the man on the ice cream bicycle who now lay on his side in the road. And it wasn't just the people. At least two of the trains were derailed. The town was falling apart and death was everywhere. It was as though Quentin Tarantino had just turned up. Don't take your children. You'll give them nightmares.

After such horror I needed to calm my nerves. I took

myself to the Royal Oak Hotel and had a pint of Snowdonia Ale while all the walkers around me had tea and cakes. Fine, I thought, but they hadn't been to the Railway Museum.

Back at my tent I cooked up some food. A robin came for a fallen piece of instant noodle. I think he was disappointed it wasn't a worm. And then it started to hail great pea-sized stones. It sounded like they were trying to blast holes in my tent. I didn't have a hope in hell of hearing the radio. I opened the tent flap to look outside. The world had turned into a Nick Griffin wet dream; everything was completely white.

*

I awoke to a bulging roof. Was it possible to suffocate under the weight of hailstones or snow gathered on top of a tent? I checked online in a mountaineering forum. Someone said they'd never heard of anyone suffocating in such a way. Another asked how likely it would be that you'd hear from someone who'd actually suffocated. He had a point.

Last night's hail had been replaced by the default setting for Welsh weather, light rain. I set off towards Dolgellau, but hail quickly returned and so I took refuge in a trailer café full of truckers. During a chat with one of the guys I realised I wasn't on the road I thought I was. If I turned right at the next opportunity though, it would put me on a quieter and less hilly route to Dolgellau. I sipped my coffee and waited for the weather to improve, but this was Wales and so it didn't.

I set off again, made the turning and headed across naked moorland beside the River Conwy. The road was entirely free of cars. And then the weather went a bit bonkers. First, heavy rain came, the sort that hurts your head, and this was followed by hail and then snow, a proper blizzard, powder swirling confusedly in all directions. My fingers, or at least the two exposed by my gloves for doing fiddly jobs, were getting numb. I had visions of arriving at tonight's destination with blackened stumps.

And then, all of a sudden, through the grey-white powdery murk a patch of blue sky appeared in front of me and the white snow clouds overhead peeled back like a magic curtain. The falling snow was illuminated by bright sunlight, the straggling flakes from the cloud that had now passed overhead. The site was surreal, snow appearing to tumble from a blue sky. Three sleek, black stallions in a field beside the road, still wet from the last twenty minutes of mad precipitation, gleamed as though they'd gone a bit pervy and donned latex outfits for a bit of horseplay. The sun shone brightly for half an hour, the road ahead clear but the hillsides only metres above me covered in snow. Millions of tiny lambs appeared and disappeared as they played around the snowline. The frosted moorlands were beautiful, like no landscape I'd seen anywhere in the world.

By now I'd reached Gwynedd, the Welshest of Welsh counties, where 64% of locals are able to speak the local language. It is home to Snowdonia National Park, placed 181st in the Lonely Planet's World Top 500 Highlights. It's misplaced. Granada's over-rated Alhambra, with the repetitive Arabic scrawl on its internal walls because human figures are banned by Islamic dogma, comes in at number nine. Snowdonia is worthy of a much higher position than that.

My map of British stereotypes depicted Gwynedd as an area of both hillbillies and nervous sheep. You might think the sheep are nervous of the hillbillies, but apparently they've got bigger problems. In 2001, a mutilated ovine was found just outside Beddgelert, about ten miles west of my current location. But this wasn't the work of dogs or foxes. The animal had a large, oval-shaped hole through its left hip bone, cut with the precision of a surgeon. A bunch of over-excited amateur investigators got together, calling themselves the Animal Pathology Field Unit (APFU). They discovered another case in Wales where six ewes had their jaws ripped off and tongues severed with barely a drop of blood. Spooky, eh? There was only one obvious conclusion the APFU could draw. It was absolutely definitely the work of aliens. I mean, if you'd spent decades and billions of space dollars creating and navigating a vessel to discover inhabitable worlds somewhere in the infinite parsecs of the universe, wouldn't your first action once you arrived be to mess up some sheep? That's what I'd do.

As I approached Ffestiniog from the west I could see the next ominous weather system moving southwards. I was on its path. I'd originally planned to have some lunch at Ffestiniog but it was three miles in the wrong direction and would have taken me into the storm. I turned south and, believing myself to have a superhuman power that I clearly don't, decided to try and outrun it.

The weather was gaining on me but seemed to be moving off to my left. I figured I could take a break and followed a sign for a café into the village of Trawsfynydd, but when I asked an old woman where it was she told me it had long since closed down. It wasn't just English villages that were withering away. She recommended one at the Coed-y-Brenin Forest Park Visitors' Centre. I returned to the road, a few snowflakes dancing around my head.

After twenty minutes I arrived at the visitors' centre, a beautiful, semicircular café made of wood and glass, its huge windows looking down on the wooded valley far below. The place was full of walkers and bikers, taking a break from their exploration of the surrounding forest. Inspirational quotes lined the wall, in English and Welsh. One by Thoreau said life isn't about keeping busy – after all, ants are busy – but it's what we do with our time that's important. Ordering something from their menu seemed like a good use of my time. I chose a wonderful venison burger with redcurrant jelly, the deer taken from these very woods, and then followed that with a great flapjack, real cycling food. That dodgy weather system passed overhead and released its load on the windows in the roof. It was the sort of weather that favoured people called Noah. I was glad I wasn't out in that. And then the snow returned, and then a big, bright blue sky.

I finished my coffee. It seemed safe to return to the road, but the Weather Gods weren't going to let me off that easily. It immediately clouded over again and for the whole remaining six miles to Dolgellau it poured and poured, like God was chopping onions, or being forced to watch the entire back catalogue of Chuck Norris. Which seems unlikely, especially as the only person hard enough to force God to watch the entire back catalogue of Chuck Norris *is* Chuck Norris, and he isn't in heaven yet.

I opened the door to the campsite's reception and dripped on its floor.

"Camping!" I said with a big grin and outstretched arms as water trickled down my face and pooled at my feet.

The woman behind the desk wrinkled her face.

"Can't you stretch to a pod for one night?"

I wish. We completed the formalities. She put on her raincoat and made for the exit.

"You haven't been here before, have you?"

"Yes, about three years ago," I replied.

She smiled and took off her jacket.

"Good. Then I don't need to show you where everything is."

I opened the door to pouring rain but by the time I'd found my pitch and set up my tent it had stopped. The clouds cleared and for the rest of the evening the sun shone. I sat on a picnic bench slurping another Welsh beer, a lovely SA Gold from Brains brewery in Cardiff, staring at the distant peaks, until it got too cold and I climbed inside my tent and cooked

95

something warming.

Today had been about weather and its many varieties. Tomorrow, unfortunately, I'd get just one variety, the one Wales is most famous for.

*

I woke up to drizzle, the sort you know is going to hang around all day. I packed the tent away in the rain, the wetness adding to the weight of my luggage. Today I was going to find the Welsh branch of my family, some of whom I'd never met before, but before then I was going to get wet, very wet indeed.

Just outside Dolgellau, as the town turned to countryside, there was a sign at the side of the road: "Please Take Your Litter Home". Someone had decided to ignore this in grand if environmentally-selfish style. On the other side of the road's barrier was a mountain of rubbish bags topped by a bright pink Peppa Pig armchair.

Over the next hour, the rain didn't stop, but became harder and harder. Between Dolgellau and Dinas Mawddwy there is a slope with a fourteen per cent gradient. With the weight of my bike, anything over about eleven per cent saw me pushing it uphill. But today the heavy rain had lubricated my brakes to the point of uselessness and so, annoyingly, I also had to push the bike *down* the hill, otherwise I would've just kept gathering speed until I broke the sound barrier and then crashed into a wall and died.

To hide from the rain I rolled into the village of Dinas Mawddwy and headed for the very old Red Lion.

"Oh dear me," said Ange, the barmaid, as I entered the bar. She immediately went to the fireplace and set ablaze its pile of logs for me. While it gained momentum I leant against a radiator with a pint in my hand trying unsuccessfully to dry off.

The pub had a lot of character. It was built in the 12th

century and the main room has a 500-year-old, woodworm-eaten table.

"The health department said we couldn't let people eat off it," Ange said. "But we had it sealed and so it's alright now." I looked at the deep grooves in the wood. "It's a pain to clean if someone spills something though."

In the 16ᵗʰ century this area had been famous for the Gwylliaid Cochion Mawddwy, a gang of red-haired bandits, a bunch of outlaws exiled from elsewhere. Ange explained how the Red Lion had dealt with them.

"A while back the fireplace was ripped out and they discovered sickles embedded in the chimney. It stopped the bandits from getting in that way."

The fire started to roar and the room heated up. I was slowly drying off. A bloke entered the pub and sat at the bar. Behind him a delivery guy was rolling in barrels.

"That was you I just saw on the road pushing your bike, was it?" the first man asked. "You were lucky. Only saw you at the last minute."

I'd been wearing a luminous yellow slip over my jacket but the day was exceedingly murky and the strong wind frequently twisted it around. Obviously it wasn't up to the job, especially when numpties were driving in a rainstorm at seventy miles an hour, as the bloke later admitted. The delivery guy overheard him and disappeared to his van before returning.

"Here you go," he said, dropping on to my table a fluorescent orange jacket, one that zipped up. "I've got loads. Better safe than sorry." That was kind of him.

I got talking to Speedy Gonzalez. For a long time he and his wife had lived on a barge. Maybe he had just got sick of moving so slowly.

"We moved here a few years back and we love it. I love the peace."

I asked him what it was like living on a boat.

"It was great," he smiled. "But it wasn't all good. Sometimes idiots would untie the barge and it'd float away. More than once we came back from the supermarket to find the barge in the middle of the canal."

I told him I'd watched the fella negotiate that lock a few days ago. I didn't mention the psycho in the wheelchair.

"I remember a while back a group of Australian girls were on a boating holiday. They didn't have a clue. They got drunk and left a series of fourteen locks wide open. It took me hours to sort that mess out."

I had another pint and a lovely ham and horseradish baguette. I was completely dry by now, the weather had calmed a bit and so I ventured out. I was only two minutes down the road when the clouds burst again, this time even harder than before. And then, although it wasn't actually possible, it pumped up the volume, and just when I thought the skies couldn't throw a greater capacity of water at me, it turned out I was very, very wrong. I couldn't have been any wetter if I'd fallen in a lake.

I crossed into Powys, my fifteenth county, but I didn't actually care. What I wanted more than anything right now was a snorkel and some flippers.

Powys is the largest county in Wales by some considerable margin. It's over twice the size of second place Gwynedd. It's also the least densely populated area of anywhere south of Scotland with only 67 people per square mile. That's similar to a rainforest-filled nation like Brazil, or the audience of anything starring Joe Pasquale.

This county is the location of one of the few cases in British law when a chosen name has been deemed unfit for a new-born. The mother in question wanted to christen her daughter Cyanide, which she thought apparently to be a "lovely, pretty name". It didn't help that she also wanted to call the baby's twin brother Preacher. Not only was she prevented from christening her kids as she wanted, they got taken off her and put into care, which seems a bit harsh. Maybe sparsely populated places have a knack of choosing wayward names. The authorities in New Zealand have clamped down three times, blocking the names Anal and Sex Fruit and, for twins, Fish and Chips.

Eventually I reached Llangadfan and my aunt's café, Cwpan Pinc, the Welsh for Pink Cup. It's a family affair, run by my aunt Eirlys, uncle Malcolm and platinum-blonde Louise, their daughter-in-law. I was given a cup of steaming tea to warm my hands while I made puddles all over their floor.

The café was a great little place that also had a mini-supermarket in one half and tonight it was the venue for a talk. Eirlys and Louise were supposed to be working here then but they really wanted to take me to the pub and so they got the youthful 78-year-old teetotaller Malcolm to stand in for them.

In the pub, Wayne turned up, Louise's husband and my cousin. He preferred to be called Smudger. I'd met him just once before, when I was about six. He had a truly magnificent beard, a huge thing that made him look like he was eating a marmot.

Louise was telling me a story.

"I went to a *Body Shop* party and came home with a pig," she said.

"Eh? Was it just there, nestled amongst the papaya face creams and stuff?"

"No. The pig wasn't there. A woman at the party was saying she had this piglet and it was the last in the litter, and the mother pig was going for the chop, and she said if no one took this piglet it was going along with its mother."

"So she guilted you into taking the pig?"

"Smudge didn't want a pig but I took him to see her and we fell for her."

"And the mother was killed?"

"Yes. Lovely sausages, to be fair. Anyway, we went on holiday and took the dogs and there's this disease that pigs can get. And the vet said that the stress of being left alone triggered it. We nearly lost her. So the vet said, what you need is another pig. So that's how we got Albert."

"Two pigs?"

"Yes, but she hated Albert and tried to kill him. We had to separate them. And Albert had come from a big family and now he was pining."

"So he was stressed too?"

"So we had to go and get Patrick."

Now, as well as their three dogs and three pigs, they've got chickens, a lamb and all sorts of other creatures too.

Neither Malcolm and Eirlys, nor Louise and Smudger, use the Primrose part of our shared poncy surname. They are just plain old Smiths.

"You should use it," I said. "It's royal."

"Is it?" Eirlys asked.

"Probably not. But that's the story."

The tale my dad tells is that one of the Earls of Rosebery, whose surname is Primrose, knocked up a maid. Her subsequent baby would have been a little awkward for a man of his standing and so, nice bloke that he was, he kicked her out and all she could take from him was his name. The boy was christened as a Primrose-Smith. Unfortunately, no one has a single shred of evidence to verify this claim or has any idea when it might have happened. It's probably cobblers.

After the pub we went back to Louise and Smudger's house to meet the animals. Smudger gave me a glass of his home brew, which had an interesting treacly taste and was surprisingly good. I've made home brew. It never tasted like

100

that. In fact, it didn't really taste of beer at all.

It had been great to meet up with this branch of the family. I'd had a good laugh and, Malcolm aside, they appeared to possess the Primrose-Smith's dangerously enthusiastic appreciation of alcohol. After two and a half weeks of going to sleep as soon as night descended it came as a bit of a shock to crawl into bed at three in the morning.

*

The next morning I was back at the café, sitting across from Kevin – Smudger's brother – and tucking into a Big Ed, the café's mega-breakfast, named after one of Smudger's friends and the breakfast's biggest fan who'd died way too young in a road accident.

As a leaving gift, Eirlys packed me a food parcel that included some lovely, thick ham sandwiches, three hard-boiled duck eggs, some more bacon and sausage – as if the breakfast hadn't been enough – two flapjacks and a cellophane-wrapped assortment of crisps. It also contained a card for my birthday in three weeks' time with strict instructions not to open it until then.

We said our goodbyes and Kevin and I cycled off. He was going to cycle with me as far as Llandrindod Wells, the county town of Powys and one-time drink-driving capital of Britain.

Kevin is a keen cyclist and has the lean physique of one who puts in the miles. Over the forty or so we did today, he developed a catchphrase: "I don't remember it being as steep as this." He guided us away from the main roads and patched together a bucolic route I'd have struggled to find on my own, mostly because I would have gone around the hills rather than over ever single one we could find.

The last 23 miles on the A483 from Newtown, Kevin's home, had a wiggly beginning and so Kevin suggested a shortcut to bypass the bends. It wasn't long before he was back to his old theme.

"This is a lot steeper than I remember."

Cheers, Kev.

The route to Llandrindod Wells was gorgeous. The weather had finally sorted itself out and a weak sun shone in the sky. The road was lined with tall pines deep into the hills.

"This could easily be Canada," I said, taking in the scenery.

We pulled up in town. Kevin would have to turn around and repeat these 23 miles but, in order to respect its dubious "capital" honour, we first stopped for a pint.

It was in 2014 that Llandrindod Wells was named the drink-driving capital of Britain. Obviously, the deep shame meant the locals had to raise their game and do something about this. They put a plan into action that clearly worked. In 2015, after all their effort, they were no longer the worst offenders in the country. No, in that year they came second, pipped to the number one spot by Cheshire's Crewe. To be fair to the residents of Llandrindod Wells, I suspect the only reason the police catch so many drink-drivers is because it's the only crime committed around here. It's a very quiet place.

Kevin turned around and headed home while I went to find a campsite in nearby Howey. It was another desperately cold night, wearing everything I had with me. What was going on with the weather? It was nearly May and winter didn't show any signs of relenting.

I'd already seen some lovely parts of Wales but the prettiest road yet was just around the corner. That is, if I could get there without being attacked by White Walkers.

Chapter 5: The Pass of Lost Existence

Ceredigion, Pembrokeshire, Carmarthenshire, Swansea, Neath Port Talbot and Bridgend

After a breakfast of coffee and hard-boiled duck eggs I set off into a beautiful if chilly morning. I was heading westwards towards Aberystwyth, Britain's most neurotic town, according to the Gloucestershire Echo. Just south of Rhayader I passed the site of the Landed festival. A young woman standing at the entrance was dressed in a large carpet. Since very little of my wardrobe is made of floor coverings I figured it probably wasn't my kind of event.

I turned on to one of Britain's loneliest and loveliest roads. Coaches and HGVs are banned entirely from it and it seemed to be shunned by motorists too. It was just me, my bike and the wind. I climbed over the Cambrian Mountains through the Elan Valley. The contours narrowed and I had to push, but it didn't matter. The scenery compensated. A series of waterfalls lined the roadside, and then there came a collection of humps, hills of green, yellow and brown. At the top I stopped and surveyed the land. Apart from the road, dry stone walls and the odd wind turbine there was no sign of humanity. For eighteen miles the world was mine alone. The route took me into the county of Ceredigion, Wales's second least populated region, but with a headcount per square mile almost twice that of Powys. Wherever these heads were, they weren't here.

Eventually I stumbled upon mankind in the form of the village with a vowel allergy, Cwmystwyth. Remnants of the old silver, lead and zinc mines lay at the side of the road. This area had been mined for 4,000 years but the industry reached its peak in the second half of the 19th century. This brought prosperity to Ceredigion, a necessary injection to replace farming that had been in serious decline for some time. The work was hard and the average lifespan of a miner was only 32 years, most suffering an early death from lead poisoning. As seems to be the theme for the toilers of Wales, the good times didn't last long and the metals soon became unprofitable to mine. Many people moved to south Wales where there was at least some work mining an equally dangerous commodity. These hills were left emptier than a politician's promise.

The road started to climb again. At the top of the hill at Penbwlchbodcoll I came to a stone archway, imaginatively called The Arch. To be honest, it's not that impressive since it spans nothing and just sits pointlessly at the side of the B4574. It was built to commemorate the golden jubilee of George III who, to show his gratitude, instantly went raving mad. But forget the arch. The best thing about this bit of Wales is that this hill crossing has a name right out of *Lord of the Rings*. It's called The Pass of Lost Existence. I'm not sure whose or what's existence was lost although, given the frosty wind, it could soon be the end of my nose.

I cycled down to Devil's Bridge, a village that takes its name from a series of three bridges built on top of each other, a 1901 iron bridge over a 1753 stone bridge over the original 12th century one. We'd come across a bridge supposedly built by the devil in France last year on our £1-a-day ride. This was another. Satan was quite the architect.

There was an ice cream shop in the village. Its sign asked passers-by "Do you want an ice cream?" From the lack of customers on this frigid morning, the answer was an emphatic "Sod off!"

I now turned south along a wearying road of ups and downs. I stopped in Tregaron in what felt like the first proper town I'd seen all day, but I'd clearly been deprived of human contact since it only has a population of a thousand. Not much seems to happen here although in 1977 a huge stash of LSD was discovered in a nearby cottage. Oh yes, and the Talbot Hotel pub supposedly has an elephant buried in its back garden. Maybe those two things are connected.

I needed to find somewhere to stay and so I asked two old women if there was a campsite nearby. One of them replied in Welsh. I said I didn't understand.

"You should speak Welsh," she replied.

"But I'm English."

"Oh, I thought I heard a Welsh accent," she said.

But she had a point. While cycling around Europe I'd tried to learn a little bit of every language I'd come across. Why hadn't I done the same for Welsh? Probably because everyone speaks English. But then again, that's almost true of the Netherlands and Germany.

I popped into a newsagent's. The bloke in charge said the campsite in town had closed down. I told him I remembered one from a trip long ago near Lampeter. He said he drove the Tregaron-Lampeter road every day and had never seen it. Maybe I'd made it up.

I went through the long, drawn-out process of booting up my Samsung and, with weakening batteries, searched for the site. Sure enough it was there, just where I thought. So I did some shopping and added extra weight to the panniers.

Outside the shop were two other cyclists, the lean and Lycraed type. They were doing an organised, one-day, four-hundred kilometre ride from and to Chepstow. They told me they'd finish at around six in the morning, fourteen hours from now.

"Is that fun?" I asked. "It doesn't sound like fun."

"Some of it is Type 1 fun," he replied. "It feels like fun while you're doing it. But most of it is Type 2 fun. It's only fun when you look back on it."

"But not while you're actually doing it?"

"No. Absolutely not."

I knew what he meant. I thought this trip had been Type 1 fun from start to finish – see how quickly you forget the drenchings and the busy roads – but previous trips hadn't. You don't remember the bad bits, which is good news for the cycle touring industry because otherwise no one would get beyond their first ride. I lost my cycle touring virginity in 2009 over 1,600 miles from the Isle of Man to the south of Spain. I remember it now as one of the best months of my life. I recently found a comment I'd made on a cycling forum at the very moment I'd finished it. I'd written that I wanted to smash my bike into a million pieces. It must have been mostly Type 2 fun.

I cycled down the road to the campsite and went up its long lane. There was no one about. Two dogs appeared and barked angrily at me. One of them looked like he meant business. I adopted the pose of Tarzan and shouted "Ungawa!" a few times but he clearly didn't speak the language of the jungle. He just kept barking at me.

I knocked at the farmhouse door but no one was in. The field that had hosted tents when I was here last now sat fenced off, full of cows. I went to the site's bathroom and found a visitor's book. There were no entries since the end of last summer and the sinks had more cobwebs than Bruce Forsyth's joke book.

I decided to use the last of my battery to phone the site's number. Perhaps they just hadn't found anyone stupid enough to want to camp at these temperatures this year. Unfortunately, there was no phone signal. I hung around for twenty minutes but realised this was pointless. I could wait for three hours and then be told the site had actually closed down. Then I'd have to hunt for somewhere else in the dark.

Or maybe they'd never come back. Perhaps there'd been a zombie apocalypse.

I continued on to Lampeter. On the way I saw another cyclist doing that organised four hundred kilometre ride. He was considerably chubbier than the other two and looked absolutely knackered. He didn't look as though he was even having Type 2 fun.

"I won't get home until eight in the morning," he said.

"Don't you need to sleep?"

"I might grab an hour in a bus shelter," he replied.

"You make it sound so glamorous."

Lampeter is the smallest university town in Britain. It must be a shock to end up here if you haven't done your research and take whatever course you can via the university clearing system. Expecting three years of debauched city life, its population of 2,000 and six pubs might make you think you've got off at the wrong stop.

I'd already done too many miles today, and over some mountainous terrain with a strong headwind, but it looked like I'd have to do seventeen more, all the way to Newcastle Emlyn. Then, about three miles down the endless lanes of central Wales, I saw a camping sign in a garden. Officially it was only a place for caravans but since no one else was here the friendly owners let me on. I set up the tent in the field next to their house under the watchful eye of two hundred sheep. I opened the tent's flat, collapsed inside and slept the sleep of Rip Van Winkle.

*

The campsite had been a bargain £4 and the weather forecast for today, the first day of May, was awful. After yesterday's extra miles, and while I was already stationed somewhere so cheap, I decided to have a day off, my first in three weeks.

The campsite's bathroom was in the house and, when I

went inside, Emyr the site owner spotted me and asked if I wanted a cup of tea. To this was added toast with his wife Gillian's home-made rhubarb jam. I sat at their kitchen table with the couple and their daughter while they gave me suggestions of local places to visit. This was already my favourite campsite so far.

I did very little all day. During a rare dry spell I popped out to visit a lovely, little church in Llanwenog that Emyr had recommended. It was full of wooden carvings made by a Belgian refugee, Joseph Reubens, during the First World War. But mostly I slept or listened to the radio or, when this was impossible, to the foul weather outside. I'd chosen a great day to do nothing. Riding in this would have required a wet suit.

*

In the morning it was still raining, just as it had done all night long. I got going late when it seemed to ease off a little but it redoubled its efforts shortly after I set off and I got another lovely Welsh soaking.

Emyr had told me the road was pretty much flat all the way to Newcastle Emlyn, and he was right as long as you ignored the repeated 16% up-and-downs, one for each river the road crossed.

Lots of gardens I passed had posters up for the imminent local elections. Many of them supported the Welsh Conservatives. I didn't think Wales had any conservatives. And there were even signs for the Welsh Liberal Democrats. I didn't think *anywhere* had LibDems any more.

The weather brightened up, little patches of blue in the sky above me. A few miles short of Newcastle Emlyn was one of Emyr and Gillian's suggestions, the West Wales Museum of Children. It was run by a large woman, a farmer's wife type who barely opened her eyes as she spoke. At first I thought she was blind but then she made some derisory comment about my appearance. In her defence, I was a bit of a sweaty mess.

She told me what I'd find in each room and also about their collection of lovespoons, a tradition dating from the 17th century when a suitor would carve intricate designs in lime, birch or oak to impress the local pretty girl. Who needs Tinder when you know the way to a woman's heart is massive wooden cutlery?

The museum's toy collection was expansive and the displays covering each decade of the 20th century brought back a Tonka Dump Truck full of memories. There was a large collection of Action Man figures. My brother Dave and I had owned a few. With no babies in the family left to provide for, one Christmas my grandma knitted us some outfits for our little plastic fellas. The blue and white jumper was fine – it made him look like a sailor – but ours were the only Action Men in the world with pink berets and cerise woollen underpants. He really didn't have the knees for it.

There were plenty of other action figures too. It was clear little effort had gone into making the Spice Girls dolls. The band members all had identical faces, their hair and outfits – the Union Jack dress or the leopard print leggings – the only thing to set them apart. And there were loads of Sindy dolls, the low-rent Barbie. The Virgin Atlantic Flight Attendant Sindy also included a bikini. #everydaysexism

Some of the action figures were baffling. Under what circumstance would anyone want a figure of The Osbournes except maybe to melt its heads with a blowtorch? And why did Gillian Anderson's X-Files doll come with an additional figure wrapped in a white body bag with the ankles and neck creepily cable-tied? And was a Barry Gibb action figure ever necessary? Maybe he just existed to give Action Man someone to beat up between unnecessary Middle East regime-changing campaigns.

They also had two bits of electronica that I'd raved about.

Merlin was a 1970s red moulded thing about the size of an early mobile phone on which you played crap games. It had the processing capability of a door bell. And the Stylophone was wrong even before you attached the name Rolf Harris to it. I'd once used mine to perform *Amazing Grace* for my primary school's Christmas show. I don't know why I didn't get my head kicked in. It sounds terrible, like an electronic bagpipe that's simultaneously nasal and scratchy, the noise your fillings would make if you were creatively electrocuted by the Stasi.

There were thousands of tiny toy soldiers, some I remembered owning but had completely forgotten about, and enough scary dolls to fuel a lifetime of nightmares. For an hour I was whisked back to my childhood and it was wonderful.

The sun was properly out by now, a very un-Welsh gesture on this Bank Holiday Monday. I cycled under its warming rays through Newcastle Emlyn and then on to Cenarth. I'd planned to reach Fishguard today but figured an afternoon in the sun on this freak warm afternoon would be a good opportunity to dry out my sodden tent as well as uncrinkle the ends of my fingers for the first time since I'd hit Wales.

Right in the centre of little Cenarth was a campsite. I rolled inside and looked for reception, and then I saw the sign. The reception was half a mile away, and for the gradient involved to reach it it may as well have been half a mile straight up. When I finally found the farmhouse in question they wanted £15, a bit of light robbery after yesterday's bargain site.

But it was a nice spot, with the River Teifi running beside it. A man was standing in the water, thigh-deep, fly-fishing. Over the river was an attractive, old stone bridge. It had large circular holes cut into its supports so that flood water would run through it rather than over the road.

Cenarth is famous for coracles, that unstable craft made of willow that's supposed to sit on the water rather than in it. They are best used when winds are light and tides are elsewhere. The National Coracle Centre is here in Cenarth but, as this was a Bank Holiday, it was closed. It wasn't the only thing. The nearest open shop was all the way back in Newcastle Emlyn. Even the garage was shut. But luckily, after the previous two nights of cheap camping, there were a few coins to spare for dinner in the White Hart pub. I chose a chicken breast covered in bacon, cheese and barbecue sauce with fat home-made chips washed down with a couple of pints of real ale. This was definitely Type 1 fun.

*

Last night's campsite was the first one to provide a key to its toilet block, as well as being the only one whose reception was at the top of a mountain and, of course, the key had to be returned. I packed away and pushed the bike up the hill for a second time. A woman answered the door. It had been a fella last time.

"When I heard we had a cyclist I was going to come down for the key," she said.

I thanked her, though I'm not sure why, given that she didn't actually come down.

My map showed several options regarding my route to one of today's destinations.

"What's the easiest way to Fishguard?" I asked.

"On a bike? There isn't one. It's a hill whichever way you go."

"Oh well."

She thought for a second.

"Stick your bike in our pickup and I'll take you to the top," she said.

"Nah, thanks, but that's cheating."

"Go on, no one will know."

I smiled.

"I'll know."

The hill was big but not terrible. It wasn't made any easier by my back wheel. I'd discovered one of its spokes was trying to remove itself and the wheel was buckled enough to rub, adding extra friction. However, the effort was alleviated by my surroundings. Flowers were beginning to emerge by now, speckling the grass verges along the side of the road with purple and yellow, like a bruise, but, y'know, nicer.

I had entered one of the loveliest parts of Wales, a county in the south-west corner whose entire coast is a National Park, Pembrokeshire. Soon after, I arrived at Castell Henllys, another one of Emyr's recommendations, where an iron age fort has been recreated.

"That's bad timing," said the young woman on the till. "The actors have just this minute gone for lunch."

That was a bit inauthentic. They should have been up there roasting a wild boar or something.

It was a lovely place to be on a sunny afternoon. A path through a herb garden took me to five yurt-like huts with woven roofs built exactly on the site of the original settlement. Inside, the roofs of the huts were black with soot. They realised that if they put a hole in the top then their fires grew too large, so they didn't bother. Instead the places just filled with smoke. As a bonus, the roof space collected carbon dioxide that killed the woodworm but, occasionally, the human inhabitants too.

One hut was much grander than the others but it was still amazing to think that the chieftains who ruled here lived in such squalor when, at the same time, Greeks had classical Athens. While lowly Socrates was philosophizing in the vast, Doric-columnned marble of the city state's forum, the chieftains of Wales were here playing "Whose Bone Is This?" and eating cockroach fritters.

I continued on my way and arrived at the pretty lower harbour of Fishguard. It was nice to see the sea for the first time since Abergele. The sun was gently heating the day to something approaching actual warmth and, as a result, I fancied an ice cream. I popped into a café and bought a small tub called Celtic Crunch. I looked at the ingredients, which included Amaretto, butterscotch and chocolate, none of which were available to my Iron Age friends, but never let authenticity get in the way of marketing.

My dodgy back wheel wasn't my only mechanical problem. I was five miles the other side of Fishguard, far from any settlement, when my chain snapped. Deep joy! It was still ten miles to St Davids. I hadn't seen a campsite nor a bicycle shop in Fishguard whereas I knew St Davids had at least somewhere to pitch up. I decided to push forward.

After whizzing along with the wind in my hair at a consistent twelve miles an hour for the last few weeks, the sudden slow plod of walking was tedious. Within a mile I was bored and suddenly remembered I'd bought a spare chain link a few years earlier. Was it still in my pannier? Amazingly, it was. I leant my bike against the dry stone wall of a farm, put the chain into position, attempted to click the link shut and then, moronically, dropped both pieces of it into the dust and gravel on the ground. I found the first half of the link almost immediately, but the other piece was nowhere to be seen. It had clearly fallen through a worm hole and was now lying on the surface of a distant planet.

Over the farm wall some blokes were messing about with a car. I approached them and told them what I'd done. I wondered if they had a metal detector but because this wasn't 1973 they obviously didn't. They did, however, come out to help me look, but after five minutes they gave up, clearly thinking I was some sort of time-wasting nutter. I kept searching. It didn't help that I'd moved the bike out of the

113

way to make it easier to search the ground and now I couldn't remember exactly where I'd dropped the link. In the end I scraped all the dust and gravel from a two metre wide circle into a big pile and searched the whole lot, millimetre by millimetre. An hour later I found it.

I clipped the chain into position. It was as good as new, except that there was a weird rubbing sound. I looked at the chain and couldn't see where the noise was coming from. But at least now I wouldn't have to push the remaining nine miles.

Since 1994, St Davids is officially Britain's smallest city by both size and population. In reality it's a village with a cathedral. You walk through quaint streets filled with little shops and then suddenly you see it below you, a building out of all proportion to its surroundings, like someone deciding to build the Gherkin in a window box.

Some believe the cathedral contains the bones of St David, the patron saint of Wales, although carbon dating says they're only 12th century whereas St David lived six hundred years earlier. Disregarding such trivial detail, the cathedral became an important pilgrimage destination, worth 50% of a trip to Rome or 33% of one to Jerusalem in God's eyes, according to the people who knew these things, or made them up on His behalf.

As far as sainthood goes, young David got off to a good start by being the child of a holy-sounding king called Sanctus and a nun. He was also supposedly born during a violent storm, but then again so is everybody in Wales.

To become a saint you must have performed at least two miracles. By rights, for keeping Blackburn Rovers in the Premier League during the 2008-9 and 2009-10 seasons, Sam Allardyce is in with a shout. St David had a bagful. He did all the normal, mundane stuff like resurrecting kids by splashing them with tears and de-blinding old fellas but his most famous one was quite showy. He was addressing a large crowd but couldn't be heard. A dove landed on his shoulder and then the ground beneath him rose up to form a hill to aid his performance. That would have been pretty impressive back then, but he would still have had a problem with amplification. Surely a more effective miracle would have been to magic up an auditorium and a decent Powerpoint presentation.

A sign outside the cathedral said that visiting time was until five thirty. Thanks to examining a massive pile of dust all afternoon it was now six. I stuck my head in the door and could see a service, an evensong, in the distance and decided to leave them to it.

Outside, in the cathedral grounds, a guy was playing a ukelele. I hung around and listened for a bit but it was clear he wasn't going to do any George Formby.

At the campsite I tried to fix the rubbing chain by turning the bike upside down, but the back wheel was buckled too badly to turn the pedals by hand. This bike needed professional attention, or at least the attention of someone who knew what the hell they were doing.

*

The sixteen miles to Haverfordwest and the nearest bicycle repair place took a slow two hours thanks to a strong headwind, the rubbing wheel, plenty of hills and frequent rubbish surfaces. Annoyingly, the route went from being relatively high all the way down to the coast at Newgale although there seemed to be nothing there to warrant the descent but a surf shop. Still, there was no denying the Pembrokeshire coast was spectacular.

In Haverfordwest, in the absence of any easy-to-find local bike shop, I stumbled upon a Halfords. It put its car spares on the ground floor and its bike repair on the first floor, which was hardly convenient with a loaded bike, especially when it wouldn't fit into their tiny lift. I removed the panniers and hid them in a corner of the store before lugging the bike upstairs. They were going to see what was wrong with the chain and, at the same time, replace the back wheel. I had to come back in an hour.

The guy on the bike desk had recommended Morrison's café next door as somewhere cheap and nearby to wait. I got a coffee and a pastry, and then saw they did eggs Benedict - one of my favourites – and so had that as well. I still hadn't killed enough time. I bought a newspaper and returned to the busy café for a Coke. With no other seats available a bloke asked if he and his wife and baby could share my table. They sat there for a few minutes but as soon as another one became available they scarpered. I suspect my now funky trainers were responsible for their hasty departure.

I returned to Halfords but the bike wasn't ready. It was hardly surprising. They had two guys on the desk to answer the phone and serve customers as well as do bike repairs. They were constantly interrupted.

"I'm not sure how you got here," said the repairman. "When we took the tyre off, your wheel fell to pieces."

I spoke to another member of staff there after he'd asked about my ride.

"There's a local tree around here that's supposedly the birthplace of Merlin," he said.

"But Merlin didn't actually exist, did he?"

He shrugged his shoulders and continued.

"There was a legend that if they chopped the tree down then there'd be a great flood."

"And did they chop it down?"

"Yeah, and there was a flood and it killed a few people."

"So the prophesy came true?"

"Yeah, it was great!" he laughed. Then he realised what he'd said and sobered up. "Well, not the dead people part."

The bike was eventually finished and I set off. With a fully functioning back wheel I floated along the roads. There was still a noise coming from the chain though and life on the A40 was fairly miserable for cyclists. It had a grate every ten metres or so, but they'd sunk over time and the tarmac around them had cracked, making each one a little death trap and forcing me farther out into the traffic than any life-loving cyclist would ever want to be.

County number eighteen was Carmarthenshire. Having discovered there were two campsites nearby I loaded the bike with some shopping at St Clears. Unfortunately, after lugging myself up a hill, I found the first site had closed down and was up for sale. The sign showing the way to the second one looked discouragingly old. Despite there being only one road on which it could've been, over loads of steep hills, I never found it. With no other option I cycled the additional ten miles into Carmarthen and a few miles beyond to find a field covered in caravans. I knocked on the door of the attached house. An old fella answered it

"Could I camp here for the night please?"

"Eh?" said the old man.

"Camping?"

He looked blank.

"Is this the house for the campsite?"

"The campsite?"

"Yes, there's a campsite just there, behind your house."

"What?"

"A campsite."

"Oh yes, the campsite," he finally said.

"So this is the right place?"

"Yes."

I didn't know what all that was about. Maybe I'd just woken him from this winter's hibernation, or perhaps he'd been doing meth.

117

"Have you got showers and stuff? I didn't see any."

"Nah. No shower. There's a toilet."

"Ah, right." It had been a warm day and after all the hills I needed a wash but it'd have to wait. "How much is it?"

"Fifteen pounds."

"Wow, that's a bit steep for a site with no showers."

"I have to pay rates for that field. And you're paying for the location," he replied.

To be honest it didn't seem like a great location.

"Is there a pub nearby or something?"

"No."

"Any shops?"

"No."

"Anything?"

"There's the castle."

"That's miles away," I said.

He shrugged. I thought for a moment.

"I can do it for fourteen," he said.

It was still too much but I didn't want to cycle any further after today's hills and headwinds. I paid up, set up the tent and realised there was no one else in any of those caravans. It looked like I was paying his rates for the entire site.

*

Oh, what a beautiful morning! The sun was shining and the birds celebrated that – at last – spring was finally here. Only a few miles down the road was the National Botanical Garden of Wales. I popped inside for a look.

On its 568-acre site they have a vegetable garden, an apothecary, a double-walled flower garden, a tropical greenhouse and that giant bubble dome thing that enclosed Springfield in Simpsons The Movie. At 95 metres long and 55 metres wide it's the largest single-span greenhouse in the world and houses rare and, in some cases, lost species of plants from each continent. It's mightily impressive.

Unfortunately, in 2015, the site made a £300,000 loss and its funding is to be reduced further still. It needs more visitors. Go and see it while you can. It's well worth it.

I learnt about the dragon tree and its bright red sap, that Cape Town's Table Mountain has more plant species than the whole of Britain, that the chaparral and its dormant seeds can survive fire, and that a mobility scooter can go really fast on a slight downhill. The old fella even screamed out an exhilarated "Wheeeeee!"

The whole place made me pine for the garden we'd had as children. Although it was obviously nothing on this scale it had seemed huge to us as little kids, the top part a flat, well-manicured lawn about the size of half a tennis court with shrubs and flowers and then a slope of semi-abandoned land terminating in a pond my then ten-year-old brother had dug and filled with frogs and newts. One of my more morose, early teenage friends, Mark, used to go down there by himself and stare into the black water for hours contemplating the misery of existence. Those were happy childhood memories of Britain. Well, probably not for Mark.

After a couple of hours of smelling flowers and watching death-defying geriatrics I continued. The route took me up a giant hill through a village that would have been aptly named had I been travelling in the opposite direction, Tumble.

Through an afternoon of lanes and woods I arrived just north of the town of Llanelli and found a campsite farm up a hill. I set up my tent and then walked into town. I was looking for a beer and I found some in the Greyhound, next to its brewery, Felinfeol, pronounced "Feeling Foul", perhaps an appropriate name for anyone partaking too excessively.

There were a few people dotted around inside including a large Welshman, Justin, sitting at the bar.

"Yes, see, I did Land's End to John o'Groats 'bout five year ago," he said in a strong Welsh accent. He was very enthusiastic and showed me photos he had on his phone. "Course I were a lot slimmer then. Great fun though."

The lounge was slowly starting to empty. Eventually Justin had to leave too.

"Bet you're glad he's gone," said another fella. I didn't manage a response before he continued. "He's a pillock."

Another man entered the pub. He was wearing orange hi-vis and was very tanned, as though he worked outdoors in a country considerably warmer than this one.

"Who are we talking about?" he asked.

"Justin."

"Yeah. He's a right dick."

He'd seemed alright to me.

"Anyway, you'll be fine on your bike," he said. "We've got this sunny weather for a month."

The last time I'd cycled through this land and experienced a so-called Welsh heatwave it had managed a single day.

*

I set off at ten and, on flat roads, an hour and a quarter later reached Swansea. This city is a whole host of British capitals: the bingo capital of Britain, the cooked breakfast capital, the knotweed capital, whatever the hell that means, and, more amusingly, the casual sex capital.

Swansea was my first of the eleven new, tiny counties in Wales's south-east. Although it's one of the largest of these, it's still smaller than Rutland, the smallest county in England outside of the City of London's square mile. In order to see them all, the next few days would see me cycling a more wiggly route than of late, up and down the Valleys.

Approaching the city I was nearly wiped out by a bus. So far, the driving in Britain had been unusually terror-free. My mum, who has predicted my death before every other bike ride, hadn't given this one a moment's worry despite Britain's statistically murderous roads; it's second only to Portugal for the number of deaths per cycle journey made. And as always, as in this case, the commercial drivers, the ones supposedly with the most experience, were the worst.

That stretch of dual carriageway on the way into Swansea was once the location of possibly the most heinous crime in British history. In 2011 a man called Andre Varciana threw a chicken bone at his friend. Unwisely, he launched it across the two-laned road in front of an unmarked police car, which performed an emergency stop and caused a four-car pile-up. The bone thrower got off lightly. He only had to pay £85 costs in a case the judge described as the most bizarre he'd ever known. I looked online expecting a headline writers' field day – y'know, things like "Why Did The Chicken Cross The Road?", "Chicken Man Given Poultry Fine" or "All KFC'ed Up!" – but it seemed the press weren't going to be egged on so easily.

It wasn't the only interesting crime to happen in Swansea in the last few years. In 2013, a newly married couple, the Barnetts, went on a bender before returning to their room at the five-star Morgans Hotel. They then proceeded to steal just about everything inside it, including slippers, dressing gowns, linen sheets, the entire contents of the minibar, the telephone and the paintings on the walls. They even passed the flat-screen telly out of the window. They'd have taken the bed and carpet too if only they'd had a bigger van. Their plan was rumbled when, checking out, they were presented with a bill for a pay-per-view movie.

"But our room doesn't have a telly," Mr Barnett argued. Which was true. But only since very recently.

The condition of the roads into Swansea is awful, the worst yet, broken and cracked and giving the bike a right hammering. That future Prime Minister in the double-decker bus café just before Ludlow had told me Wales took loads of EU money for roads – he was pro-Brexit and so I wasn't sure why he was so down on money finding its way back here, but he was – but if that were true then none of it had ended up in Swansea.

In the town centre I saw a short bloke in a massively oversized, dark flak jacket wearing a black face mask. He looked like he was auditioning for a part in a new Mortal Kombat movie, a sort of goth Scorpion. I figured I'd give him a wide berth. I've played that game. I didn't want him grabbing my head and pulling my spine out of my body.

Cycling along the coastal cycle path through Swansea and out past the marina was joyous. And then it turned into what seemed like a giant industrial estate and, oddly out of place, there was a museum with a sign that said something like "Go Back In Time To 1940", which seemed a bit cruel. If I were going back in time, 1940 wouldn't be a year I'd have chosen.

I paid a fiver and went into the war museum. I was the only one there. Its Anderson shelter, with an air raid siren blaring in the background, was chilling. But as well as bringing home the horrors of war it also made you realise the horrors of 1940s houses and their grim furnishings.

There was an interesting collection of wartime posters. One of them seemed to put a little too much trust in God for my liking. I mean, even if He existed, how would you know He was on your side?

"The secret of steadiness and inner strength is to listen to God and do what He says. God speaks directly to the heart of every man and woman who is prepared to listen and obey. Write down the thoughts He gives you. His voice can be heard wherever you are, in the home, in the factory, in the air-raid shelter, in the first-aid post."

I think the author was confusing God with schizophrenia.

There was another one about wasting food that said, "Better Pot Luck with Churchill than Humble Pie with Hitler." That wasn't exactly confidence boosting.

They had a nice collection of kit, shells and gas masks and a cookbook detailing recipes that could be made from war rations, like the original Jack Munroe.

I continued into Port Talbot, in the next countylet of Neath Port Talbot, the largest of these little sections of Wales. The town was once dubbed "the wife-stealing capital of Britain" although it was only described thus by one bloke who was sick of being cuckolded rather than by any scientific body like, say, The Sun. Port Talbot is also one of the five places in Britain you're most likely to find a blonde. Its Superdrug apparently sells double the amount of blonde hair dye than any other product.

From a distance Port Talbot is a fairly hideous place, despite all the blondes, but rather than cycle past as I'd done when we came this way last year, this time I wanted to find another museum, one I'd suspected to be a myth, the Baked Bean Museum. I found its location on my phone and headed to it, but the route took me into a road that contained nothing but council flats. Maybe the museum was just some bloke's spare room housing a collection of tins, but without a sign outside, I'd never know which one it was. Or maybe my phone was playing up. But at least I was now back on the coast and the front of Port Talbot was a vast improvement on its other aspects.

I contemplated stealing a wife or two but time was getting on and I decided instead to return to the cycle path I'd followed since Swansea, National Cycle Route 4. In the past, some of these NCR paths have had a tendency to throw up some weirdnesses, like ridiculously steep hills when a flatter option is just around the corner, or a three-mile detour to miss a one hundred metre stretch of quiet A-road. Today would be no different. After cycling around a labyrinth of urban decay, I found myself on a boulder-strewn path and then through some woods before being presented by an iron gate so narrow I had to remove all the bags from my bike. The route continued high on a hill on a tiny path that didn't seem like cyclists should be on it, before another iron gate had me stripping the bike for a second time.

Eventually I reached another town and county, Bridgend. Sadly, it's another place reported as the suicide capital of Britain, but here with good reason. In the ten years to 2006, there was a fairly normal average of three suicides a year. However, over the next six years, 79 people in this tiny county committed suicide, mostly young people and almost exclusively by hanging. None of the deaths are linked, except by the possibility of copycat behaviour, but it hasn't stopped people reaching for more occult explanations.

I appreciate I've finished this chapter on a bit of a downer. I'm sorry about that. Maybe it'll cheer you up to learn that tomorrow I have a run-in with the police.

Chapter 6: Crashing the time machine

Vale of Glamorgan, Cardiff, Rhondda Cynon Taf, Merthyr Tydfil, Caerphilly, Blaenau Gwent, Torfaen, Newport and Monmouthshire

On a grey morning I packed away my tent, left the campsite and cycled to the end of the lane. I was meeting Sarah today and because she was coming from several miles away I was expecting to have to wait for a while, but as I reached the junction, there she was, a few metres down the road and fast approaching, a pretty blonde woman in pink Lycra on a sleek racing bike. I knew nothing about her except that she was a cyclist. She was going to give me a tour.

I rode beside Sarah as we cycled towards Porthcawl. She told me about a special local event there. Just as you might expect for a small Welsh seaside town, Porthcawl is the venue of one of Europe's largest annual Elvis Presley conventions. Thousands of fans of The King descend on the Porthcawl Elvis Festival every September and get all shook up. Sarah knew it through her work; she'd experienced just about the most dramatic career change it was possible to have.

"You went from primary school teacher to policewoman?" I asked, amazed. I've never understood why anyone would want to be in the police force.

"Yes, for six years now."

"You must have seen some unpleasant things?"

Sarah told me a story of a suicide. He'd thrown himself in front of a fast train.

"We were picking up bits of him for a mile." I pulled a face. "Finding a foot in a shoe is something I don't really want to do again." But other events were even more terrible. "The

125

worst thing was telling the mum of a six-year-old that he was dead. He'd run out between two parked cars."

She still wasn't convincing me that this was a wise career choice.

Despite her slender figure Sarah was a tough cookie.

"I've just had a replacement crown," she said. "Some charmer head-butted me and cracked my tooth."

She'd done some riot control and the police weren't against using sex appeal to calm things down.

"They tend to send the women in first to talk to an angry crowd."

"And what if it's a crowd of women?"

"I don't like dealing with groups of women." Her looks were useless against them. "They usually send in a good-looking fella instead."

"But you enjoy it?"

"Yes, but I really want to train in firearms."

Oh, bloody hell.

After a visit to Porthcawl's Rest Bay, Sarah took me to a huge sand dune not far from Ogmore Castle. I leant my bike against a tree and I looked up at it. Should I scramble up it to see what was at the top? I moved my foot and placed it on top of a squelchy gift from a local dog, an Alsation as big as an elephant judging by the size of it. Sarah laughed.

"Walking in a load of sand is definitely what you need right now," she said.

She was right. I ran up the side of the sandy mountain but when I got to the top there was more of it. I kept going and the dune kept expanding. I'd left Sarah at the bottom and we had more cycling to do so I descended without ever reaching the summit. But the sand had worked its magic on my trainers. Even if it hadn't then the next hurdle would have done the trick.

"We're really going this way?" I asked, looking at the

126

river, thirty metres wide.

A few people on horseback were walking across it. The horse's legs were completely below the waterline.

"Don't worry," she said. "You can get across on the stepping stones." I looked down at my bike with all its bags and then back at Sarah. "I didn't realise you'd have this much luggage."

The stepping stones were narrow. Sarah picked up her two-ounce bike and danced across them to the other side. She came back over and took my back panniers.

There was no way I could get across the stones walking side-by-side with my bike, and with the other bags still attached it was far too heavy to carry. There was only one thing to do.

I took off my socks and trainers, hooked the low-hanging front panniers to my handlebars and pushed the bike through the chilly water to the other side. Near the stones the water wasn't as deep as where the horses had crossed but it still came high up my thighs and threatened those areas that would prefer to stay clear of icy liquid.

Safely on dry land I had a quick scoot around the early 12th century, now ruined Ogmore Castle. A ghost, the White Lady, is said to guard the place but there wasn't really anything worth taking. Sarah, however, was feeling mischievous. She pointed to an information board.

"There's a knight there crying out for some googly eyes," she said.

I got out my little bag of plastic peepers and stuck two on him. He instantly looked crazed.

"I'm a police officer," she said. "I can't believe we're doing this."

"It's not real vandalism," I assured her. "They come off easily."

I wasn't worried. If I got nabbed I'd just say I was told to do it by the police.

We cycled on to Ogmore-by-Sea. There was a newsagent's she wanted to show me that was famous for its sweet treats. I was feeling hungry. I got a lemon cake, an incredible-tasting chocolate marshmallow Rocky Road thing – a welcome introduction to Britain since I'd lived here – and a gorgeously fruity flapjack. I'd had my cake *and* I'd eaten it. To be honest, I've never understood the dilemma. I always eat it.

"Are you still doing that weird food thing?" Sarah asked. She pointed to something I'd never had before, some seaweed in packets on the counter, one honey and sesame flavour, the other coconut and chilli.

"Of course."

I bought a bag of each. I saved the coconut one for later but we tried the honey one. The bag held five thin, tasty but insubstantial seaweed sheets, each somewhat smaller than a playing card. The entire pack only contained twelve calories.

What you do in life colours how you view the world. Cycling around Europe, I've met thousands of friendly, helpful people, and you're just as likely to find them in Albania as in Altrincham or in Bosnia as in Birmingham. As a result, my experience is that people are essentially good. Sarah's work pulls her view in the opposite direction.

"So what percentage are bad?" I asked her.

"Well, there are good people who do bad things, but people who are out-and-out bad," she thought for a moment, "I'd say about five per cent."

Wow, that was high.

"One in twenty people are out-and-out bad?" I asked.

"No, alright. That's too high. Two-and-a-half per cent."

But that still seemed massively wide of the mark. If I thought even 1% of people were irredeemably bad I'd never leave the house.

"I got married a year ago," she continued. "He's police

too, and ex-services. He's even more wary of people than I am."

He was even wary of me. He's a cyclist too and was originally going to come along today but couldn't get time off work. Instead, Sarah had a tracking app on her phone so that he could check wherever she was "just in case". He really had nothing to worry about. She could have kicked my head in.

The morning's greyness had been replaced by a none-too-confident sun but temperatures were pleasant and Sarah took me to a old-fashioned country pub. I had a pint in its beer garden.

"Is it true you can get done for being drunk on a bike in Britain nowadays?"

"Absolutely."

"And what's the limit?"

"It's the same as for cars."

"Really?"

"It's not just bikes though. It's a crime to be drunk in charge of any conveyance."

"A conveyance? What, roller skates?"

She thought for a second.

"I suppose they'd count. I've never heard of anyone getting done though, not even on a bicycle."

If I went back inside and got myself another pint I wondered if she'd have me sprawled over the picnic table with my arms behind my back in handcuffs. It was probably better not to risk it.

Our ride terminated at Llantwit Major. We were now in the Vale of Glamorgan, the most southerly of all the Welsh counties, sitting at the bottom of the country like one of those supporting rubber pads you find on the bottom of a laptop, or a verruca.

"Llan means 'church' in Welsh, and so Llantwit literally means 'church of the twits'," she said.

"Is that true?" I asked sceptically.

She laughed.

"No."

As well as showing me around her part of Wales, Sarah had been good enough to locate a campsite for me. I thanked her for her kindness and we said goodbye. It had been a fun day.

For the first time on this trip the site was buzzing with other canvas-based campers. The sun had slowly been donating its rays more enthusiastically as the day went on and it was now a beautiful Saturday evening. I decided to go out and have a look around this small town. It was well-served with pubs in the centre. I popped into one and had a pint while charging my phone. That was my excuse.

A bunch of twenty-something, baseball-capped American lads entered the pub and played pool. They fed the jukebox, choosing more and more eclectic songs as time went on. Johnny Cash and Bob Marley's Buffalo Soldier started well, but then it descended into *The Time of our Lives* from Dirty Dancing and before long they'd managed to find an old Victorian music hall song about buying fruit to impress a girl.

Ten songs in and the phone still wasn't charged. I got myself another pint and some pork scratchings. I read the back of the packet. Britain is going the way of America, with a public so litigious, or deemed so stupid, that everything contains a warning. The one on the pork scratchings was particularly worrying: "Although every care has been taken to remove bones, some may remain." Given that a pig's bones are as far away from its skin as it's possible to get, how could that actually happen?

*

My timing was awful. I was in the county of Rhondda Cynon Taf. I'd always wanted to see the Royal Mint, a British institution and the birthplace of each and every coin in my pocket. I'd assumed it would be a huge, grey-stoned castle with fat turrets and ancient machinery churning out buckets of pound coins deep in a dungeon somewhere, probably staffed by magical elves. Standing outside the building in Llantrisant I couldn't have been more wrong. It looks like a cross between a downmarket B&Q and a seventies low-rise office building. It's a squat, ugly thing. Still, at least I could go inside.

"You can't go inside," said a security woman sitting at reception.

"Oh."

"But there's a visitor's centre."

"Good, I'll go in there instead."

"But it's not open yet."

"That's alright. What time does it open?"

"No, you've misunderstood. It hasn't opened yet. It'll open in ten days' time."

The Royal Mint has stood at its present location since 1968. In a lifetime of over 420,000 hours I'd missed its opening by just 240. In a further ironic twist the visitor's centre opened on my birthday, almost as though it were a present for me, by which time I'd be miles away.

It had been a hard slog up the hill to Llantrisant on a hot and sunny morning. I'd sweated pints to get here. I couldn't give up so easily.

"I've cycled a long way. If it's nearly ready to open, maybe I could go in and just have a quick look around."

She wasn't going to budge.

"No, it's not finished. There are electrical cables all over the place. You'd need a hard hat."

"I've got my bicycle helmet. That's like a hard hat."

"Sorry," she said in a firm tone that indicated a conclusion to our conversation.

I took myself to a café and had to console myself with a

lemon and mustard chicken sandwich that tasted of neither lemon nor mustard. All in all, it hadn't been the best of mornings.

Still, I was feeling positive. I was on my way to Cardiff and that city was home to a unique British something I'd definitely get to see. Through heavy traffic – it is after all the most densely populated county in Wales and the sixth in the whole of Britain – I fought my way to the city's huge Victoria Park that houses a nice, little campsite within walking distance of the centre. On the desk I met Vance, a bloke my age with a nice, round, smiley head.

"I'll put your bike in our container."

"Is that necessary?" I asked.

Normally I just fastened it to a tree.

"Scum come through here at night. It's the city centre. They'll have your bike." He opened the container's heavy metal door and my bike disappeared. "Before we got this we had sixteen go in one week."

I think I'm making this campsite sound a lot ropier than it is.

"What are you up to anyway?" Vance asked.

I told him.

"Right then."

For the next twenty minutes he and his colleague in reception racked their brains for recommendations in Cardiff.

"I'm going out for a drive this evening, around Cardiff," said Vance. "Come along if you like."

Until then, I thought I'd take advantage of the sunshine. I pottered off to Y Mochyn Du – the Black Pig in Welsh – a pub on the edge of the park, with dozens of people outside enjoying the springtime warmth.

Sitting in a beer garden is a different experience in Britain than it is in a normally sunny country, such as Spain. Here there's an air of excitement and a smile on everyone's face at

132

the unexpected joy of such a day. It's the knowledge that this won't last very long, probably not until tomorrow, maybe not even for another hour. But while it's here, it's glorious. It isn't taken for granted because it *can't* be taken for granted.

I tasted my pint. While living in Austria I'd regularly drunk mid-5% lagers but after my four weeks of weaker British ales my taste buds had changed. The 5.7% Target IPA I sipped here tasted too strong, although its power matched that of the bar snack I'd bought, another bone-warning packet of pork scratchings – British tapas! – this time The Snuffling Pig's Hot-to-Trot Habanero flavour.

I finished my pint and returned to the campsite. Vance was almost ready to go. I climbed into the passenger seat of his blue, open-top sports car.

"Everyone likes the car except my ex," he said. "That says something."

It probably did, but I'm not sure what. I immediately got on with Vance and his accent seemed familiar. It turned out he was also from Blackburn. He lived across town from me but had gone to the school on the council estate, Shadsworth, next door to the giant estate in Knuzden on which I'd grown up.

"The kids from Shad were scary," I said. "We'd look up the hill from Knuzden Brook towards Shad and it was like Mordor."

But Vance wasn't scary. He was a friendly bloke. He'd been in the army for a little while but he was a pacifist. He'd only joined up to travel but he ended up training in Blackpool. That wasn't much travel; it's only 25 miles from Blackburn.

He'd had other jobs too.

"I was an entertainer in Tenerife," he said as we zipped through the streets of Cardiff.

"What sort of entertainer?"

"Fire eating, guitar."

"Wow, guitar eating? I'd pay to see that."

He drove through town and parked up at the huge and remodelled Cardiff Bay, formerly rough old Tiger Bay. Nowadays it's very clean, almost Scandinavian, and reminiscent of Oslo's own seafront. Stray bits of wonderfully pointless bits of art lie about the place.

We got an expensive pint from The World of Boats, looked out across the bay and chatted. Vance was currently single. He'd been going out with a woman for years. They'd had a child, got married and almost instantly split up. Vance didn't want to remain without a partner.

"I'm going to try speed-dating on Wednesday." He smiled a little nervously. "It's my first time."

It's a pity I'd be gone by then. I'd like to have heard how he got on.

"Do you go back to Blackburn much?" I asked.

He shook his head.

"I can't. It depresses me."

I'd made my peace with the place but I still didn't feel a desperate need to go back there. There were no plans to see it at all on this Britain-wide trip. And besides, in my hunt for the best place to live in Britain, I knew from experience it wasn't Blackburn.

Vance took me back to the campsite. It had been a useful tour to orientate myself in Cardiff. Tomorrow the weather forecast had predicted rain and so I was giving myself a full day to explore Cardiff properly and – who knows? – maybe some other distant corners of the universe.

*

I was peering through the window of a tourist shop opposite Cardiff Castle. I'd been told to find a particular world record holder here. There it was, on the wall, the world's longest lovespoon, those tokens of affection I'd first seen at the toy museum. I wondered if the recipient of this one had liked her gift or read a deeper meaning into it. After all, it did sort of imply she had a massive gob.

Today was going to be much more exciting than bits of tree carved into insulting presents. And not because Cardiff is the booze capital of Britain. I walked back down to the bay where Vance had taken me the day before and located my goal. The reception area seemed empty but they couldn't fit me in until eleven thirty, fifty minutes from now. I would have to wait.

To kill time I wandered the bay, looking at the street art. One was a small, whale-shaped wooden house. It had a window you could look through. Inside was a tiny kitchen with a kettle. This, apparently, was actually a kiosk called "Love Me or Leave Me Alone" that sold food and drink inspired by Tiger Bay's multicultural heritage. Today though it was empty. Another piece was the wrecked body of a ship but whose hull was actually a face turned towards the ground. A tourist train came past driven by a middle-aged pirate and full of infant school children, laughing and shouting "Hola!" at me. Their accompanying teachers laughed along with them. It was a welcome splash of colour on an otherwise grey morning.

By now it was close to eleven thirty. I returned to my appointment and got in line with about twelve others. I was suddenly six years old again.

A young blond woman, not much older than twenty, appeared ahead of the queue, wearing a bright red cloak. She would be our guide. We were about to go on a quest through the universe.

To be honest, the interactive bit of the Doctor Who Exhibition was a bit rubbish. The TARDIS was under attack from giant space squid, a challenge frequently faced by NASA, and, as a team, we had to cross the cosmos and collect three crystals for reasons that now escape me. Peter Capaldi's

Doctor would appear on a monitor from time to time and take the piss out of us. Finding the crystals wasn't very difficult. On whichever world we appeared, Skaro or wherever the hell those Weeping Angels live, they were just lying about the place.

Bless her, the guide worked her socks off and had the crack-addled enthusiasm of a children's television presenter, geeing us up and clapping her hands like a SeaWorld seal. Whatever she was paid, she was worth double.

The best part of the whole experience was when we entered the TARDIS itself. Six of us then got to control the time machine as we hurtled towards the surface of a planet. Lights flashed and the floor shook as the Doctor screamed instructions from a screen and the planet drew closer and closer. In the end we crashed. But that's always likely to happen if six different people try to drive the same vehicle. Given the events and the speed of our approach, it was a remarkably soft landing. In real life there'd have been a few casualties. I didn't care. I'd flown the TARDIS!

It was the next part of the day I was more interested in, the exhibition of props and costumes. It was great to see the evolution of the TARDIS interiors, the oldest one with home-made Dymo labels on its control panel saying ridiculous things like "YEAR-OMETER".

And boy, were some of the early costumes rubbish. A black and white bee character from what is generally considered to be the worst Doctor Who story ever, The Web Planet, looked like the sort of thing a five-year-old would knock together for a school fancy dress party. Its eyes were clearly made from an old pair of tights.

Each Doctor had his own look and their outfits were all displayed next to each other. The old Doctors started off dour but classy and then descended from there. By the time we got to the mid-1980s – Colin Baker and Sylvester McCoy's era –

the pretence of the time traveller's style had evaporated completely along with the BBC's enthusiasm for the show. You could almost hear the production department screaming, "Let's sink this ship as quickly as possible." Sylvester McCoy in particular looked like he'd been dressed by a committee of asylum inmates.

But the creatures old and new, like the Daleks, the Ood and the Sontarans, were great. And if you wanted to, via an instructional video on a loop, you could learn to walk like a Cyberman, or like one of those freaky scarecrows from the Family of Blood episode. Today though, nobody seemed particularly interested in adding this talent to their CV.

And then to the gift shop. Christ, there's a lot of Doctor Who crap. Fifteen quid for a sonic screwdriver was out of my budget, and it probably didn't work anyway, but I'd have taken a Cyberman's head mug if it hadn't been so heavy.

On the way out I noticed our bouncy guide was now on the ticket desk. The whole massive enterprise seemed to be run by a staff of about three.

"How many times a day do you have to do that?" I asked her.

"Depends," she said with an enormous grin and perfect teeth. "Usually eight or nine."

Bloody hell.

"And how do you keep up that level of enthusiasm?"

Drugs. Say lots and lots of drugs.

"The people," she answered. "They're great. And every group is different. It's best when they come here dressed up as The Doctor or something."

None of our group had dressed up. I felt we'd probably been a bit of a disappointment to her, merely a smelly cyclist and a handful of chubby, middle-aged Americans.

It was lunchtime. Cardiff's Caroline Street is locally known as Chippy Lane for the simple reason that it hosts a lot of chippies. It also contains Colin's Books, an adult magazine store with, ironically, the least sexy shop name on the planet.

I was told that a meal was invented on this street by Dorothy's, the oldest chippy here, and it's now replicated by all the others. Don't get excited. It's called "chicken off the bone" curry. It's a mass of shredded chicken and chips swimming in a rich curry sauce. It was very nice but, c'mon, it's chicken curry and chips.

On my way back to the campsite I had a look around Cardiff's indoor market. It's like a smaller, less chaotic version of the old monster in Budapest but with more foreign influences. I bought a couple of Welsh cakes for 30p each, a crumbly, half-thickness scone. They were alright but I suspect they should have had butter on them. It took me a good half hour to regenerate any saliva.

A little farther through town a muscular black bloke with dyed blond dreadlocks played bongos on a street bin in a repetitive and awkward 5/4 time while the people staffing the street stalls nearby looked on uncomfortably. I think they were just hoping he'd go away. It would have to be of his own volition. No one was going to challenge him.

Back at the tent I cooked up some food and listened to Radio Four. There was a series of travel programmes called Crossing Continents. Written down, that name looks fine, but spoken on the radio I was expecting a show about people who were angry at their lack of bladder control. Does no one think these things through?

*

Yesterday's predicted rubbish weather actually arrived this morning. Today I was supposed to be heading towards Merthyr Tydfil but I didn't fancy another Welsh drenching and I was just glad I was at least stranded in a city that still had places to explore.

In this weather I couldn't even boil water with my

porchless tent and so I moved into the site's laundry room and made coffee. Vance came in.

"What's with those animals around the castle?" I asked him. Cardiff Castle has a series of stone beasts peeking out from over its wall. "I mean, the lions and bears make sense for a castle but what's the story with the seal?"

"Ah," he said. "It's Billy the Seal. I named my son Billy."

"You named your son after a seal?"

"No, just a coincidence."

Billy though wasn't just a stone seal. She, for Billy was a female, was tangled in fishing nets and brought to live in Victoria Park from 1912 until her death in 1939. She was always popular but never more so than when the River Ely overflowed and Billy escaped and went swimming down Cowbridge Road East.

With breakfast eaten and coffee slurped I shuffled to the town's large museum through a blanket of rain. It's one of those places where you start by carefully examining each item. You then start to speed up, walking faster and faster, once you realise that if you spent as long on everything as you had on the first item you'd actually die of old age in there.

There was some chilling art relating to Mametz Wood, a First World War battle that saw the end of several thousand Welshmen, as well as a modern art installation containing five huge video panels, each showing a person – doctor, barmaid, orchestra conductor and other walks of life – each rotating in darkness. The work was dedicated to the memory of the Aberfan disaster in which 116 children and 28 adults died in a landslide in the sixties. The museum wasn't as grim as I'm making it sound. They also had the world's largest known leatherback turtle, weighing nearly 1000 kg and washed ashore in north Wales. It had died tangled in discarded fishing nets. No, that's still grim, isn't it? Let's move on.

After walking about ten miles through the museum I went back into town, still under a leaking sky, and headed to Rummer Tavern that claims to be the oldest in Cardiff. I ordered a pint of ale, Sleeping Brew Tea, from the barmaid.

"Will that be a straight glass or with a handle?"

I didn't care. Why would I?

"Whatever. A straight glass," I said. "Does it make a difference to the flavour?"

"No," she replied, "but the hipsters like handles. You'll have to grow yourself a beard and get one with a handle."

From there I went back to Dorothy's for an early dinner, this time for another local speciality I'd never tried, chips, cheese and gravy. I'd no idea how big it was going to be and so I asked the lady behind the counter – Dorothy? – if I needed a pie with it as well.

"I don't think so, babe," she replied, as though I'd asked a stupid question.

She brought the huge brown and yellow splat to my table. It wasn't awful, but it's less a meal and more a sloppy, incoherent mess.

*

This morning the weather was even worse. The continents had shifted. Wales was suffering a monsoon. Would I ever be able to leave Cardiff? I liked the place but there were other counties I needed to see. This would be my last day here no matter what tomorrow threw at me. I was leaving Cardiff then even if I were required to swim. As it turned out, staying was the right choice. Today I'd have drowned.

Back in town, dripping wet, I was approached by a young fella in a suit. Ah bugger, I thought. He's going to try to sell me something.

"I'm doing a business project," he said with a smile. He pulled an item of stationery from his pocket. "And I have to trade this paper clip for anything you have on you. But it can't be money. And then I'll trade whatever you give me and see how far I can go."

The only thing I had on me – apart from my jacket and he wasn't getting that – was my bag of googly eyes.

"There you go," I said.

I gave him a small handful. God knows what he was going to get for them, but I estimated he had at least quadrupled his initial investment. I still have his paper clip. It's the favourite one I own.

I've sometimes thought back and wondered what was the final value of the item he ended up with. He looked like a capable sort of bloke, but I could have been very wrong. Maybe he was rubbish. Perhaps he'd begun a couple of hours earlier with a flat screen telly and twelve trades later all he had was that paper clip.

I wandered around, ducking from shelter to shelter. I had a look at the menu for The Clink, a restaurant run by prisoners from Cardiff Jail, but it was out of my budget, although as far as prison food goes it all sounded pretty good. I wondered if they served it to you on compartmentalised moulded plastic trays, one sloppy ladleful here and there, while the cigarette ash of the kitchen staff dropped into your mash potato. Probably not.

By eight in the evening the rain had stopped for the first time in fifty-odd hours. My journey wouldn't end in Cardiff.

*

It was Thursday morning. I popped into reception to say goodbye. I felt like Vance had become a friend in the time that I was there. He'd enjoyed his speed-dating the previous evening. There was one woman he'd particularly liked but if it didn't pan out – he would find out what she thought of him that evening – then at least he wouldn't be quite so nervous next time. I hope he finds someone. He seemed like a nice bloke.

Unfortunately, my bike developed a new malady. On the edge of Cardiff I stopped for a break. When I set off again the chain jammed. One link of it was now twisted. This was causing the chain to jump off the cogs as I pedalled.

I cycled out of town on the Taff Trail. Like most cycle paths it was far from direct but it was taking me in the direction I wanted to go and beside a pretty stretch of river. I decided to stick with it for a while, at least until it took me somewhere daft. This occurred a few minutes later when I went on a circuitous tour of a housing estate in Caerphilly. Abandoning the official route I arrived at its famous castle – the largest in Wales and second largest in Britain – an impressive building with a collapsed, leaning tower. A tour guide was telling a large bunch of Americans he'd seen a Welsh leaflet claiming it leant at an angle "steeper than the Leaning Tower of Pizza".

Caerphilly was the first Anytown I'd come across in Wales. The cities aside, the country seemed to have done its best to snub the chains. At least there was a local baker, Glanmer, next door to Greggs. I bought two pasties, a chicken and ham, and a beef and Stilton. They were twice the price of their large chain rival but, then again, if you put pieces of meat in your products – not something that concerns Greggs - it's going to get expensive. They were worth every penny.

And then I hit county twenty-five, Merthyr Tydfil, just over a quarter of the way through this Britain-wide quest. This is not to be confused with the sick note capital of Britain, the town of Merthy Tydfil.

Climbing towards the valleys, in the village of Senghenydd, there's a painful memorial to those lost in the treacherous industry for which this area is famous. An explosion here in 1913 killed 440 miners. The negligent mining company was fined a mere 55p per death. The website whatsthecost.com tells me that, in today's money, this is something like £50, about the cost of one quarter of a cheap coffin, which, sadly, is all they would have needed if the crooked company had bothered to gather up their remains. The garden has a sort of circle of death, detailing the fatalities elsewhere throughout Welsh mining's history. It's grim reading. What's even sadder is that this bleak period, when sons and fathers went off to their doom for the privilege of extracting a fuel that would ultimately devastate the Earth's environment, is seen around these parts as "the good old days".

From Trelewis I headed east over a large hill and moors with a strong headwind but pretty views looking down on to distant towns. At least the sun was finally out again. Arriving in Markham it was easy to see why this place is called The Valleys. Two deep, tree-lined channels, one main road in each, disappeared northwards. More valleys run parallel off to the east. It was like the whole world led to this bit of Wales.

The next tiny county, Blaenau Gwent, is the smallest in Wales although it's also one of the most densely populated. It has a couple of claims to fame. Its county town, Ebbw Vale has Britain's highest number of people on anti-depressants, according to the Daily Mail,. And it's also the town with Britain's cheapest rents. Just think how many pills they'd be popping if they had to pay London prices.

There might have been an air of gloom around these Welsh hills, especially when you consider its tough history and what the Daily Mail reports as its medical solution, but the surprising thing was that, for such a ruggedly attractive area, there appeared to be little tourist infrastructure. Campsites were certainly in short supply. I carried on northwards to Tredegar to the only campsite I'd seen around these parts. They had to put me on a special field because their normal one was under water from the last three days of rain.

143

I decided to look at my bike again. The chain was still making a rubbing noise. And it was then, under closer inspection, I realised it was fitted incorrectly. When I'd relinked it ten days ago I'd fed it through the wrong part of the dangly down bit whose name I still haven't learned. Now, I'm a technical buffoon, obviously, but why the hell hadn't the so-called professionals at Halfords spotted it when they checked the gears over? I unclipped the link, put the chain in the correct place and the rubbing stopped. The mangled chain still jumped off the gears though. You can't have everything.

*

Today something truly horrible was going to happen. It was horrible when it happened to me, and it will be horrible when you read it. Or funny. That depends on you. But if you are currently eating anything covered in a thick gravy or, say, chocolate sauce I'd skip this bit until you've finished your meal.

I woke up to a lovely sunny day. I left my tent and had a stroll to the lake at the campsite. Several pairs of Canada geese were swimming about, followed by their little, yellow-green, fluffy chicks. What a scene of bucolic loveliness, I thought. One of the chicks came ashore and walked with a limp before falling over. The foxes'll have him, I thought. It didn't seem so bucolically lovely any more.

After breakfast I headed into Tredegar to see what I'd heard was a "dominating clock tower" in the main street. So undominating was it that I couldn't even find it.

I popped into a hardware store to buy meths for my stove.

"I bought some myself the other day," the man on the counter said. "I like to use it to clean light switches. Maybe I should stock some."

Like every other hardware store in Britain, yes, Alan Sugar, maybe you *should* sell meths.

I knew there would be hills today to begin with but

144

nothing terrible came my way. On the outskirts of Ebbw Vale I found the rock monument to Aneurin Bevan, the designer of the NHS, the place where he once made a great speech. The main rock represented Bevan himself, and there were three others, one for his home town Tredegar, his constituency Ebbw Vale and another, probably to represent the perceived weight of the NHS as it hangs around the Tories necks.

The route took me across beautiful, wild moorland. The sun was shining and the riding was great even with my gears failing as they did. All was well.

In Blaenavon I saw the old, now closed ironworks and decided to stop for lunch. I walked into a very full chip shop. Everyone was standing around; no one was being served.

"If you want chips you'll have to wait," said the woman in charge of the fat.

I waited and waited and several more people came in behind me. Eventually the chips were ready and we all walked away with our own paper packages, mine containing a fish cake too. I sat on a bench on a little square and ate my meal in the sunshine. The fish cake was tasty but some of the chips were a little underdone. Perhaps they'd rushed them to feed the queue as quickly as possible.

For almost the entire ride to Newport I barely had to pedal. I freewheeled downhill with a lovely cool breeze evaporating the sweat from the earlier hills still on my forehead. Life couldn't have been better. My stomach gurgled in a way it sometimes does. It was nothing to worry about. Nothing at all.

I'd entered the county of Torfaen and passed close to the village of Varteg that had recently seen a battle between local residents and Welsh language campaigners. Varteg, y'see, isn't Welsh – its alphabet has no letter 'V' – and there was a proposal to Welshify it. Unfortunately, this would have meant changing the village's name to Y Farteg. A number of dismayed locals described their horror and humiliation if having to give their address as Fart Egg. The residents came up trumps. Of all the town names the campaigners wanted to localize, they let one go.

The rural joy ceased in Newport. It's sadly one of the burglary capitals of Britain as well as the McDonald's capital of Wales. Maybe it's because the robbers have nicked all their pots and pans that they have to eat manky takeaway. It's not a pretty place at the best of times and today the dense traffic made it worse. I weaved around the cars, heading to today's campsite, roughly five miles away. My stomach gurgled again and suggested a toilet break was necessary but not yet. It wouldn't take much more than twenty minutes to get there, even with the queues. Traffic jams are no obstacle to a bicycle. I had plenty of time.

I hit the bank of the Severn Estuary. There were now only two miles to the campsite and then the horrible thing happened. My stomach suddenly and without warning went mental.

"You need to find a toilet," said my gut. "And I mean right now!"

I looked around frantically for a pub. The few that I passed were shut or closed down completely. OK then, maybe a café or a supermarket. But I was in the middle of an industrial estate. Out the other side there was a Lidl but, from past experience, their toilets are usually behind closed doors and you need to ask someone, and I didn't have time to negotiate.

I was getting desperate now. I was clenching with all my might. Stomach pains were bending me over double. Sweat poured from my head. I saw a KFC in the distance and pedalled towards it, throwing the bike against its wall, leaving it unlocked. I felt another stab in my gut. I couldn't stand up straight in my attempt to hold my insides where they needed to be. I was ten metres from the door of the KFC when my body gave up.

"Oh shit!" I thought, quite literally.

The pains stopped instantly but I now had a different problem. At least the hem of my Lycra cycling shorts would prevent my biological mishap from exposing itself to others, I thought. They would act like a huge pair of incontinence pants, wouldn't they? Surely? Please? I looked down. The elastic hem had given up far too easily. The rapidly digested fish cake and those underdone chips had been converted into something far less palatable and it was running thickly down my legs. Whatever happened now, embarrassment of some sort had to ensue.

Luckily, no cars were passing this part of the road, the only people about were some kids in the far distance, and the windows of the KFC were mercifully tinted. People inside might have seen me but at least I couldn't see them. I apologise if you were there having lunch that afternoon.

What to do? What to do? I could see a wide grass verge on the other side of the road. I'd get myself there as quickly as I could, sit down with my bike as though stopping for a rest, of no interest to passing cars or people, and work out what to do next. I shuffled across the road, sat down with a squelch and started to think.

I suddenly became Benedict Cumberbatch's Sherlock Holmes. You know whenever he meets someone new and little graphics appear to pour from them providing him with all the clues he needs to work out who they are or what they do? This happened to me. I scoured my surroundings for anything that might save the day.

The grass had been recently cut and it had rained in the night. Small piles of damp grass lay around me. On the other side of the verge was a banking descending downwards, although it was covered in nettles and thorns. I quickly grabbed handfuls of cut grass and cleaned my legs. It was amazingly effective, like a sponge, much better than the toilet paper I didn't have. Now at least I looked clean. But I still had to get out of these shorts and while in full view of anyone passing by. Going back to KFC wasn't an option. Standing up would have caused further leakage and I can't imagine I smelled too great either.

I fished into my pannier for my clean pair of cycle shorts. This bit was going to be tricky. It's not easy to remove cycling shorts in a hurry because of the shoulder straps beneath your shirt. I slipped my hand under my top, slid down the left shoulder strap and bent my arm awkwardly to free it, and did the same with the right one.

A ten-year-old kid on a bike cycled past, saw me and decided he wanted a conversation. He shouted something towards me. I yelled that I couldn't hear him over the traffic. I didn't want to approach him and get too close in case he said, "Oh mister, why do you stink?" He got bored at the loud, unproductive chat and cycled off.

What I needed now was a swift, single action: shorts off, clean up, new shorts on. Two school kids were walking by. It would have to wait a minute or two. I gathered another pile of wet grass, this time larger than before. The two children disappeared but were replaced by three more. They were walking slowly down the road in little groups. I waited for about ten minutes.

Then, at last, the pavement was empty. I slid down the banking, into the nettles. The shorts came off, the plants stinging my backside. I looked up the road and could see three Asian girls walking towards me. Please no! I didn't want to be charged with exposing myself to Muslim pre-teens. I'd get murdered.

The damp grass was put to good use and I also rubbed my arse on the nettle-covered ground like a dog with worms. I was done! The fresh shorts came on and I jumped out of the nettles towards my bike like a man reappearing from a magic trick. The Muslim girls were still just a little up the road. No one had seen a thing.

I hooked the straps back on to my shoulders, threw the old shorts into a nearby bin and was back on the road, trembling slightly at what had been a near miss. No one need ever know about this, I thought. Except you, obviously. And all the people in the KFC. And everyone with a CCTV camera in the vicinity.

I very nearly didn't include this story – you probably wish I hadn't – but I did for two reasons. The first is that it was entirely out of my control. I mean, it's not like I deliberately curled one off on a pub's pool table, is it? It's no more a reflection on me than my brain haemorrhage back in 2009 or the last time I sneezed. But the other reason to include it is as a friendly warning. If you're out on a bike sometime soon you might want to steer clear of fish cakes and partially cooked spuds.

Now what I wanted more than anything was to have a shower. I arrived at the campsite a few minutes later feeling surprisingly composed. The registration process took forever. I noticed a second woman, in her fifties, come out of a back room and look at my legs. I'd already had a couple of people comment on them. They're the only muscles in my body and after a spring in Spain they were nicely tanned. While I was checking in, she was checking me out. It was only once I'd left reception I noticed I'd missed a large, shitty smear on the side of my left leg. That's what she'd been staring at.

After a shower and the confidence that I was sparklingly clean I walked to the local supermarket. In the car park at the front of it a cat fight broke out. A woman in a big, blue car leaned out of her window.

"Watch where you're fuckin' going!" she yelled at a

woman in another car.

"It was your fault!" screamed back the second woman.

"Fuckin' cow!" blasted the first.

The second one thought for a moment. She clearly wasn't quite as used to public slanging matches.

"Cow!" she shouted back a little weakly, knowing she could have been a bit more original.

What a palaver, I thought. If the women of Newport were going to act like that then I didn't feel so bad about shitting all over their town.

*

As a county Newport is just outside the top ten most densely populated. Cycling eastwards through this urban hell, the jumping chain got worse and I knew I had to do something about it. I passed a Halfords but one that only dealt with cars. A guy working there gave me directions to a bicycle branch. I followed them and realised it was on the same shopping park as yesterday's KFC. Oh, such happy memories!

The morning's greyness had been replaced by bright sunshine. Fully repaired I headed across the transporter bridge, one of only eight still working on the planet, to avoid the worst of Newport's busy roads. I now cycled the quieter, wider roads of southern Newport.

Now in Monmouthshire I passed through Undy – half a pair of pants – Caldicot and Chepstow. As well as Undy, it's got a handful of other nicely named places: Mardy, Jingle Street and Bullyhole Bottom.

Now free of the tiny counties of south Wales, larger Monmouthshire deserved a more thorough exploration but the rain delays in Cardiff meant I was already going to have to chop a day off both Gloucestershire and Wiltshire to stay on schedule even if I breezed through Monmouthshire without stopping. That was a shame because I quite fancied

150

having a pint at the Skirrid Mountain Inn in Abergavenny, supposed the oldest and most haunted pub in Wales. It had an interesting story attached.

Skirrid is a version of a Welsh word for "to shiver". Apparently, in the hours after the crucifixion of your fella in Jerusalem, the entire mountain on which the pub stands shivered. No one knows how powerful a shiver it was because, of course, this was in the days before we measured shivers on the Richter Scale. We should also consider that no one in Wales would have had a clue who Jesus was or when he was supposedly killed until several centuries later and so – who knows? – perhaps they were out by an hour or two.

Anyway, Monmouthshire mostly and sadly ignored, I cycled on to the old Severn Bridge, a wonderful ride on a blue-sky day like today, crossing the wide expanse of the Severn Estuary and rolling once again into England. Farewell Wales! You were at times beautiful, frequently bleak but always bloody soggy. And sorry about the Newport thing.

Chapter 7: The sanctuary of dead elephants

Gloucestershire, Wiltshire, Bristol and Somerset

Back in England after my near-three week tour of Wales, I relished my re-entry into a world that permitted the use of vowels. Being able to pronounce the names of the places through which I was cycling *and* a third sunny day in a row was a little bit special. I celebrated in a Thornbury beer garden with a pint of pale ale and mild sunburn.

Just down the road from the pub, I was given a vision of England in the form of a live cricket match. I leant against a dry stone wall beneath a tree adorned with pink cherry blossom determined to soak up a dose of Englishness on this lazy, hazy Saturday afternoon.

Perhaps this area of Gloucestershire was an area of wide ethnic diversity but I doubted it. Thornbury had seemed as white as a Ku Klux Klan convention. Therefore, Thornbury Cricket Club must have been playing a bunch of visiting Asian lads.

The bowler ran languidly towards the stumps and released the ball. The batsman swung and missed. He didn't seem too disappointed by this. It seemed to be absolutely normal. And indeed it was, as this inaction was repeated several times over a period of five minutes. The batsman managed to nick the ball once but sent it scurrying along the grass back to the bowler.

I've never watched cricket. I mean, I might have seen a bowl or two on telly but then it would get turned over, or off, because why would anyone want to watch cricket?

But here on a warm, sunny afternoon, with little birds

singing in the tree above my head, I could see its appeal. It's hypnotic in an exceedingly dull way, like spending hours entranced by a tropical fish tank. You know nothing is going to happen but it's nice just to focus your eyes in its direction. But more than that, it's sunny. I assume that's why they don't play in the rain. It's not because they couldn't – every other sport continues during a shower – but could you really be arsed to experience so little action if you were getting soaked at the same time?

A few miles down the road from Thornbury I saw a little supermarket, the first shop I'd seen all day down these flowery lanes. I bought some things for dinner and a Millionaire's Flapjack. It didn't say which millionaire, but I hoped it was Piers Morgan's and he was really angry that I'd snaffled it.

I crossed the M5, a world away from the tranquillity of my route. As the din of the cars subsided, the land started to fold. The hills were at the limit of what my legs could manage. The lanes were lined with garlicky ramsons and I got a little lost. On one steep ascent I saw a father and son walking as I snailed my way upwards.

"Is this the way to the campsite?" I asked.

"Yes," the dad replied, "but if you go at that speed it'll take you four hours."

"Thanks but sod off," I didn't say.

It didn't take four hours. It took five minutes. I set up my tent and sprawled out in the sun with my phone charging via my solar panel. This was lovely weather, certainly better than the kind they had just up the road in Berkeley in 2013 when it rained seaweed. Even Wales isn't *that* mean.

I was hungry. I looked at the can of sausages I'd bought from the shop and then realised its tin was one of the old-fashioned ones that need an opener. I popped to reception and asked the warden if he had one.

"No," he replied. "But it's no problem."

He took out a huge knife, like the sort a Hutu would own, and proceeded to attack the tin. I got a bad feeling.

"I can hear the theme music from Casualty."

I spent the evening eating sausages and bits of severed finger while listening to the Eurovision Song Contest on the radio. It's not as much fun when you can't see 'em prancing around in their daft outfits and you just have to focus on the music. Once again, the United Kingdom did terribly, receiving 5 points and coming 24th out of 27. It's almost as if they think we have no respect for the competition.

*

I set off on a glorious morning, meandering over the hills of the Cotswolds. This lumpy land and this sun-warmed, wind-cooled air is what bikes were designed for. I wanted to put on a dress, swap my bike for an old bone shaker and scream down the hills with my legs on the handlebars, the pedals spinning recklessly and showing my pants to the world.

The intermittent trees provided both a strobe effect and a temperature oscillation. Hot and bright, cold and dark, hot and bright, the heat a welcome source of warmth after the coolness of the shade, the refrigerated air a welcome chill after each blast of sunshine.

I passed through cutesy North Nibley, which sounds like a place middle-class rabbits go skiing. I had a hill to climb. A dead baby deer lay in the road. The cars coming down the hill steered to avoid it. Just as I passed the poor animal, a descending car hit it full-on, splatting its bloated carcass with a dull explosion that would have covered me in putrid venison and liver pâté had I been five metres farther down the hill.

I arrived in Wotton-under-Edge, a lovely village with a beautiful, well-attended church this Sunday morning. Two

154

young girls walked past me, speaking French. Suddenly, rather than Britain, I was in Brittany and that other land of lovely villages just over the Channel.

Village after village, the place was gorgeous. Alderly had another attractive church. I passed the Somerset Monument, a lighthouse-like structure in memory of Lord Edward Somerset as opposed to a hastily erected tower accidentally built in the wrong county, and cycled through Sopworth, a village called Dunkirk and another called Petty France.

I stopped in Sherston, a perfect English village just over the Wiltshire border. It has the appearance of a film set, its few pubs, shops and businesses all thriving. What were they doing differently here than in the rest of Britain's dying settlements? Maybe the community had decided to buy locally rather than drive to the nearest large town and give all their cash to the shareholders of Sainsbury's. That'd be a good start.

After a morning of villages and lanes I hit the town of Malmesbury. The place has a couple of interesting firsts for Britain. In 1703 it was home to Hannah Twynnoy, the first person in the British Isles to be killed by a tiger on home soil. She'd been working as a barmaid in a pub exhibiting wild animals. The tiger didn't take too kindly to her teasing and so it gobbled her up. Hannah was also Britain's first ever pub meal.

Between Malmesbury and Royal Wootton Bassett I inadvertently participated in a bike race. The police made me pull over to one side while the real cyclists came screaming through. A mile down the road I passed a race marshal. He looked at my bags and gave me a clap.

"You're way behind the pace," he said with a smile.

My campsite was just the other side of Marlborough, my second cigarette town of the day, but only if you allow me the Sopworth Camel from earlier, which you shouldn't because it isn't even spelled correctly.

Marlborough itself seemed wealthy, a very Waitrose-y kind of place, the sort of town that might, and indeed does, host a jazz festival. Among the local shops on its wide shopping street, a Greggs sat conspicuously out of place, a little bit of Liam Gallagher amongst Marlborough's Miles Davis.

I'd loved my first full day back in England, and despite its short distance away from Wales the two places felt so different. Wales is at its best when folded, rugged, the scars of recently dead or dying industries visible, preferably with a brooding sky. England is better when flatter, laid out like a patchwork quilt, rapeseed and pasture by turn, genteel to the point of repressed, with distant spires poking over clumps of trees. Wales is thick arm muscles and a pint of Brains followed by a lusty belch. Wiltshire's England is a vicar, a nice cup of tea and people pretending they don't fart.

*

According to my British stereotypes map I was moving out of the zone of the Self-Satisfieds into the land of Hippies. Today was a day for druids and mystical nonsense. This area of Wiltshire has a whole host of such features. I wasn't heading to the most obvious, Stonehenge, because I'd been there before and it felt a bit overrated. Besides, I'd recently been told it cost £16 to visit and I'd flown a TARDIS for that much.

I set off in yet more beautiful sunshine, wondering whether I really could be this lucky with the English weather or perhaps I'd cycled through a rip in space-time and ended up in Mediterranean Italy.

The first stop was The Sanctuary although perhaps The Field With Little Bits of Wood and Stones In It would have been a more accurate name. It took some stretch of the imagination to picture what it might once have been. Rocks and poles denoted the structure of, well, no one is really sure.

While staring and mentally-picturing I met a group of walkers who were out strolling the ancient sites of Wiltshire. The group's leader looked at the field and tilted his head.

"I was expecting more," he said sadly.

"You have to use your imagination," I replied.

He looked a little longer.

"I reckon if you join those rocks up it'd make a picture of an elephant."

I looked but couldn't see it.

"Maybe the archaeologists got it wrong. Maybe it wasn't an ancient house or temple, but the druid police's rock outline of an ancient pachyderm murder scene."

He looked at me and wrinkled his brow.

"I don't think England had elephants back then," he said.

"I don't think they had druid police either."

"So that's stupid then, isn't it?"

"Yes," I said, chastised.

I moved on to the slightly more satisfying 129-feet tall Silbury Hill. No imagination was needed here. Silbury Hill is, well, a hill. The odd thing is that it's man-made and no one knows why anyone bothered. It was built between 2400 and 2300 BC. Over successive generations more and more people lugged more and more soil to the top and it grew and grew. But why? That's anyone's guess. There probably wasn't much on telly back then.

Next up, a stone's throw up the road, is West Kennet Long Barrow, an ancient burial chamber, one of the longest in Britain and well over 5,000 years old. Its side chambers are perfect isosceles triangles, built thousands of years before the Greeks even devised the word 'geometry' and ruined the lives of millions of school children. At least the archaeologists know what this one is.

Today's star attraction, though, was Avebury, the ancient

site of Britain's largest stone circle. In a misty twilight I imagine this Neolithic ring of stones could be nicely spooky, but in bright sunshine in the middle of the afternoon it was less so. The serenity wasn't enhanced by hundreds of school kids running about the place screaming as though someone had set their hair on fire. I also couldn't help thinking the site's mysticism levels might have been higher had they not built a sodding road right through the middle of it.

When the kids had gone it was a nice spot to linger. The huge standing stones must have taken some shifting. Sheep wandered between them, although one or two looked a bit diseased. If this place had any magic it wasn't rubbing off on its ovine representatives.

I went to the Henge Shop, the typical sort of place you see anywhere druids, witches or gullible tourists have ever gathered. It sells a collection of things vaguely connected to the site and the word 'spirituality' in general, such as jewellery twisted into ancient shapes and books on magic, Nostradamus and crop circles. Less mystical, although perhaps more apt, were the Lambs Whoopsies, chocolate buttons masquerading as delicious sheep turds.

Just before I arrived in the town of Calne, my tent's grassy home for tonight, I passed the Cherhill White Horse, a 40 x 43 metre hillside equine cut out of the chalk landscape in 1780. There are loads of them around here – from my map I counted at least seven in an eight-mile radius of Avebury. This must help trade in the local Tesco's as people wander the country lanes, see one of the horses and then think, "Mmm, I really fancy a burger."

But if anything, today was one of regret. Although the last few hours had been stuffed full of bona fide tourist attractions, even if no one knew what most of them were actually for, I later discovered I'd missed two places just off my route. Castle Combe has been called Britain's prettiest village. Missing this wasn't such a big deal. Wiltshire is gorgeous. Just about every place I cycled through could have been a contender for such a title. More annoying was missing out on my growing collection of strange place names. Near Castle Combe is an eight-cottage hamlet called Tiddleywink.

This highlights something about the diversity of Britain's attributes. You could do a ride like mine, visiting every county without ever actually experiencing a single road that I cycled and still see some great stuff. In fact, you could get luckier than me. You could see the land's prettiest village and the hamlet of Tiddleywink instead of a field full of sticks and stones, a circle of rocks populated by rabid children and mangy sheep and what may or may not have been the final resting place of a murdered elephant.

*

Shortly after Stockley, I reached the top of a hill and could see welcome flatness ahead. I tumbled down the other side into a village, the unfortunately named Lacock, whose moniker didn't match its genteel ambience. It was home to four lovely streets and a handful of pubs, which for any village these days is impressive, as well as Lacock Abbey, a building used in TV's Wolf Hall.

I cycled on to Box and scored me a sausage sarnie from a petrol station. One change from when I lived in Britain is that, for many small communities, the only place to buy anything seems to be the petrol station. It's no longer just a place to fill up the car but a snack bar, a newsagent, an off licence, a mini-supermarket and a coffee shop, all these once local facilities hoovered up by the garage chains. I'd rather not have shopped there but the alternative was to eat nothing, get all light-headed and fall off my bike. So I donated some money to Shell, or whichever company it was, to help in their ongoing project to burn the world.

This morning there was a story on Radio Four about a

severed foot found in a park in Bath. I wasn't looking for dismembered limbs but it was Bath that was the next place on my route. Unfortunately the blue skies and sunny weather of yesterday had been replaced by a grey murk that wouldn't have helped any town, no matter how beautiful. I couldn't complain. I'd had half a week of sunshine. From memories of my youth in Blackburn, that's two summers-worth.

I cycled around a bit and found a park, mercifully free of body parts. I'd been hoping to locate a cycle-path tunnel that someone had told me about, Britain's longest apparently, but no one knew where it was. Instead I'd ended up here.

Sitting on a bench were an old couple. She was played by Ab Fab's Patsy Stone's great-grandma, her shrivelled body wrapped in designer shades, while he was the amiable old drunk from The Fast Show. They called me over, as though I were their man-servant. They were both incredibly well-spoken, like the Queen used to be in the fifties before she let herself go.

They'd lived in Cambridge and spent years in California but had come back home.

"Where's home for you?" she asked.

I shook my head.

"It isn't a place. It's people."

As soon as I spoke, Mr Fast Show descended into a comedy Yorkshire accent, all ee-by-gums and ecky-thumps.

"I can't help it," he said.

But I think he probably could.

"He just loves a northern boy," said Granny Stone. "Where are you going?"

"I've got no route."

"We have no roots either," she replied.

Their hearing wasn't as highly polished as their accents.

"No, not roots," I corrected. "No route."

"You've got no food?"

This was getting me nowhere. They didn't know where the tunnel was either. In fact, the question seemed to confuse them. They thought I was asking for a funnel. It was time for me to move on.

According to The Telegraph, Bath is Britain's cultural capital but it has a less appealing claim to be Britain's personal debt capital. As of 2014, each person in the BA1 postcode owed on average £2,311 in personal loans. It was costing them an arm and a leg, quite literally for those unfortunates who had their bits scattered around Bath's parks.

It had taken me longer than expected to get to Bath and so, with the weather closing in, it was time to find a site for the night. The grey sky grumbled over my head. The canal towpath I'd been told about as a pleasant escape from the city was closed and so I was forced on to busy roads. The rain came down, not really adding to the general mood.

On the soggy campsite there were a couple of motorcyclists visiting from Australia. One of them was originally English although you'd never have known from his accent. The other had never left Oz before. I looked at his immediate surroundings, the verdant trees, emerald lawn and khaki bushes and compared it mentally to his antipodean deserts.

"Is this the first time you've ever seen the colour green?" I asked him.

He smiled.

"We have some in Melbourne," he replied, "but today I came over a hill and I said, 'Faakin' hell, mate, now that's green!'"

I left them there, drinking Fosters, obviously, as I popped to yet another garage – the only place for miles around – to buy my dinner. While there, another motorcyclist paced around, looking a bit sheepish. I asked him if he was alright.

"Not really," he replied with a southern Irish lilt. "I used the green petrol nozzle thinking it was unleaded."

"And it was diesel?"

"Yup," he said sadly.

His accent made it sound less tragedy and more comedy but he wasn't laughing.

Inside the garage supermarket I bought ingredients to make a pasta sauce but, back at the tent, the rain returned, buggering any plans to cook and so I had to make do with a couple of Scotch eggs I'd bought as a starter. I was living the dream. So far on this ride, trying to eat British where possible, it wasn't so much Five-a-Day as Five-a-Month, and I don't think I was even achieving that sorry target.

*

It was the 18th of May and my birthday. As on most of my previous birthdays while cycle-touring I was being met by Nina. In the past she'd come to find me in such wonderful cities as Berlin, Rome, Athens, Madrid and Istanbul. Today she would top them all. She was coming to Bristol!

At the end of the last ride, it had seemed like this relationship was over, and indeed it was for the four months following that trip. But in January we got back together and, this spring, I'd spent a lovely three months in Nina's mountain village in Spain. All was well.

The forecast rain waited until I'd packed the tent away and got myself about one hundred metres down the road before it unleashed its swimming pool-sized load on my head. It stopped soon afterwards but it was in damp clothes that I peeled my way through the layers of main road and dual carriageway to arrive at Bristol's main railway station. The externals of Bristol hadn't given much hope as to what we'd find inside, but, then again, that's true of most cities. Nina got off a bus and my birthday party could begin.

Bristol is also a county and, at 42 square miles, is the equal second smallest in Britain, tied with Blaenau Gwent. It's been given such diverse titles as the street art and graffiti capital of Britain, the UK's most bike-friendly city, the green capital of Europe, the musical capital of Britain and, a little dubiously, within that region of the world second most likely to see a tornado. Don't get excited; we didn't see any twisters.

The little apartment we rented was near the Cabot Circus shopping centre. I tend not to visit shopping centres unless it's absolutely necessary, and I hadn't experienced any on this trip so far, but haven't they come on? I mean, this one still sold the same old shit and the food on offer was mass-produced pap but at least the building was interesting, like an indoor version of the town in Bladerunner but in English and with not quite so many replicants running about the place. That said, how would I know?

Over the next three days we checked out all the city had to offer. It's a damn nice place. It has great street food at the St Nicholas market, where you can get grub from all four corners of an oddly-shaped globe, from huge Middle Eastern pittas stuffed with freshly-frazzed falafel to strange African fish. And Millennium Square was an interesting space with its solar-panelled tree from which you could charge your phone, as well as a solar-powered music machine and raised beds growing fruit and vegetables for a project called Food for Free. A huge silver ball the size of a house dominates the square. And then there are the people. A man passed by on a mobility scooter wearing a pirate's hat.

We popped down to the harbour. It was here not long ago that a monster alien, something that looked like a flashing radioactive squid, was caught on camera. You can find the video on YouTube. But this wasn't a job for that Animal Pathology Field Unit in Wales. It turned out to be just a P.R. stunt for a new TV programme that no one can remember. Maybe that's a lesson. Never make your stunt more exciting than your show.

Walking around town one day I was accosted by an activist for Amnesty International, a hipster with a waxed moustache, a look that, when adopted by a recent contestant on Great British Bake Off, caused the internet to explode with rage. The hipster was angry that the Tories wanted to drop Britain's commitment to the Human Rights Act. I should have just nodded and said, Yeah, mate." Instead, I mentioned how human rights are meaningless unless they're enforced. For example, what's the point of insisting people have a human right to clean water if there are humans who don't have clean water and yet it's no one's job to sort that out? So I got a fifteen-minute lecture when I'd rather have been seeing what else Bristol had to offer.

The debate had put me in the right fighting mood, however, when I was stopped a few minutes later by a film crew who asked me my opinion on the forthcoming EU Referendum, just over a month away. As someone who's lived and worked in Austria and Spain and benefited from the single currency while travelling everywhere in Europe, it won't be a surprise which side of the fence I was on.

"To me," I said with a camera in my face, "seventy years ago we were all killing each other. Every step since the end of the war has been a positive one, moving towards where we are today. If we keep moving forward, keep working together, eventually there'll be a United States of Europe. I know that worries a lot of people, but I'm not sure why. I mean, it worked pretty well for America. If Britain leaves the EU, then that's the first step backwards, the first step away from the European peace project."

The reporter shook my hand and said, "You're a star," but I suspect he would've said that even if I'd drooled incoherently and shouted, "Send 'em all back!"

We continued on to the M-Shed, a building offering

various oddball exhibitions. At one such collection I found Nina stroking her chin and perusing an assortment of toys scattered on the floor.

"What do you think it means?" she asked thoughtfully.

A four-year-old child appeared, picked up one of the building blocks and threw it. I looked at Nina, who appeared to gasp.

"It's a play area," I said.

The penny dropped.

"Don't you dare tell anyone about that," she replied.

"I promise."

One of the most original things in the M-Shed was Briswool, a model of the city that had been hand-knitted by, I'm assuming given its scale, absolutely loads of people. There were woollen houses by a woollen river on which bobbed woollen boats. A woollen cathedral looked down from a woollen hillside. Woollen cars drove down woollen streets, one of which went to that huge woollen silver orb we'd seen on Millennium Square. Unfortunately they'd forgotten to complete the scene with a woollen nutter in a pirate hat.

My quest to find foods I'd never eaten before wasn't turning up the culinary treats that my ride around Europe had done, but in Bristol we found a Chinese supermarket and I bought a jar of waxberries. I'd never even heard of them. Imagine a large currant within which is a stone approximately the size of a large currant. That's a waxberry. Don't bother. They're a lot of work for little reward.

After a final evening in the apartment that included a bottle of tequila and a supermarket pizza that was reduced to a lump of charcoal in the flat's nuclear-powered oven, it was time for Nina to pack up and return home, and for me to continue on my road trip. Bristol had been fun, a British city well worthy of a visit. Go and see it, maybe on a mobility scooter in fancy dress.

*

The weather in Bristol had been generally murky, grey with rain and little sunshine, but that hardly matters when you're visiting markets and woollen cities and pondering the artistic merits of a child's play area. Now I was back on the road, things were different. I'd been promised three more days of sunshine. And it was British sunshine, the most valuable sort of sunshine in the world because, like gold and the talents of Kanye West, it's a scarce commodity.

I was now in Somerset, a county that feels like it should be different to the ones around it, full of farmers and bales of straw and people with cider-related cirrhosis of the liver. I'd left the city behind and cycled to Cheddar.

There's no more famous British cheese than the one produced here and I wanted to know what sets it apart from its competitors. I headed to the Cheddar Gorge Cheese Company's HQ. It's the only place in town that makes Cheddar, and in their visitor centre you can watch a video of the entire process. If you prefer your cheese-making a bit more rock 'n' roll, you can watch its manufacture live, although they'll almost certainly kick you out each evening with the rest of the groupies. The performance goes on for days, like a Chris Rea song seems to.

The milk is heated until it separates into curds and whey. The whey is poured off and the curds are sliced into chunks and then compressed to release more whey. This is the process for all hard cheeses. The Cheddar difference is that the compacted cheese is then sliced into pieces and stacked on top of one another in higher and higher towers, a process called Cheddaring, that squeezes out even more whey. It's then put into moulds and aged in nearby Gough's Cave, a two-kilometre-deep cavern in which, 15,000 years ago, cannibals lived. Cannibals don't like cheese, although they're quite partial to Kurds.

The visitor's centre included some cheesy facts. Apparently, Captain Scott took 3,500 lbs of Cheddar on his Antarctic expedition. When Oates famously left their tent saying that he may be some time, perhaps he was just popping out for some crackers.

In the centre's accompanying shop, I sampled their Vintage Cheddar, one matured for a full sixteen months. It's wonderfully strong. It reminded me of a description I'd heard for Casu Marzu, the cheese from Sardinia to which fly larvae are added from which sprout maggots that munch the cheese and excrete, I suppose, maggot poo. Apparently, Casu Marzu has such a strong ammonia taste that a nibble can linger in your mouth for up to twelve hours. You've also got to watch for the maggots throwing themselves at your eyeballs. Vintage Cheddar wasn't as powerful as Casu Marzu but it definitely had a tiny hint of ammonia. Anyway, I blessed the cheesemakers with a fiver and carried off a packet of Vintage. If I wanted to take it to the next level, I figured I'd have to find my own maggots.

Cheesemaking isn't the only demonstration in town. Just around the corner a sweet shop has its own. The next session wasn't for half an hour and so I decided to get some lunch beforehand. I nipped into the local chippy for a chicken and mushroom pie.

"Just a pie? No chips?" the shop owner asked sadly.

"No, it's alright."

I was still wary of undercooked chips after the Newport Poo Disaster.

He took my money, got a pie from his freezer, pinged it in the microwave, put it in a Styrofoam container and handed it to me. Then he adopted a tone you'd normally reserve for talking to three-year-olds.

"I've given you a few chippies anyway," he said in his

soppy voice.

It didn't matter. Today's chips were properly cooked and so Cheddar was spared a potato-based horror.

With the pie eaten I was back at the sweet factory although, in reality, it was a room about the size of a single car garage, a rope slicing the place lengthways, one half for the audience and the other for the staff. A long bench on their side of the rope hugged the wall. On a stove, a sugary solution was boiling away like a little witch's cauldron.

The boss man was a chubby old dude whose presentation skills felt a little, well, autistic. He worked at his bench, hunched over, mumbling inaudibly into the far wall. He then went to the sink in the corner, washed his hands and did some more talking.

"...and we'd be delighted...mumble, mumble...next time...mumble, mumble...questions."

Beside him, the majority of the work was carried out by a young woman who kneaded the cooked toffee. She then cut off an eighth and repeatedly threw it over a knackered-looking hook on the wall, pushing air into the confection and causing it to lighten in colour. Strips of this paler toffee were placed on top of the darker slab before she folded it a few times and then loaded the entire thing into a large automated metal press. Boss man flicked a switch and helped to feed the machine's output – a thin sausage of sweetness – into a little hammering device that squished the sweets into their traditional peppermint humbug shape. The lightened toffee provided the stripe running through the darker whole. He finally turned around. That bit was quite dramatic. It was the first time we'd got a look of him. Was he actually going to talk to us face-to-face?

"That's it," he said drably. "As you're leaving, can I remind you to follow the arrows. It's down to health and safety."

No, it wasn't. The arrows led into the sweet shop. We

could just as easily have gone out the way we came. But that was fair enough, since the demo was free after all. I bought a stick of cider rock. I mean, it was Somerset after all.

Full of cheese, pie and sweets I rode up Cheddar Gorge. It must be one of England's most stunning roads, the sheer, tall rock faces hemming me in on both sides of a narrow track. Indeed, it's not just my opinion. The book 100 Greatest Cycling Climbs puts it at number one.

It got steeper and steeper and so I thought I'd take a breather. I noticed a climber at the base of a cliff roping up a section and so I found a rock to sit on and stopped to watch him. But instead of climbing he walked to the corner of the rock face and had a piss. I didn't know if I was supposed to applaud or something.

Twenty minutes later I'd reached the top of the gorge. It had been a lovely climb. A bloke stood by his car at the side of the road.

"How far is it to the nearest village?" he asked in an Eastern European accent.

"Dunno. About two miles," I said. "And it's great. You can watch cheese-making and sweets being made," I added like some tourist information twonk.

"Thank you," he replied a little weakly.

It was only after I continued that my mind filled in the details of the scene unfolding behind him. His family was standing outside the car while another bloke had his head under the bonnet. He wasn't looking for local places of interest. He needed a mechanic.

Once out of the gorge, you progress along a reasonably flat hill top and then happen upon a stunning vista, the plateau on which sits the city of Wells with, in the distance, Glastonbury Tor, a little, round hill containing a tower that stands proudly and commands the eye. The newly confident sun helped to colour the world a rich green. It's the sort of scene that would make me set up an easel and paint a landscape if I didn't have the artistic skills of a spaniel.

I rolled down the hill into lovely little Wells. Outside the cathedral, on an information board, it proudly says "England's smallest city" although if you read the text beneath, it sneakily confesses that the City of London is marginally smaller.

The cathedral is beautiful, with its wide front and large central tower. I stood there in its grounds captivated by it for a while. A young family sat on a bench nearby. For the sake of your visualisation you may as well populate this mental scene with the actors from Outnumbered, so perfectly cast would they be. Dad and daughter Karen were playing Rock-Scissors-Paper repeatedly. Dad seemed to be winning every game, which, in a random game like this, suggests Karen was picking the same object each time. Then young Ben came jumping in to spoil it.

"Rock-Scissors-Paper!" said Karen.

They all declared their weapon of choice simultaneously.

"Rock!" said the daughter.

"Paper!" said Dad.

"Nuclear bomb!" shouted Ben.

This sparked an idea in Karen's mind.

"We should play a different version," she said. "Cheese-Cat-Mouse!"

"How would that work?" asked Dad, while Mum laughed to herself.

"Mouse would eat cheese."

"Yes?"

"And cat would eat mouse."

"Good."

"And cat would eat cheese."

"But that's not going to work, love," he said.

"Yes," she said earnestly. "Yes, it is."

170

"OK then."

"Cheese-Cat-Mouse!" said Karen.

"Cat!" shouted Dad, while Mum sniggered, and he did this for the next ten games until Karen realised the flaw in her game's rules. It was really quite lovely.

I wheeled my bike around town, hunting out the old streets. I found an absolute gem in Vicars' Close, a narrow cul-de-sac terminating with a chapel, each house with a tall chimney. It's supposed to be the oldest purely residential street with original buildings still intact in the whole of Europe. It was built between 1348 and 1430. Sometimes Britain can be amazing.

As I pushed my bike up the middle of this lovely lane, a bloke at the chapel end got out his camera to take a picture. It wasn't me he was interested in but there was no way I could get out of the way. I felt it was the least I could do to move slightly to my right and occupy the Golden Mean to aid his composition.

I continued ever onwards. Six or seven miles down the road, near the Tor I'd seen earlier, I found a campsite. It was the most organised one I'd seen so far, with its own off licence that loaded its shelves with Glastonbury Real Ale beers and, for the Guardian readers, labelled each item with the food miles that had brought the beer to the shop. Since Glastonbury is just down the road, each bottle had only cost five food miles, which is pretty environmentally friendly until you factor in how far the hops, the other ingredients and the bottles had to travel to reach the factory in the first place. But the thought was there.

The campsite also had specific foodie nights, for Chinese, Indian, pizza and fish and chips. You placed your order and they organised the food from a local takeaway. Unfortunately, on Sundays they organised nothing and you can guess what day it was today. But at least the weather was nice enough for me to cook something for myself. I popped to the site shop, bought four different Glastonbury Real Ales and a packet of crisps.

"That looks like a fun evening," said the woman behind the counter.

Yes, it did. And she was right. The beers were excellent, especially their Hedge Monkey that described itself as "bold and ballsy" as well as being "dangerously drinkable". I don't think this brewery bothers with all that Drink Aware stuff.

The beer made me philosophical. Outside my tent I looked across the flatish English countryside and examined the sky. Clouds are everywhere in Britain but are one of the most overlooked features of the landscape. Maybe they don't count because they're constantly changing, but they can be more beautiful than the ground. In a blue sky I watched cotton wool clouds bubbling into odd shapes, a squashed, elongated cumulonimbus. One structure must have been twenty or thirty miles long, but stood alone in the baby blue sky, moving eastwards and carrying moisture to rain eventually on someone else's head. It was magnificent. Or maybe it was just the beer.

*

After a breakfast of two not very British *pain au chocolates* from the campsite shop I cycled into Glastonbury. If you're the mayor of a town worried that yours is being sucked into the chain-filled tedium of an Anytown, you should come to Glastonbury and take note. Towns with character don't have chains. No, they have a theme, a theme unique to themselves, and Glastonbury's theme is "spiritual shite" and good on it.

I got off my bike to look at its shops. On one side of the street was a place called Natural Earthling and another called Enlightenment, while on the other side a Meditation Centre was having a sale on Buddha Maitreya Etheric Weavers. I had to do some research to find out what the hell they were. It's a "quartz crystal meditation vibrational healing tool that transmits the monadic, soul-filled light and healing blessings of Buddha Maitreya the Christ to awaken the soul and heal the personality". Hmm. Later, a shop with the supernaturally corporate name of Witchcraft Limited was advertising tarot healings. What, they can heal as well as accurately predict the future? Amazing. It would take a large glass of water to wash a couple of them down though.

Glastonbury Abbey was getting in on the otherworldly nonsense too although, being an abbey, I suppose it always did. It claims to be the burial site of King Arthur.

The warden of last night's campsite had described Glastonbury as "like Marmite".

"It's not for everyone," he said. "But it's full of people who want to do you no harm".

A warming smell of joss sticks hung in the high street air, or was it marijuana? Two blokes with long beards and guitars sang folk tunes. I didn't believe a single syllable of what the town was trying to sell to me but, Glastonbury, I like your style.

I was a little sad to leave Witchville but I had some miles to do. I stopped at Burrow Mump, an artificial-looking hill with a knackered church on its summit. From the top I could see for miles around, a flat patchwork of fields in muted greens now that the sun was hiding. Low hills rose in the distance, ones I'd be tackling shortly.

And then I reached Taunton, the county town of Somerset. I was expecting the stereotypes, Worzles-style locals sitting at picnic benches quaffing huge tankards of scrumpy and belching amiably outside rough-looking houses made out of old cider casks. Unfortunately it wasn't as much fun as all that. Taunton was an über-Anytown, with barely a non-chain to be seen.

I cycled around the pedestrianised centre. I could hear

people talking. This accent is the closest Britain gets to the American Appalachians; it's Deliverance on a river of cider.

I stopped at a place called Henry's for a Somerset sausage baguette with cheese and a pint of cloudy cider. Across the street was the British Heart Foundation's furniture and electrical store. A bloke, who had this really been America would surely have been called Cletus, leaned his head out of the shop and warned a potential customer, "Do vat again, mate, an' I'll knock your block off!" It wasn't the only whiff of violence in the air.

As I ate my sandwich, a conversation carried on behind me between a local lad and another who was the bar's doorman. Was security really necessary at 2pm on a Monday lunchtime?

"I only gone an' got moiself barred, in I?" said the lad.

"What for, mate?" asked security.

"Foighting at Fever. Took four bouncers to pull me orf."

The security didn't seem too impressed with this. After all, had it been here rather than the other nightclub this doorman would've been the one pulling him orf and he was probably sick of silly little sods like him.

They discussed the failing state of the town's nightclubs. Soon there'd be no foighting because there'd be no clubs, the lad whined. Security mentioned a place he used to go.

"Nah, that place is going dahn, mate. It's the boss there. He ain't the brightest spark."

In front of me, two Vicki Pollards threw a small baby backwards and forwards between themselves while each puffed away on a mouthful of fags. The mother looked at her baby boy and then her friend.

"He's doin' my head in," she said.

"You shouldna 'ad 'im," her friend replied.

The mother shook her head.

"Wish ah 'adn't."

Taunton's town centre wasn't the sort of place to be if you wanted to focus on positive Britain. I cycled down the road a little and found myself a nice campsite. I sat in the sun and watched a middle-aged man who had the look of a Bond villain spend a couple of hours trying to rescue his drone from a tall tree with the aid of a picnic bench and a telescopic broom handle. Various people occasionally offered to help, but no one managed to rescue it. The man returned to his caravan looking broken. He would have to find some other way to take over the world.

Chapter 8: Gnomes, fairies and wizards

Devon, Cornwall and Dorset

I woke up to an utterly beautiful sunny day. The trees swayed in a gentle breeze, even the one with a drone still stuck in it.

As I packed away I saw the campsite owner.

"Sleep well?" he asked. I had. "It wasn't too noisy for you, was it?"

He was talking about the nearby motorway.

"Not considering how close it is," I said. "It's just a distant hum."

"I pretend it's the sea," he said.

Now that's thinking positively!

I cycled out of Taunton and along lovely country roads, stopping at Wiveliscombe for a bacon, egg and sausage bap. A woman was complaining to her friend.

"You know in this silly bloody country they don't have competitive sports days any more," she said.

"What happens then?" her friend asked.

"They're *all* winners. Everyone wins."

"Mmm."

"An' our Jack, he's a good little runner. He wants to win. But they say it's not fair."

"Yeah."

"But Jack's dyslexic and he's constantly tested at words. There always has to be a winner with words."

She had a point. Surely it's better to lose at a running race at an early age than to reach sixteen riding on a wave of life's inability to disappoint and then commit suicide because the WiFi's gone down for twenty minutes.

Along a B-road of rural loveliness I crossed the line into

Britain's fifth largest county, Devon, and according to Cambridge University, the friendliest one outside of Scotland.

After further refuelling at a garage in South Molton I asked the woman behind the counter how far it was to Torrington.

"It's about fifteen miles away," she said.

"That's alright then."

"But it's all up and down," she said.

Bloody hell, she wasn't telling fibs. The land concertinaed. I'd experienced a similar sort of nonsense in this part of the world before, repeated ascents and descents with 20% or 25% gradients. Last time I just assumed we'd chosen a lousy route. I didn't realise the entire county was like this. Devon's motto is "With God's help" but even He wouldn't have been able to get me up these hills. I had a lot of pushing to do.

Torrington isn't really a place. There's Great Torrington, which is shortened to Torrington, and then, just down the road, there's Little Torrington. There's also a Black Torrington, presumably where all the local outlaws live.

Once there I popped into a Co-op to do some shopping and talked to the young woman on the till. I was lacking some travel information.

"Which direction is Little Torrington?" I asked.

She shook her head.

"Little Torrington?" she asked a young lad beside her like I'd requested directions to Uranus.

"I've no idea," he said.

"Really?" I continued. "I thought it was only about two miles away."

The woman shrugged her shoulders and walked off, leaving me with this local mine of information. He just looked blankly at me.

"Do you live here?" I asked. Maybe he was someone who commuted in from miles away and had good reason not to know any local geography.

"Yeah."

"Oh. All your life?"

"Yeah. But I don't go out there," he added mysteriously.

Maybe Little Torrington was the Voldemort of villages, the one that Must-Not-Be-Named, even less visited.

"You've never been two miles away from the town?"

He looked wounded.

"Yes. Just not in that direction."

There are only three main roads out of Torrington. And I suppose the A-road to Little Torrington, that turned out to be slightly less than two miles away, does venture further into deepest, darkest Devon rather than in the direction of the bright lights of Bideford on the sexy northern coast.

Outside the Co-op was a large woman with a pram.

"Good way to get a nice tan," she said, looking at my lower half. "To get the legs out."

"Yeah, but beneath these shorts is the body of an anaemic albino."

"Maybe you should ride around in a mankini."

I smiled and shook my head.

"No one wants to see that."

"Oh, I don't know," she said, chuckling and wandering off. "I don't know."

No, really, I *do* know.

I cycled another horribly steep hill to Little Torrington and its campsite.

"Why are your hills so steep?" I asked the site owner. "I mean, it's not like you've any mountains around here. What do you do if it's snowy or icy?"

He shook his head.

"It doesn't snow that often." This was west England, famous for its wet weather. "I've lived here fifteen years and it's only snowed three times."

This is at odds with the weather statistics websites that claim Devon has between eight and fifteen snowy days each and every a year. Maybe he forgot to mention that he spends each winter on the Costa Blanca.

*

The next morning I cycled back into Great Torrington and finished off the B3227, the lovely country road that had already carried me the fifty-odd miles from Taunton. At Stibb Cross I leapt into a maze of tiny, traffic-free lanes and got utterly lost. I navigated by compass for a while until I stumbled upon what I was looking for, passing a road sign saying "Slow" beneath a red triangle containing a gnome.

We think of garden gnomes as a very British phenomenon but the statuettes as we know them today originated in Germany in the mid-1800s. One of the fellas in the first batch of gnomes to reach these shores from Germany, Lampy, still survives and is insured for £1 million. They are still popular in Germany, with an estimated population of 25 million. Here, unfortunately, our love affair with garden gnomes is dwindling. Sales have halved in the last ten years and there may only be around five million left in the entire country. At least they were safe here at the Gnome Reserve.

I walked into the reception area where the elderly lady at the desk was already serving another woman. She saw me and stopped.

"Just let me deal with this," she said to the woman. She looked up at me. "Yes?" she asked.

"What?" I said. "Aren't you dealing with this lady first?"

"Aren't you delivering something?"

"No, I'm here to see the gnomes."

"Oh."

I suppose it was the high-vis jacket I'd been given on that rainy day in Wales, or perhaps grown men don't usually turn up to a place like this by themselves.

Eventually the other customer was served and I paid my money.

"Go and take a gnome hat from the other room and then see the Gnome Reserve. Then come back in here and I'll give you a quiz to go fairy spotting."

In the adjoining room was a wide range of gnome hats – apparently the gnomes don't like it if you enter their woods under-dressed – and I selected a natty, rainbow-striped one.

I wandered the reserve, the sunlight dappling the pathway, birds tweeting in the trees. There were hundreds of gnomes: gnomes on a fairground, gnomes at a beach, gnomes on a chessboard, a gnome airport and gnome farmers, one of whom was riding a pig, although not in a David Cameron sort of way; this was mostly for children after all. There was a gnome motorbike race, what appeared to be a gnome court passing judgement over another gnome taking a dump, gnome spacemen, the Gnome Olympics and a sort of gnome cemetery where the little fellas had gone green with the moss that had grown over them.

Finally, there was the Ottery Pool full of hook-a-ducks. The idea was to pick your lottery numbers by selecting six yellow plastic birds at random – the bottom of each contained a number – and yanking them out with a big stick. I don't do the lottery and so I decided to use the ducks to select my next Chinese meal. I got number 38.

I popped back to the office for my fairy quiz and asked how many gnomes there were.

"We're in the Guinness Book of Records," said the lady at the desk. "If you include all these pixies inside as well there are about two thousand."

"And do you make them all yourselves?"

"We make the concrete ones but the themed ones, like the Olympic gnomes, we buy them in. Do you have gnomes yourself?"

"No, I don't have a garden."

But really that's a rubbish excuse. A gnome would be equally pointless in a bathroom. She gave me my fairy quiz and pointed me in the direction of the Wild Flower Garden.

"And you can put your hat back now if you like."

"Why? Would it offend the fairies?"

I was trying to get into this.

"Not really," she laughed, "but you don't need it."

I ambled around the flower garden looking for fairies, failing to find most of them. A young mother and her daughter were on the other side of the looping garden path, eyeing me suspiciously. Why the hell would a middle-aged man be here counting fairies all alone? Well, because I'd been sent here, obviously.

Since I was in Devon I stopped at the site's café and had myself a cream tea. I took my scone, split it in two and added the jam and then the clotted cream. I later read that only a moron does it in this order, or someone from Cornwall. In Devon you're supposed to put the cream on first.

I'd enjoyed my afternoon at the Gnome Reserve and I'd learnt something. By forcing myself to look at every nook and cranny of that little flower garden I noticed things I wouldn't otherwise have seen, like tiny flowers and weird little insects. It was an exercise in extreme and accidental mindfulness. Maybe we should always be on the lookout for fairies; we'd see so much more of the world.

I continued westwards into Bude. It was a warm late spring day and all was right with the world. Things were brightened still further, admittedly childishly, when I passed a plumber's van with the workman's name on the side; he was called Cobbledick.

I had now entered Cornwall. Despite being the most scenic county, according to the BBC, it was, by the Independent's reckoning, the poorest in England. Indeed, it was England's only county to receive emergency EU funding. As they say, man cannot live on views alone.

On our pound-a-day trip the campsite at Bude had been good enough to sponsor us a free night. I wanted to return to it and pay this time. Unfortunately I couldn't remember where it was.

I cycled around Bude and, passing a Chinese, remembered the gnomes' meal suggestion. I looked at the menu in the window outside. Number 38 was ten battered prawns. But with no sauce that would be dull. The gnomes were clearly idiots. But then I remembered I still had some on-the-turn sausages in my bag. The gnomes were offering me an unappealing option in Bude so that I'd finish off the sausages before food poisoning kicked in. I could accept their suggestion at a future Chinese when number 38 would be something amazing. Clever little gnomes!

I found Bude Holiday Resort. It wasn't the place we stayed last time but I was beginning to wonder whether I'd invented the other campsite. The young girl on reception looked at me with suspicion.

"Are you a contractor?" she asked.

"No, why?"

"Because of your jacket."

"I wear it to stop cars hitting me."

Do building contractors walk around town in cycling shorts? I don't know. Maybe they do.

"It's just contractors aren't allowed to stay here," she said.

"Well, I'm not a contractor."

She bashed the keyboard on her desk for a bit.

"That'll be twenty pounds," she said.

"Really? That's expensive."

She looked blankly at me.

"That's the price."

"It's ironic," I said. "If I was a contractor I could afford to stay here."

"But you're not a contractor."

"No."

She shrugged her shoulders.

"That's the price."

Twenty quid to sleep in a field is ridiculous and tonight there was an alternative. I wasn't making the other place up. I eventually found it. They only wanted eight pounds, which is just about right.

*

I woke up to yet another totally lovely day. Was this really England I was cycling around? By half eight the tent was already too hot and had to be opened to let in some cool air. I made coffee, ate chocolate-covered macaroons for breakfast and made a leisurely start around half ten.

It was a wonderful pootle down towards Widemouth Bay with its craggy cliffs, decorated with tiny flowers, falling steeply into the sea. Down below, in the coves and caves, ancient smugglers squirrelled away their ill-gotten bounty of wine and brandy and, if duty-free shops are anything to go by, those massive Toblerones.

Moving downhill I cycled through a swarm of flies three hundred metres long. The swarm was three hundred metres long, not the flies; that would've been terrifying. Coming out the other side I found something in my mouth. Was it a shred of coconut from this morning's macaroon or a creature from that swarm? I was coated with the little buggers, the sheen of sweat on my brow acting like fly paper.

It wasn't long before I was in Boscastle. We'd cycled through this Cornish coastal village last year and I'd looked longingly at its ridiculous museum without the funds to go inside. Now I was back and I had more than a quid in my pocket. Today nothing could stop me entering The Museum of Witchcraft and Magic.

There are two ways a museum of magic can go. The first is with a knowing wink, hinting that, yes, of course it's all a load of nonsense, but it's fun so enjoy yourself. The other way is to take it very, very seriously indeed. Today's museum took the second approach.

There was an interesting collection of items, including a pentacle the size of a small pizza made out of matchsticks by a Pagan prisoner called Bill, who was serving life. The attached note said Bill had used it in his cell for many years, but it didn't say how. Probably as a coaster or something.

I learnt about the Book of Shadows. It's a home-made collection of spells, recipes and magic formulas copied by hand from a coven's master copy. The initiated witch is then supposed to add to the book when she discovers her own spells that work, or her own recipes, like that delightful fruit cake she made for the WI. The museum's own Book of Shadows had originally belonged to an elderly gentlemen who gave it to a witch in Lincolnshire.

"After twelve years and an unfortunate incident with the elderly gentleman, the witch decided not to use it any more and kindly donated it."

I love the vagueness of the statement. What was the incident? Is there now an old fella hopping around Lincoln in the form of a frog?

Another star exhibit was the Time Machine. But this was no TARDIS, merely a metal disc attached to a battery. The museum was honest when it said, "Details of how it worked are sketchy." Apparently a Mr Alex Saunders would stand on the disc and enter a trance while his mate Derek Taylor transcribed what happened, like an episode of Quantum Leap but without any actual time travel. Or even anything as exciting as leaping.

Some of the items in the museum were presented in a way that made you wonder how its label typist kept a straight face. Here's a caption for a painted broomstick:

"Owned by writer, artist and sensitive Olga Hunt from Manaton; on a full moon she delighted in leaping all over Haytor rocks with her broomstick, much to the alarm of campers and courting couples."

Yeah, of course she did. And if she delighted in interrupting couples shagging on Haytor rocks then she wasn't *that* sensitive.

Still not convinced by the magic on offer here? In 1998 a small yacht was becalmed outside Boscastle harbour. The sailors approached the museum and apparently asked to "buy the wind". Don't ask me how but the wind was then tied in three knots on a rope and sold to the gullible lads. And guess what? "The boat sailed the following morning." The most unbelievable thing about this story is that the Devon coast had a day without wind in the first place.

I cycled up the hill away from the museum of magic and out of Boscastle, and before you could say abracadabra I was in Tintagel. I got myself settled on a cheap campsite in a huge, weirdly sloping field and went out to find the town's star attraction.

According to legend, Arthur was conceived at Tintagel Castle. To be honest, to call it a castle is a bit of a stretch. It's merely a few low walls on a dramatic cliff top. Since the 16th century, bridges and steep staircases connect the mainland to the rocky outcrop on which the castle's remains stand. It's worth a look but don't go expecting round tables or anything.

As someone who's not much of a fan of the Royal Family, I think we should hold up Arthur as an inspiration. I'd prefer all our monarchs to go around not actually existing. And the old pro-monarchist argument about queenie bringing in more than she costs is also true of Arthur, despite his non-existence. Tintagel Inc. is coining it in, charging nearly nine quid a pop to visit the place. If people are interested in viewing an imaginary king's castle, just think how many tourists would still want to see the Queen's gaff once she's out on her ear.

I was after some more local food but it couldn't be found. I hunted the menus outside Tintagel's bars and restaurants for Stargazy Pie but no cigar, and no pie.

Stargazy Pie is like a normal pie but instead it has a number of pilchards' heads protruding from its crust. The macabre-looking dinner is actually from a village called Mousehole, but it's in the far south-west of Cornwall and I wasn't going that far for a pie full of bones.

I fell into the King Arthur's Arms, bought a pint of eye-wateringly strong Rattler cider and looked at their menu. It included fish pie and so I asked the barman.

"Is this fish pie Stargazy Pie?"

"No."

"Do you know where can I get some?" I asked.

He shook his head.

"None of the pubs around here have it."

"Have you ever tried it?"

"No."

"Would you?"

"No."

Maybe it was just something people made at home when they wanted to scare the grandkids.

*

It rained in the night and I awoke to a grey, misty and overcast day, the sort of morning Morrissey would probably write a song about.

I cycled on to Camelford, the location of Britain's worst mass-poisoning event. In 1988, twenty tons of aluminium sulphate were accidentally added to the water supply. It eventually broke down, but then only into sulphuric acid, which didn't really help. The contamination was not initially acknowledged. At the time the water industry was about to be privatised and an investigation into the mass poisoning of an entire town's water was considered by Michael Howard, then Minister of State for the Environment, as "very distracting". In fact, authorities said the water was safe to drink, but that people might want to add cordial to mask the unpleasant taste. No one was told what had really happened until sixteen days later. Short term effects included the usual diarrhoea and vomiting but also more disturbing stuff, like the victim's hair turning blue, as though the whole town was slowly morphing into Smurfs. No one knows how many died as a direct result of what happened but, over the years since the leak, autopsies have revealed abnormal amounts of aluminium in the brains of the people who lived in Camelford at the time. But at least there was a happy ending: Michael Howard was made a Lord. So that's alright then.

Avoiding the water, I left Camelford behind and from there took the A39, a big mistake. It's a horrible road for cyclists, both narrow and busy. I escaped its traffic by heading off towards Padstow but since I'd seen it on the last ride – it's little more than a shrine to Rick Stein anyway – I continued onwards to Newquay, the surf capital of Britain.

Entering the town came as a surprise. I'm not sure why, but I was expecting a long, wide beach with a few old VW camper vans on it and buff, long-haired dudes in knee-length shorts riding the waves. Instead the beautiful coastline gave way to Watergate Bay's admittedly lovely sand surrounded by hideous hotels. A lorry was holding up traffic, its advertising pitch "Eat More Chips!"

All in all, Newquay seemed run down. As well as its surfing credentials, it's Britain's stag night capital. Vice.com describes it colourfully as a place of "puke, herbal ecstasy and endless fingerings" with "feral children roaming in packs...making Vines of each other eating glass and drinking alcohol through their eyes". In 2009, two teenagers died in separate drunken cliff falls in what was branded the "fortnight of shame". The town has tried to clean up its act. For one, it's banned the mankini, although I can't imagine it's the garment of choice for many teenagers, otherwise you'd find more 1970s Top of the Pops presenters holidaying in Newquay.

Cycling through town, the hills kept on coming. I wanted to head a little further down the coast but the road fizzled out at Towan Head, a cliff where no more progress could be made by bike without turning back. So I stopped and sat in the sun, making up for this disappointment with a honeycomb and caramel swirl ice cream. An old couple came to rest nearby.

"Do you want to go any further, Alan?" asked the old woman.

"No," he replied sourly.

"What do you want to do?"

He looked her right in the eye.

"I want to drink," he said.

It wasn't just the kids who were on a bender.

*

The choice in Cornwall is a busy A-road with a steep hill or a non-busy non-A-road with a *stupidly* steep hill. This lumpy south-west corner of Britain is a gorgeous place to cycle but I'm just not sure there's enough beauty to justify the pain of its gradients if you're carrying heavy bags. And the roads, even the A-roads, are too narrow for cyclists and motorists to happily co-exist. Even when I stopped and dismounted to allow traffic to pass me there wasn't enough room to do so until nothing was coming in the opposite direction. I imagine even driving around here is a massive pain in the arse.

Newquay had been the western terminus of my British journey. For the next few weeks I'd be heading east. I decided

I'd avoid the cars of the A30 and found a quiet road running almost parallel. This route brought me to Castle-an-Dinas, an Iron Age hill fort, now just a ring of large channels. There wasn't much to see but the views were great, especially towards Goss Moor, a large, low forest with strange spiky hills behind. At the gate of the site someone had flyposted an ad for a dog grooming business that urgently demanded some googly eyes.

Remember Sarah the police officer in Wales? Well, her mum Jo worked at Lanhydrock, a large stately home a few miles south of Bodmin, and I'd been invited to visit. Unfortunately, today was the day that Jo didn't actually work, but I could still have a look around this nine hundred acre estate and pretend I was one of the nobs from Downton Abbey.

The house showed how people with money lived in Victorian Britain. The parents and ten kids were cared for by a house staff of thirty, including eighteen in the kitchen. That's one and a half full-time people per person just to cook stuff for you. There were also fifty people to maintain the externals and extensive garden.

"And this wasn't even their main home!" said one of the National Trust staff.

They had another place in London as well as a house in Cambridge.

The family's eldest son had been an MP, known as the best-dressed man in Parliament. It's a pity he wasn't also the best-behaved man in Parliament. He was kicked out of the place for electoral fraud. He just waited for a bit and then found a new constituency.

Lanhydrock's long hall has an elaborate plaster ceiling depicting scenes from Genesis, and the walls are lined with theological books. To give you a sense of size, the room was once used to play badminton. While I wandered around admiring my surroundings, a wedding was taking place outside and a group of well-to-do women were assessing the sartorial qualities of the gathering through a large window.

"Ooo, I don't like that black and purple thing she's wearing," said one.

"Oh, it's all the rage these days, Cynthia."

"Is it? Is it really? Well, Gemma, it's *facking* awful."

I continued on to Lostwithiel and found a campsite, as nice as any I'd visited on this journey and for only a fiver. Unfortunately, the nearest shop was back in town, down an endless 17% hill. Here's a thing: When designing a road, if you find you've had to include an escape lane then maybe throw the design away and start again. If the Alps don't need escape lanes then you can be sure Cornwall doesn't. Today's was lethal, a one-metre wide strip of sand and gravel directly beside a metal fence. The only thing it would help any out-of-control driver escape is existence.

*

I set off on another lovely day and shortly passed Restormel Castle, a pretty, round building with a proper, although dry, moat. It was so well-preserved I could do a complete circuit of the walls where the lookouts would have stood. The gardens around it were full of huge, blossoming trees. No one else was about except a dad and his son, and a large Polish family whose dog wanted to eat my shoes.

The road took me past the café of the Duchy of Cornwall, Prince Charles's place. Given his love of homeopathy I could imagine a conversation at the café's counter.

"I ordered an Americano but I really wanted an espresso."

"Oh, you want it stronger, do you? Just let me add some more water. That'll do the trick."

I decided to bail on the A390 to Liskeard because of the traffic and I headed into the lanes, which were often nice but always painful.

The route took me through the tiny village of Herodsfoot, one of a number of Britain's special places. In England and Wales there are 54 of them and they are known as Thankful Villages. They are grateful because every single man they sent to the First World War came back alive. You might think 54 death-free villages is a lot but it isn't when you consider that there were 16,000 distinct settlements in Britain and every one of those 15,946 unthankful villages lost at least someone, and in some cases hundreds or thousands.

Such lucky places weren't dished out equally. While Lancashire, Merseyside, Greater Manchester and Cheshire don't score a single village, there are nine in Somerset alone. You might think this was maybe because their soldiers just hung out in the trenches drinking cider and not getting shot at, but it was more likely because of the idea of the Mate's Brigade, where groups of friends went off to join the same battalion, and if that battalion found itself in something as lethal as the Battle of the Somme, not many were coming home. Likewise, if your village's battalion was lucky enough to be sent to guard something nobody wanted in the first place, then you'd all come back.

At the time I was cycling around, Darren Hayman, a singer-songwriter, was also visiting every Thankful village to write and record a track about each. He's releasing the songs on a trilogy of albums. It's not a project about war, but about the villages themselves. Talking of one village, he said:

"...when I was walking down the high street you were just seeing buildings that used to be something else. It's marked in stone: the school house, the police building, the community hall...It's a problem. Villages have diminishing young populations. The village is in trouble."

This was something I'd already noticed, no pubs, no shops, let alone a school. But if the villages were in trouble, and most of the towns were being converted into chain-identical Anytowns, what was left of Britain?

The road in and out of Herodsfoot was another sixteen-per-center. I was beginning to hate the street planners of Cornwall. But at least by now spring had fully sprung. Flowers of all colours grew in the hedgerows on either side of my single track lane and, at one point, trees grew over the road to form a perfect, green tunnel. It was like cycling through the gateway to an elven wonderland.

The onward roads to Torpoint were absolutely knackering and took an hour and a half longer than I'd expected. I turned up at half three and headed for the marina. I was on the lookout for a boat called Excalibur. I couldn't see it. It didn't help that I didn't know what sort of boat it was.

I popped into the marina's office, but no one was about. A large whiteboard with a drawing of the marina was on the wall, each boat with a berth labelled, but there was no Excalibur.

Outside, at the Torpoint Mosquito Sailing Club, a weekend-long beer festival was in full swing, live music booming out on to its picnic-tabled terrace. Despite taking my time to get here, I was still too early for my appointment with Excalibur's skipper, if indeed I was even at the right place.

I cycled back into town for a look around but there wasn't much happening on this lazy Sunday afternoon. A ferry arrived from Plymouth, just across the water, and spilled its load of cars and vans and the occasional cyclist on to the peninsula on which Torpoint stands. This brief flurry of life quickly subsided.

There's never any place better to wait around than at a pub. I opted for the King's Arms, near the port. I sat outside with a pint of cider and looked towards Plymouth. The ferry goes every fifteen minutes during the day. Torpoint is one of its commuter towns.

A couple in their forties bearing a bottle of red wine came

to sit at the next picnic bench, the fella eventually spilling himself on to mine. He looked at me and smiled. He had mad eyes, like Brad Pitt's in 12 Monkeys, except that Simon's eyes were alcohol-induced. He asked me what I was doing. I told him.

"You'll see some good stuff," Simon said with a mild slur.

"Yep. There are some fleas I want to see."

"Eh?"

"They're Mexican."

He looked confused but then managed to focus for a second.

"I'll get you on The One Show!" he screamed emphatically.

"Shut up, Simon," said his wife Helen.

"Do you know anyone on The One Show?" I asked.

"No." He swivelled his eyes. "Green Army!"

He punched the air joyously. He was celebrating Plymouth reaching the Division One playoffs.

"I'll collect some money for you," he said, jumping up.

"Sit down, Simon!"

"There's no need," I said. "But thanks."

He got up anyway and went from window to window of the cars queuing for the ferry.

"He's been out since eleven this morning," said Helen wearily.

"Green army!" we heard him shout.

He came back empty-handed.

"Have you seen this?" he said, showing me his elbow.

"You had an accident?"

"I can't believe you're telling him this," said Helen.

"I got pushed. I was at a campsite and talking to this Canadian, a black fella. About football." He mentioned a West Ham player whose name escapes me. "I called him a big, black bastard."

"Who? The Canadian?"

"No, the footballer. The Canadian didn't mind. But a woman there did. She screamed at me an' called me a racist. To be honest, we were all a bit drunk. An' she pushed me." A wave of mild discomfort crossed his face, and then he smiled again. "I'll get you on The One Show."

"No, it's alright."

"Green army!"

He went for another wander and I spoke to Helen. She had only met up with him about ten minutes earlier and appeared to be trying to catch him alcoholically, although she had a long way to go. Although I didn't catch her true job title, she was a sort of school bouncer. If any trouble kicks off it's her job to go and extract the offending pupil from the classroom. It's unbelievable that someone is needed full-time for a role like that.

"How many kids do you pull out a week?" I asked.

"Depends. Usually it's around ten. But it's always more the day after a full moon."

"Really?"

"Yeah. I don't know why. It just is."

"You need to go to The Jetty," said Simon, returning.

"Where's The Jetty?"

"There," he replied, pointing to a pub across the road. "It's got a great view from the terrace."

The view appeared to be the same view we could see either side of the pub building, but he was adamant.

"It *is* nice," said Helen.

We went across the road, they bought me another cider and another bottle of red for themselves.

"If you're looking for weird places you should find the gallows in the docks of Plymouth. But they're difficult to get into," said Simon.

"Why?"

"I dunno. Green army! Did I tell you I can get you on The

One Show?"

"Shut up, Simon!"

"Have you always lived around here?" I asked.

"Nah, a long time ago I used to live in London," replied Helen. "Across the road was a squat. Boy George, Marilyn and Steve Strange lived there."

"Did you ever speak to them?"

"Well, we taunted Boy George once and he yelled, 'Fuck off, you slag!' But that was all. It's my claim to fame."

Helen and Simon had been a fun way to fill in the time before the real reason I was in Torpoint, to meet Lizzie, captain of the good ship Excalibur. She'd said I could spend the night on her boat. Other than that, like that time machine in the Boscastle witchcraft museum, details were sketchy.

At seven, I returned to the beer festival at the marina and met Lizzie.

"Do you know anything about the gallows at Plymouth Docks? Apparently they're hard to get into."

"Yes," she replied, "because that's where the nuclear subs are serviced."

"OK, really? I'll forget that then."

Lizzie wasn't alone. With her were Tim, Theresa and another Simon. Tim's sleek 35-foot yacht was in the marina. I wouldn't be staying on that one. But Lizzie's 21-foot Excalibur was in open water on the other side of the harbour wall. She'd bought it recently for a few hundred quid, covered in mould, and was slowly cleaning and restoring it. That's where I'd be sleeping.

Lizzie's a primary school teacher who had done plenty of cycle touring of her own. She's harder than me. She doesn't even use a tent, just a bivouac, the nutter.

"So, do you like the pointy end?" asked Theresa, referring to Cornwall.

I asked if this is the local way of referring to it. It isn't.

I know we had a laugh that night but details are fuzzy. I was three beers ahead before they arrived, they caught me up very quickly and then together we sprinted off into the beery distance.

We got to the end of the night and I still wasn't sure what the sleeping arrangements were. As it turned out, Martin rowed Lizzie and me out in a rubber dinghy to Excalibur, where she showed me around – it doesn't take long on a 21-foot boat – and gave me a bottle of elderflower cider. They then got back in the dinghy and left me to float in the water all alone, the bright lights of Plymouth to my right, the more muted ones of Torpoint to my left. I sat there, bobbing in the sea under a black sky, sipping the cider and watching distant lighthouses twinkle. I don't think I've ever felt so peaceful.

*

I slept the sleep of a womb-housed babe, floating in the amniotic fluid of Plymouth Sound, on a tranquil, windless night. The cider helped as well.

I was told to text Lizzie when I woke up and a few minutes later a very splashy dinghy appeared, oared this time by Theresa, perhaps not as experienced a sailor as Martin, with Lizzie as cox and taking a circuitous route roughly but not entirely in my direction. As they approached, the still morning air was filled with giggles and mild swearing.

Eventually they pulled alongside and I climbed aboard. I took over on the oars for the trip back to land and made an even bigger hash of it than Theresa.

We had a cup of tea on Simon's yacht while everyone else nursed their hangovers – my brain haemorrhage-based hangover-less superpower remains – and then walked into town to score ourselves a great full Cornish breakfast. Outside the café, four blokes were attempting to change the wheel on a ropey-looking, black sports car. On the back of it was stencilled "No Fucks Given!" and, more bizarrely, on the

196

boot it simply read "Her tits". As we passed, their car jack collapsed, slamming the partially tyre-less car to the ground with a crash and, audibly at least, one fuck was given.

As I rolled off the ferry the heat was on as I headed up into the hills north of Plymouth. It was Monday 30th of May and summer was coming. The traffic of the A386 wasn't pleasant but short of doing a massive detour it seemed the easiest way to reach the gateway to the Dartmoor Forest. Today I would cycle across the entire thing.

Dartmoor Forest is a bit of a misnomer. It's mostly open nothingness, moorland with the odd clump of trees. The B3212 should have been lonelier than it was but as the only east-west route across the middle of this 368 square mile National Park it sees more traffic than is ideal.

Dartmoor is a place of ghost stories, of pixies, spectral hounds and a headless horseman. And then there are the Hairy Hands. These disembodied mitts supposedly grab steering wheels and force drivers off the road. It's one explanation for the disproportionately high number of road accidents around here. Another explanation is alcohol.

The moorland was studded with sheep and cows and the famous wild ponies, mostly chocolate brown, wandering about the place. Trees aside, nothing grew very tall, the moorland dotted with the occasional low shrub and the odd single stone, standing all alone, like Katie Hopkins at a party.

I expected there to be a surprise campsite somewhere around Moretonhampstead but I was disappointed. And I'd also expected the hills to stop near Exeter, but I had no such luck. I kept going and found a camping ground four miles the other side. It was a bit dilapidated with no facilities except a toilet. A mouldy caravan sat rotting in one corner opposite a bank of equally dead-looking camper vans. It was like a graveyard for Breaking Bad-style mobile meth labs.

I set off into the surrounding lanes to find the only

supermarket around but couldn't. I did, however, find two grown men hugging each other and weeping inconsolably. Eventually I worked out where the supermarket was but by then it had gone six and it was already shut. Seeking help, I was directed to the grocery-shop-of-last-resort, a secret non-motorway entrance to the M5 Services. Finding something to make for dinner was like the most depressing episode ever of Ready Steady Cook.

*

I woke up to a day that promised sunshine but then broke that promise, clouded over and delivered a sharp wind, fortunately from behind. It was another day of climbing and inadequate roads for the quantity of traffic. All pretence at remaining positive about the current infrastructure had long since been abandoned.

I started late and decided to make a lazy day of it. Tomorrow I had an appointment but today I would end the day at the coastal village of Beer, if only because of its name.

The afternoon was hills and more hills, and then I saw a sign for the National Cycle Route No. 2, directing me off the main road, down a web of lanes towards Beer five miles away. I liked the idea of following a sign for Beer. As on previous NCR paths it made an effort to seek out the least bike-friendly terrain.

The ride took me through Branscombe on the south coast with its pretty St Winifred's church up on the hill and then into the village itself, a Best Kept one from a few years ago. Maybe it had let its standards slide of late or perhaps they share out the awards equitably over the years.

In the centre of this dot of a place is an old bakery and a blacksmith, who hung around outside his forge, pondering whether there really was enough work to keep this type of thing going. The beer gardens of the roadside pubs were full of happy punters enjoying this hidden-away corner of Devon, drinking themselves into that summer ale-oblivion that would end with one of them crossing the road to the blacksmith and asking him how much he'd charge for a suit of armour.

It was here at Branscombe that the MSC Napoli was beached in 2007, resulting in a mass-looting of some of its 2,394 containers. The Daily Mail wrote that looters arrived from "as far away as Liverpool", in no way reinforcing any stereotypes. As well as biscuits, nappies, perfume and car parts, some people zoomed off on salvaged BMW motorcycles. In the same article, one drinker from the village pub said, "The locals didn't take anything – maybe a few souvenirs. It was northerners who took everything." That said, if you live in Branscombe, everyone in Britain is a northerner.

Before I could reach my destination there was of course another huge hill to ascend, and then I tumbled down the other side, passing Beer Quarry, and then obviously had another climb to the campsite on Beer Head, the town's high cliffs with Seaton in the distance.

The place itself is small but it's amusing to see the word 'Beer' attached to each business's name. The Beer Pharmacy suggested all ills cured by ales. The Beer Church was one at which even I could worship.

After a delicious supper of fish, chips and gravy in the local chippy I finished the day the way that every day should be finished in this attractive little village, at The Anchor Inn supping a beer in Beer.

*

Today I was going to visit Dave. If you read *Hungry for Miles*, you already know Dave. Depending on your opinion, he was either 'the loveable one', 'the indecisive one' or 'the mental one'. All three descriptions fit him equally well.

One or two of the readers of that book seemed to get the

impression that Dave, and the other rider Joe, were in some way mistreated. Believe me, if Dave had been mistreated he was big enough to have dealt with it himself. There was no direct animosity between any of us. There may have been times when they both annoyed me, as I'm sure I annoyed them, but that's what you get when you bring a bunch of strangers together and starve them to death while cycling great distances. We each dealt with our grievances in a very British way, by repressing it and pretending it wasn't happening.

En route to Dave's I passed into county 37 and Dorset. The road to his home took me on an uneventful ride under a grey sky. I was expecting more of Axminster. Given the perceived qualities of its carpets I imagined its town would be equally plush, but that wasn't the case. It felt more like a piece of lino.

I did, however, see a genuine first. You know how a normal cake is a tenner but call it a wedding cake and it's suddenly three hundred quid, or to deliver a washing machine to your house is thirty quid but to deliver Uncle Jeff to the cemetery costs billions. Well, in Axminster there was a funeral and outside the church, to prevent inconvenient parking, they had special funereal traffic cones, not orange or red, but black ones. They must have cost the deceased's family a fortune.

I took a series of grey and green lanes from Axminster, up and down dale, passing near a place called Fishpond Bottom, which sounds like a condition that requires Imodium. I eventually rolled into Beaminster, another one of those towns whose pronunciation isn't obvious. It's Bemster.

Dave answered the door of his flat wearing his cycling gear and with his trademark smile wider than Brad Pitt's telly. It was great to see him again. We popped to the Red Lion, a pub just five minutes from his house. It was only after three pints that he told me he thought we were going cycling today, hence the cycling outfit. I just assumed he'd already been out. We figured it was probably safer to leave it until tomorrow now.

He was going to leave with me and start his own tour of various British Cycle Quest (BCQ) sites. Basically, the aim of BCQ is to visit six pre-selected sites per county and answer a question about each that you'd only be able to discover by turning up in person. He didn't have time to do the whole country but he planned to cycle for three months. He had a bigger budget than on our last ride. This time he had a full five pounds a day.

On the way back we stopped at the supermarket for more cider and a couple of pizzas. While his oven cooked the food he played me his record collection on a tiny, ancient deck. The evening felt nicely retro, listening to his heavy rock staples of AC/DC and Iron Maiden with the occasional Eurythmics thrown in to provide variation and then to spoil it all, his pride and joy, an album by The Worzles.

"Here," he said, coming out of the kitchen. "I got this for you."

He handed me a bottle of local porter, Black Ven from Lyme Regis.

"Thanks, Dave."

"I bought you a four-pack but I drank the other three last night."

It was good stuff. We had our pizzas and worked our way through the cider. Then Dave started to talk excitedly about his fat bike, basically a monster truck driver's rebuild of a BMX. Its tyres are almost as wide as a car's.

"People think I'm stupid spending money on this," he said. After all, he wasn't earning much. He was back as a pot washer at the pub he'd been working at before last year's ride. "But I don't care what people think. If I want to spend £1,100 on it, I will do," he grinned. "It's up to me. In fact, if I want to spend £1,100 on *drugs*, I will do."

He showed me his bike. It really did look a little bit ridiculous.

"Your bike looks like the sort of decision you'd make after taking £1,100's worth of drugs," I said.

The huge tyres are under-inflated to allow you to ride on soft sand. They're not much use on the road. With the cider all gone and drunkenness maximised Dave wanted to give me a demonstration of his monster bike. What better time to do it? It was, after all, gone midnight. He opened his front door, pushed the bike outside and mounted it.

"Ready?" I said.

He nodded, his smile splitting his face. The cider had made him happy, but the idea of cider and a fat bike pushed him over the edge. He disappeared down his short pathway, through his gate, over the quiet residential road and bumped the front wheel up the opposite pavement on to a small grass verge.

Now, at this point, he'd planned to turn, do a half-circle on the grass and return to where he'd started. Instead, he kept going straight on, through a huge clump of nettles and down a steep banking. I ran out to see if he was alright in time to hear a splash, a "Ouf!" and then hysterical giggles.

A few seconds later he emerged from the nettles, his light grey t-shirt now charcoal thanks to the water in the river at the bottom of the banking and his track suit bottoms soaked.

"You dick," I said, failing to hold back a smirk.

His huge beamer was wider than any smile I'd ever seen before.

*

After my night sleeping on Dave's living room floor we set off together the next morning, Dave on his road bike rather than his fat bike. We were heading towards the Cerne Abbas Giant on roads that Dave had described as "not very hilly" but which were, in reality, very hilly indeed. It wasn't as bad as Cornwall but I still needed to push.

After an hour or so we arrived at the viewing point to see the chalk giant. He stands 55 metres tall with an impressive 11-metre erection. Apparently, postcards of the giant are the only image of an erect penis that can be sent legally through the English Post Office.

The village of Cerne Abbas was keen to use the commercial power of the hillside nude for its own benefit and a lot of the local businesses included his image, phallus and all, as a part of their own logos. It was all very unBritish. After all, no UK company has employed such a massive knob in its advertising since Iceland fired Peter André.

The sun was out that morning but it certainly wasn't a given around here. Only seven miles south from here is Martintown, Britain's wettest village. It's not generally damp but holds the record all the same. On July 18 1955, 279 mm of rain fell in 24 hours. That's three months' worth on a single day!

After lunch we continued over a huge hill through Piddletrenthide. A strong wind blowing from the deep blue sky rippled the long grass on the hillside, creating impressionistic waves of pale green. As our route collided with the A354, we bade each other farewell. Dave was heading north-west to his sister's forty miles away while I had some martyrs to see.

The towns and villages in this part of Dorset are oddly named. There is a puddle of Piddles and a piddlingly large amount of Puddles. There's Piddlehinton, Affpuddle and Briantspuddle. Puddletown, which stands on the River Piddle, sounds like a CBeebies show about a village of animated ducks. To maintain the urination theme, there's also a neighbouring village called Tincleton, but my destination today was Tolpuddle.

The Tolpuddle Martyrs were a bunch of young men who, without intending to, started the trade union movement. They campaigned to increase the wages of the average worker and for such insolence were shipped off to Australia and sentenced to hard labour.

One local landowner complained the workers were trying to determine their own wages, which was "against the natural order of things", and shows that nowadays, in an age when unions have less and less power, little has changed.

Although the Tolpuddle museum is free, I was the only person in there. More popular, and not far down the road, is Bovington Tank Museum. If the Tolpuddle museum is about making life better for the workers of the world, Bovington is about building machines that do the opposite.

Before reaching the museum proper, there was some sort of racing track for tanks with an information board to show you the types of killing machine flying past. They all seemed to have names like condoms. There was a Trojan and a Titan and a Centurion. There was even one called a Mastiff, for the bestiality lovers out there.

To justify the thirteen quid entrance fee the tank museum says you can come back any time you like within the next year, but they know there's more than a yearful of tanks in a single visit to the place.

The first tank I saw was from 1915 and called Little Willie. Presumably the tank designers back then had more confidence in the size of their own wedding tackle rather than bluster with the big penis names of modern tanks.

Next came a cute, little, white death machine used by the UN. It had originally been named Fieldmouse, but this was deemed too dainty and so was changed to Ferret, which isn't much better. If the opposing forces of European nations had spent as much effort on diplomacy as they did dreaming up imaginative names for their hardware perhaps they wouldn't have needed tanks at all.

The museum didn't shy away from describing unfortunate tank design issues. There was an Italian Carro Veloce, a tiny, flame-throwing tank, that suffered its own problems. Its cannon frequently backfired and cooked alive its own crew way past *al dente*.

The museum glorified war and soldiering, which perhaps isn't so surprising this close to Bovington Camp's army base. But some parts were unnecessary, like the stick-your-head-into-the-scene-and-complete-the-picture of you holding a massive bayonet, presumably just before stabbing it into someone's head.

The models of the trenches were uncomfortable and the cutaways of the tanks showed just how tightly the soldiers were packed in there. They must have wished they'd done a GCSE and joined the RAF instead.

It was best to walk around this place without thinking too deeply about it, lest humanity take a mental kicking for its ability to excel at such sadistic creativity. Every single machine in that huge hangar – and there were hundreds – was designed with one aim in mind: to blow other human beings to pieces.

Feeling slightly ill about the whole place wasn't improved when I turned up at the nearby campsite in Wool.

"It's £24," the bloke said.

Bloody hell.

"Is that for the week?" I asked.

He ignored me. There was no alternative, or at least that's what I thought. Popping out to buy provisions later, I saw a sign for another place just a mile away. Never mind, I could still think back to Dave's gurning, dripping-wet head emerging from a thicket of nettles and giggle myself into a better mood.

*

I cycled towards the south coast, through the lovely Purbeck Hills, along the track of a firing range. Large numbers were positioned high on the hillside for target practice. Lower down, on the flat plain beneath the hills, burnt out and partially destroyed tanks littered the landscape. Each and every fence was adorned with a Keep Out sign.

I was heading to Tyneham Village. Down a steep track from the high ridge of the hill I was in for a surprise. For a famously abandoned village it contained more people than any of the inhabited ones I'd cycled through of late, although these were all day-visitors.

The village itself was just a row of four houses, a rectory, an old school room, a church, a gardener's house and a farm with a barn that had once functioned as a local theatre. The village had been a thriving little community but was acquisitioned during World War Two. For the incoming Ministry of Defence operatives, a sad notice had been hung on the church door:

"Please treat the church and houses with care. We have given up our homes where many of us have lived for generations, to help win the war to keep men free. We will return one day and thank you for treating the village kindly."

No one was ever allowed back. It was never made clear, at least to the visitor, why the Army had needed the village. It hadn't been used as target practice. The houses remained as they had been left, minus roofs in most cases. But a community had been torn apart never to reform.

Under a melancholic sky I trundled onwards, passing dramatic Corfe Castle. I headed towards the Isle of Purbeck, which isn't an island at all. From a high viewpoint, Poole's harbour and wide bay are gorgeous.

At the end of the headland a boat avoids a twenty-mile diversion around the bay. The link from the Isle of Purbeck to

Poole is via a chain ferry that costs a pound. On the same boat were two Lycra-clad cyclists, blonde Steph and brunette Nicki. We chatted on the short crossing. Just as we hit land, Nicki piped up.

"Is my face dirty?" she asked.

"Yes, it is."

It was filthy. She left it at that and we all disembarked before she could tell me the story.

Through Poole I made my way into Bournemouth where the fire brigade had closed off a main road while they hosed down an abandoned pub that was mysteriously on fire and screamed "Insurance job!"

I was still moving east, now heading into Hampshire and the Sussexes, some of the wealthiest parts of Britain. Would all this cash lying about the place make it the most desirable part of the country to live in? Er, no, it wouldn't.

Chapter 9: Down in the Downs

Hampshire, West Sussex and East Sussex

After skirting Christchurch I was approaching the New Forest. I had big hopes for the place. I'd heard great things about it. Weirdly, as the signs appeared along with the cattle grids to keep the ponies on the inside, the trees disappeared and were replaced by withered stumps or low shrubs. It was as forest-like as a football pitch, at least for those first few miles.

In the woods of Brockenhurst I found a huge, expensive and mostly rubbish campsite where hundreds of tents were packed so closely together on this sunny Friday in early June that later we'd be able to hear each other snore. Ponies walked about the place with the kind of protection offered to the street-walking cows of Delhi, which was probably necessary since they appeared to be particularly fond of devouring tents. Given that mine had now been slept in for all but a handful of my 54 days on the road, its internal odour provided, thankfully, a measure of protection.

*

I'd always imagined the New Forest to be a rural wonderland instead of the traffic-clogged, uninspiring place that it turned out to be. I suspect I'd been spoiled by the majesty of Wales, and the occasional peacefulness of Cornwall and Devon at least once away from the A-roads and, well, just about everywhere I'd been so far bar the West Midlands.

The New Forest is in Hampshire, of course. Hampshire sounds like a place with money and if that's correct, and everyone is paying their taxes, the residents would have a pretty good case for acts of public disobedience given the crappy state of their roads. Swansea may have suffered potholes on the way in, but Hampshire's surfaces were unpleasant just about everywhere.

As I'd cycled around Britain so far, it had been relatively light on road-based teenage knobbery, the sort of driver who overtakes and then holds in his clutch slightly at the same time as accelerating to make his engine roar as loudly and aggressively as possible. But here, in Hampshire, it seemed like everyone was doing it. If you can get that angry while driving through a forest, maybe you should have a lie down. Or buy a bicycle, but just remember to ride somewhere other than Hampshire.

The route east took me through Romsey, a pleasant enough historic market town, and then on an entirely forgettable A-road to the little city of Winchester.

Winchester sounds like a classy sort of place, maybe because it usually precedes 'cathedral', and so it was a surprise to see there's a prison here. Maybe it's home to gentlemen thieves like Raffles. But then the town's welcome sign calls Winchester "the City of Kings and Priests" and so perhaps it's just a large paedo wing for the latter.

Winchester turned out to be a massive disappointment. The highlight was a woman singing in the main shopping street accompanied by a man on a little keyboard. She wailed like she was giving birth to an eighteen pound baby. And the cathedral wasn't too bad. It's apparently Britain's longest although it has a squat, not particularly attractive main tower. The more I travelled through Britain, and the more great stuff I saw, the less easy it was to be impressed. Sorry, Winchester.

But the worst element of Winchester was that, in reality, it's just an upmarket Anytown. The centre was still full of chains. They may have been more chic than Poundland, McDonald's and Ladbrokes – Joules, Fat Face and Wagamama were here – but it didn't make the place any less of a carbon copy of elsewhere.

This is supposed to be a positive tour of Britain and I feel I've done nothing but moan about Hampshire. I deliberately set out to find something wonderful. I tried typing "Hampshire" and "positive" into Google. The first search result was for a HIV support group. Oh well.

*

If I was dumping on Hampshire, Hampshire was dumping on me too. I woke up to the sound of a bird expansively unloading on to the roof of my tent. I cleaned it off with a handful of large sycamore leaves. It must have been an albatross.

The sun continued to shine. If you live in Britain, you might be thinking, "Hang on, I don't remember all this good weather in 2016" and you'd be right. I was being incredibly lucky. While I'd been bathing in the south-west's sunshine it was raining in the south-east. As I edged in the direction of London, the dampness moved westwards. I'd basically had a big hole in the clouds directly over my head since Cardiff three and a half weeks earlier.

The weather may have been nice but the roads continued to be awful and, lest you think this is just some northern rant against the south, I wasn't the only one who thought so. I bought a local newspaper, The Herald. There were two letters in it from annoyed locals on this topic, including one from Diana, also a cyclist, who'd just come back from a holiday in Somerset and realised how bad it is around here. That said, maybe these things were more noticeable on a bike than in a car. The long ruts in the side of the road every few metres might not even register with anyone sitting on big Michelins. Maybe I should have cycled around the place on Dave's fat bike.

I carried on through the South Downs National Park, the scenery ordinary after Dorset, Devon and Cornwall. It wasn't unattractive, just far from memorable. And drivers were noticeably less friendly too, not reacting when I let them pass as they'd done everywhere else. Maybe they expected a dirty, little, bike-riding oik like me to get out of their way. Perhaps I should have tugged a forelock at the same time.

I arrived in small-town Petersfield and found the sign for Steep, supposedly the location of tonight's field. Never has a village been more aptly named. As I climbed up a seemingly endless hill something in the sky above me took aim, fired and hit me squarely on the arm. Unusually it wasn't the typical hue of an avian deposit. Perhaps someone had launched a St Bernard from a cannon.

At the top of groovily hippyish-sounding Stoner's Hill I asked a man if he knew where the campsite was. He had no idea but said I was no longer in Steep and so it must be somewhere back down the hill. That wasn't what I wanted to hear.

"Beautiful round 'ere, isn't it?" he said.

I nodded but wanted to say 'meh'. He was right though. It definitely wasn't ugly. Perhaps the constant wheel-banging of the broken roads and the precision of the bird life was tainting my experience.

Halfway back down the hill I saw a woman trimming her bush with a chainsaw. No sniggering at the back, please! The campsite was, it turned out, down the lane at the side of her house although, with no sign of any kind, I suppose the only way you'd find it without her there to provide directions would be via satnav.

I cycled down the lane and came to a car park on which stood a tiny handful of caravans. Next to it was a field. I looked for an office or a toilet block but there was nothing. Maybe this wasn't the campsite at all. I carried on down the lane but I was soon faced with a No Entry sign. That field was obviously the site and so I cycled back to it. And then I spotted the facilities, a single portaloo in the corner of the field, looking like the shittest TARDIS ever. The sloping field was empty save for a single, large caravan with a huge awning attached to the front. Every inch of available space was covered with washing, an unfeasible amount for the number of people who could realistically live in such a caravan, as though whoever resided within was taking in laundry for their non-existent neighbours.

As I pushed my bike past the caravan to access the sole flat space in the top corner of the field, Jeff emerged from the inside. I'm guessing he was early fifties but I'm rubbish with ages.

"Just set up your tent," he said. "It's £10. The farmer will come to collect it. Otherwise, stick it in the letterbox at the end of the lane."

Last week I'd paid £5 for a fully-featured campsite and here it was double for a sloping field, a water tap and a shitpit. The field was surrounded by tall, handsome trees though and so it wasn't all bad.

"You look hot," he said, handing me a cold can of Coke.

He was right. I was boiling. And grateful.

I'd noticed a pub a little way back down the hill, the Cricketers, but bizarrely on this sunny Sunday afternoon it was closed. Luckily, someone had left a single leaflet in the portaloo – maybe its destiny had been emergency loo paper – and it talked of local poet Edward Thomas and a walk around Steep. There was apparently a second pub too. I set off.

The walk to The Harrow took longer than I'd expected and, when I got there, it too was closed. Another bloke examining its exterior told me it would open at seven, in an hour's time. On its outdoor picnic benches there were magazine articles about the pub – it was locally famous – one of which included a gushing recommendation for its food, beer and charm from that jovial, older fella from The Great British Menu, not Prue Leith or that younger bloke made of angles and bitterness.

I stuck around and amused myself until it opened. The articles outside had described how oldie-worldie it was, and that was certainly true. It was 17th century after all. The interior had a dark wood, hobbit hovel feel to the place and drinks were served from a hatch.

I noticed a WiFi sign on a shelf and asked for the password. The barman laughed.

"No," he said. "That's a joke."

Of course it was. The place didn't even electrically cool its drinks; why would it have internet? Silly me. I didn't mind being without Facebook but I would've preferred it if they'd stuck 50p in the meter and chilled the cider.

I took my pint outside. As I sat there sipping my lukewarm apple juice a bunch of twenty-something cricketers crowded on to the picnic bench behind me. In expensive accents they discussed this evening's narrow victory despite playing rubbish as well as the age of their girlfriends. One of them used the word "Classic!" a little too often. Tonight's shock gossip was that one of their number had acquired a girlfriend as old as nineteen.

"Nineteen. That's, like, ancient."

"Classic!"

The others had much younger females than her. No one admitted to anything pederastic but if nineteen is way too old then they weren't leaving themselves too many options. These guys didn't sound like they wanted to bowl a maiden over, maybe just a tween.

Next to the front door was what appeared to be a legal notice. A Mr Mahood Majeggings had apparently applied for a licence to take over the place and sell kebabs and pizza. It was another joke. Can you imagine anything as uncouth as a pizza being served here? That fella from The Great British Menu would never come back. Unless it was topped with

Japanese *fugu* and quails' vaginas or something.

I didn't want to stick around for more tepid cider and so I returned to my tent and sat outside. As I lit my stove Jeff appeared again. He was keen to talk.

"How often do you come here?" I asked.

"We live here. I got the caravan delivered a while back and it got stuck in the mud. Now we can't move it."

"Delivered? So you haven't a car?"

"No, neither me nor the missus can drive."

That must be awkward. The nearest shops were in Petersfield, a few miles down the hill.

"We tried living in town with the wife's sister but..." Then he called her a name or two and pulled a face. "So we came here. She picks us up to go shopping once a week." That seemed generous for someone he didn't actually like. "She only does it to make herself feel good."

We talked, or rather Jeff talked, while I cooked my dinner. He was into search engine optimization. I worked in I.T. many years ago. I didn't need to be reminded how dull it is. He was really good at it apparently but doesn't do it any more.

"Maybe I'll start again. This time I'd just charge £30 a month or something."

He was setting his sights low. I'd looked in the newspaper at property pricing around here. An ordinary two-bedroomed terraced house would set you back £1,200 a month in rent although for larger but still not massive houses this rose to £3,000. To buy a three-bedroomed house on a photocopy estate, detached in name only – a one-metre gap separated each home – would cost £400,000. I suppose Petersfield is in the commuter capture area for London but it would be a miserable old trudge to travel up there every day.

Jeff mentioned what a great area this was, how Mark Owen lived not far away, and another impressively famous couple whose names escape me now. If he was only going to charge £30 a month, he was going to need a lot of customers. And I'm sure if Mark Owen wants www.TheTakeThatImp.com at Google's number one spot then, given his tax arrangements, he could comfortably stretch to forty quid.

Jeff had been a successful businessman, he said, but then later mentioned he'd never had a bank account. I ate my dinner while he continued to talk. It started to get dark and Jeff looked at his watch.

"Sorry. I've hogged the conversation, talking about me all the time," he said. "Tomorrow I'll ask you all about your adventures."

It was alright. I didn't need to talk about my adventures.

I think more than anywhere else I'd been in Britain so far, Hampshire felt the most alien, the most far-removed from what I thought Britain is supposed to feel like. Everyone was paying an absolute fortune to live in fairly ordinary surroundings. And despite the obvious wealth around here, few people seemed happy. Drivers were angry. Smiles were in short supply. Maybe it was just too bloody expensive. Or maybe they kept bumping into Mark Owen.

*

I woke up to yet more sunshine. I hadn't been awake long when Jeff captured me again. Boy, he could talk. He told me a story of a time he went to India. A diplomat was supposed to make a speech but had been forced to cancel the engagement. The organisers cast around for someone to fill his shoes. With only five minutes' notice, Jeff pulled it off. He did a 45-minute presentation in front of a roomful of people. I believed him. I mean, he was a little David Brent-like – he'd often start a story with "Oh, and this is funny" but then it wouldn't turn out to be – but he wasn't a bad chap. I think he just desperately needed someone to talk to.

By half eleven I was on the road again. The route took me on forgettable hills and lanes full of tall hedges. It was impossible to see over them, or to see anything at all. I may as well have been fitted with blinkers. The only clue I'd entered West Sussex, apart from the road sign, was that the roads improved.

Wonderfully-monikered villages whizzed by. Although I didn't venture away from the A272 I was never far from places with names like Balls Cross, Cocking Causeway and Gay Street.

After such a late start I wasn't going to get many miles done today. Near Billingshurst I found a campsite behind a pub called The Limemakers for a tenner. While the site was fine for the money asked, I was now close enough to the capital for it to start infecting pub prices. Five quid for a pint was a little bit Scandinavian.

Today, for the first time on the trip, I felt bored as I rolled along the lanes of West Sussex. Everywhere else had stimulated the senses. I was looking forward to the day I could head north again towards wilder lands. But I wasn't despondent. I suspected my boredom would end tomorrow. Brighton was calling.

*

One of the joys of being in Britain is a breakfast of a big bag of supermarket custard doughnuts costing only 70p, knowing that throughout the course of the day you'll work off those delicious calories.

I started by moving eastwards. After West Grinstead the traffic on the A292 became seriously unpleasant. A lorry came so close it ran me off the road. Luckily, at that precise moment there was a turning to my left into which I could escape.

I ducked off the racetrack towards Henfield and could see an ominous sky ahead. The earlier blue had mutated into the blue-grey of an imminent thunderstorm.

I crossed into East Sussex, statistically almost identical to West Sussex, a similar size, a similar population and a similar amount of that teenage knobbish driving.

I'd been told to visit Devil's Dyke in the South Downs National Park. As the skies grew increasingly murderous, I headed south and up the large hill towards the dyke. I heard my first rumble. I kept going. It couldn't be far, but the more I climbed, the more the sky grumbled around me. I had no idea what the dyke was but, judging by my ascent, it seemed to be on or via the top of a hill and, generally speaking, the top of a hill is not the sort of place you want to be in a lightning storm. A flash ripped through the air with a simultaneous deafening crack. It really wasn't far away. I didn't care what the Devil's Dyke was. It could be a mountain of diamonds with a free bar on top. I wasn't going there in these conditions.

I rolled back down the slope and while on the cycle path to Brighton it started to rain. The storm was only just warming up. The route took me through a tunnel and for a few minutes I hid inside to see what would happen to the weather. Another cyclist came in the opposite direction, dripping from every bodily protrusion.

"It's worse in Brighton, mate," he said.

The light drizzle I was experiencing continued but didn't seem to be getting any worse and so I decided to move along. I eventually reached Brighton unsoaked. Britain's gay capital hadn't fared so well. Its giant potholes were full of water. They must have had quite a storm. Once again on this trip, the worst of the weather was somewhere else. Probably in Wales.

I found the campsite near the coast on the opposite side of town.

"Are you in a car?" asked the woman on the desk.

"No, I'm cycling."

"Wow, you're really slumming it, aren't you?"

It was nice to hear someone talk up their holiday camp so highly.

I left my bags and walked the two miles back into town along the sea front. A little depressingly I was asked by a couple of French kids for directions to the nearest McDonald's. Thankfully I couldn't help. Hopefully they found a proper burger elsewhere.

The storm had passed and the sky was a perfect blue but in the west an enormous, lone, aircraft-smashing cumulonimbus was growing majestically.

It was clear Brighton was better than your average British seaside resort. Its crazy golf course had its own waterfall for God's sake, and on the seafront I caught a glimpse of the world's oldest still-active electric tram.

In any coastal resort there's always a compulsion to visit that bit of scaffolding sticking out into the sea. Call it pier pressure if you like. I'd always thought of them as a very British invention but there are piers all over the world. Brighton's pier was exactly how I remembered Blackpool in the eighties but with a slightly elevated, international feel. The stalls at its entrance sold Spanish *churros*, although really they're just doughnuts in a different shape. From the bright sunshine I walked into the bulbs and neon of the arcade. Suddenly I was transported to my sixteen-year-old idiot self, shovelling in handfuls of coins to win pointless toys no one really wanted. The space was almost entirely devoid of adults. Plinky plonky cheap synthesizer sounds merged with roaring fake Formula One engines and dying Pacmen.

I was glad to emerge on the other side, back on to the wooden planks further down the pier. Various little shops sold sweets and t-shirts, and you could throw something to win something although you knew it was a fix and you'd have to spend more than the cost of the object you were trying to win. A woman in a burka examined the laminated photo choices at a Photo-In-A-Costume booth. I suspect she'd be disappointed unless they had something as unrevealing as a deep sea diver's outfit.

At the end of the pier was a funfair, although precious few were having fun. They had a special offer. For twenty pounds you could ride all day, but hardly anyone wanted to ride at all. The only machine spinning was one of those octopus things where you sit in a car at the end of its tentacles, and there were only five people on that.

I walked back down the opposite side of the pier. A group of four forty-something women in white jeans inspected the filthiness of each other's arses after sitting on various pieces of pier furniture. They pointed and shrieked like crows.

I left the pier and headed into town. A Deliveroo bike courier came past me, carrying what appeared to be a washing machine on his back, the poor sod.

Once I'd reach the lovely Pavilion, with its Russian onion domes, Brighton's character changed from Blackpool to Berlin. Tackiness was swapped for quirkiness. Diversity was its name. Various demonstrations of gayness abounded, from casual shy smiles to flamboyant Rue Paul mincing. There was hair of every colour and none, sometimes all on the same head, clumps shaved, strategically or otherwise.

Not everyone had chosen modern punk. There were the Euro chicsters, too-cool women wearing shades big enough to weld a battleship. These people weren't mouth-breathers; they weren't even *nose*-breathers. They probably had a little blowhole on the top of their heads, the only sign they respired at all was a slight ruffle of their hair every three or four minutes.

A crowd of suntanned pissheads, with rough beards and beef-jerky skin, sat cackling on a bench. No one paid them any attention. It seemed you could be what you wanted to be in Brighton. No one was going to judge you because there'd be someone more interesting along in a minute.

The Lanes were a joy to experience. The dudes and dudettes who haunted these streets were too eclectic to suffer anything as banal as modern British shopping. These stalls were two fingers to the corporate suits, dreaming up profitable conformity in their boardrooms. I'm sure in another part of central Brighton you could have bored yourself with a rubbish Starbucks coffee or had a dull lunch at Burger King but, for this part of town alone, Brighton, I salute you.

After a tour of the centre I walked back tentwards, this time one street in from the front. A young bloke was standing on the pavement ahead of me. He swallowed something from what appeared to be a prescription medicine bottle and then, with a grimace, part-wrestled his shirt from his body, giving up after a few seconds. He seemed in pain.

"Are you alright?" I asked him.

He stared at me blankly, his face two feet away from mine. I repeated the question. Nothing. I tried once more, but still he was mute and just glared with dead eyes. Finally, after a good thirty seconds and without an expression on his face, he spoke.

"What are you saying?" he said, his voice a million miles away, his pupils dilated.

Maybe he was a Jedi. He certainly seemed to be on another planet. After all, Brighton is the Jedi capital of Britain. According to the last census, 1% of residents identify with the Galactic power, almost as many people as are Buddhists. As reported in the Sussex Tab, local Abbie Betts said:

"I guess there are no rules on what can and can't be classed as a religion but, as a Christian, I'd have a hard time accepting someone as a Jedi."

They've got their light sabres and the Force, Abbie, and

you've got your miracles and resurrection. They're all as daft as each other. Let's just get along.

The article in the Tab also discussed Brighton's high levels of atheism, deducing its connection to the gay community's reluctance to embrace religion. It didn't use the expression "gay community". It said "LGBTQIA+ community". Bloody hell, I've been out of Britain for a long time. I've no idea what anything after the T stands for, but I've a feeling this inclusive acronym is just going to keep growing until it starts repeating letters. Otherwise, sexual identities will have to name themselves with specific initials in mind.

"We need a word that means fancying men from Monday to Wednesday, women Thursday and Friday and gender neutrals at weekends. Oh, and it has to begin with X."

Anyway, back on the street and Mr Dilated Pupils was still staring at me. I didn't know what I was doing. I'm no doctor. I'd just seen a human who appeared to be in distress but now appeared to be safely buried somewhere deep in the cocoon of his own mind. I figured it was better to walk on than to try to prise him out of there.

Near the campsite I stopped at Lidl. An Eastern European lad sat at the till, swiping cheap biscuits, with another set of dead eyes, his soul somewhere other than this supermarket. Is this what he really wanted? Minimum wage in an expensive town like Brighton, thousands of miles from his family and friends? Maybe he was saving up for a bigger dream, because this couldn't surely be it.

After the dullness of West Sussex, Brighton seemed the reverse, almost like it had sucked all the life out of its host county to provide it with one spot of genuine interest. And even in a town as atheistic as Brighton, thank Christ for that!

*

I set off the next morning down the pleasant coastal cycle path out of Brighton, passing the huge marina with its tall

221

towers of expensive flats. If the Sussex countryside had been dull then its seaside wasn't. It was stunning, its huge, rugged chalk cliffs dropping dramatically into the English Channel. Unfortunately, and typically for Britain, a decent cycle path can only last so long before the forces of council underfunding give it a kicking. The cycle path ran out at delicious-sounding Rottingdean, reappeared later and was then sporadic all the way to Seaford.

I was initially going to cycle to Beachy Head, another of Britain's suicide capitals. But from the coast I could see the steep climb to it, the traffic-laden A259 with no pavement or verge, and realised it would have been a long and sweaty climb, pissing off a countyful of people who often seemed fairly pissed off already. I suspect it would have been me who was tumbling from that famous cliff top and not of my own volition.

Only two places in the world see more suicides than Beachy Head. They are San Francisco's Golden Gate Bridge and Aokigahara Woods in Japan. There is a Samaritans sign on top and the area is patrolled by the Beachy Head Chaplaincy Team. There are usually around twenty jumpers per year, the majority of which come from outside East Sussex, indicating its reputation has led to the most macabre sort of tourism possible.

Instead I headed inland, through car-free lanes. I saw another hillside chalk horse and then the Long Man of Wilmington. I crossed the A27, another busy road, and decided to find a route north specifically to take me via Upper Dicker. You've got to love English village names.

I'd seen online that there were a lot of campsites around the village of Horam. The first one I came across wasn't on my list. I knocked on the door of its farm but there was no answer. A buxom blonde, Charlotte, probably about 19, was tending her horse. She said the owners weren't in and tried them on her phone but got no answer.

"I'm sure it'll be alright," she said.

She remounted her horse and I followed her to the camping field. It was absolutely massive and entirely empty bar one other tent.

"Try to find some room," she said with a smile.

The site had only just opened. It had showers that included a soap dispenser and a sink with washing up liquid – tiny frills you don't normally get at a campsite – and even a fridge-freezer to keep beer chilled and all for only a tenner, the cheapest I'd paid in a week, proving that, just because you're in the south of England, it doesn't mean everyone wants to rob you.

I checked the weather forecast. It provided bad news. My sunburnt face was predicted to fade over the coming weeks. A ten-day spell of rain was on its way. Bugger.

*

I'd always imagined the Battle of Hastings occurred somewhere near the beach in, oh I don't know, Hastings, but it didn't. It happened in a village called Battle. Spooky! It's almost as if it was destined for conflict.

As with all towns whose names double up as everyday words, the local businesses used it at their peril. Battle Cakes sounds more like a Weightwatcher's programme.

I cycled through the town to the square containing the entrance to the site of the 1066 fisticuffs. I leant my bike against its huge stone walls and my cycle computer, which had been dead for the last 52 days, suddenly sprang into life. Although my bike's wheels weren't moving I was apparently doing a solid ten miles an hour. Ticking off the clicks had never been so easy.

Inside the walls of the site a hoard of school kids charged about like Vikings who'd ingested too much of that lichen that sends reindeers doolally. It was great to see the field where Harold got one in the eye. William the Conqueror built an abbey, Battle Abbey, at the site where Harold was killed to atone for the sheer amount of death he'd inflicted upon the locals. That day hadn't been one of East Sussex's better ones.

Once done I returned to my bike and discovered it had cycled fifteen miles without me. I celebrated with what appeared to be the ingredients of a full English breakfast wrapped in pastry. My diet wasn't getting any healthier.

From Battle I chose smaller B-roads. Down a lane I could hear hooves coming from around a corner and slowed to a stop. An old wooden cart suddenly appeared, pulled by two out-of-control horses. It flew around the bend while the old bloke holding the reins whooped enthusiastically. The horses reared up at the sight of me and the driver's elderly wife nearly tumbled out of the back. They continued on their way, swerving from side to side, his wife wailing for him to stop.

I was on my way to Rye. The quiet, country lanes took me past the Kings Head pub. A large blackboard on its exterior wall offered camping for a fiver in its field. I wasn't about to pass up an opportunity like that.

I set up my tent, dumped my bags and cycled the six miles or so through Rye to Rye Harbour. I'd always wanted to see this place. It was where my dad had lived, aged about ten.

The tree-strewn road to the village was less than lovely, its small-scale industry lacing the air with the odour of refineries and solvents, but the smells disappeared a few hundred metres down the perfectly straight one-and-a-half mile track and suddenly pretty, little Rye Harbour was upon me.

Most of the pubs I'd visited on this trip had been poorly attended at best. The Inkerman Arms, on the other hand, was heaving, especially given that it was three o'clock on a Thursday afternoon. I bought myself a pint of Old Dairy and a packet of pork scratchings and found a table. I settled down to soak up some of my dad's childhood home. He'd lived in this pub.

The clientele was certainly knocking on a bit. On a table sat a pile of magazines called Golden Times, aimed squarely at the over-fifties. Next to it, a basket of eggs and a pile of greeting cards were for sale. On the ceiling hung loads of brass kettles and jugs, not like a theme pub, but as though they'd always been here. Its menu was mostly based on the fish landed just around the corner.

The harbour was a little way inland via a channel. Small boats chugged up and down it every now and again. A booth sold ice-creams for just £1. Didn't they realise it was 2016? I bought one and it was bloody good. On the other side of the main track to the harbour small dunes and salt marshes were rich in bird life. This wouldn't have been a bad spot to have been a young boy. My dad had said how a local fisherman would sometimes catch more than he could physically carry to market. He'd leave the rest on the beach in a big pile. The local whippersnappers would scoop them up and take them home. After all, times were hard. Rationing was still in operation.

I cycled back through Rye and had a proper look around. It was a town with its own personality. It deserved some sort of medal. I wheeled the bike around its streets, looking in the shop windows. A white-haired bloke speaking in a very camp voice pounced upon me.

"Have you registered for the EU referendum?" he asked.

I told him I'd love to vote but couldn't. I'd lived outside of the UK for too long. He was a Remainer but was suspicious of what the Prime Minister had supposedly negotiated with the EU ahead of his campaign to keep us in Europe. He continued in his effeminate voice.

"But I tell you what, I don't like the look of Cameron's package."

I felt like I'd slipped into a Carry On film.

Back at the pub, on a golden evening, I sat in the beer garden and spoke to the landlord. He told me how, a few decades earlier, Rye Harbour was a rough old hole with a bunch of bad 'uns called the Blue Boulder Boys and "weirdos" who lived on the marshes. Rye Harbour had been a desperately poor place back when my dad lived there.

I mentioned that, unlike many towns, Rye had at least retained some of its character but he wasn't as convinced.

"I used to enjoy going into Rye at the end of the eighties in December for that Christmas feeling," he said, "y'know, the carol singing an' everything. It's all gone now. Cleaned up by the DFLs."

"DFL?" I asked.

"Down From Londons."

Boat-owning Lizzie in Torpoint hadn't lived all the way over there in Cornwall; she lived not far from here, in Hastings, and told me to give her a call if I passed nearby. She popped to the pub in the evening. It was a school night and so she couldn't stay late.

I told her about the EU campaigner in town that afternoon. She said that over the last few weeks she'd researched every facet of the EU debate and was now a passionate Remainer. There wasn't a single credible argument in favour of leaving, she said. The landlord was of a different view, which resulted in a heated exchange.

The discussion had been intensifying of late. The country was polarising. This was particularly sad because a lot of the pro-Brexit arguments were based on lies from Boris Johnson and Nigel Farage, particularly about the amount we paid to Europe. They were also countered with nonsense from the Remain campaign, stating categorically that if we left we'd all be an exact number of pounds out of pocket. Since when were government figures accurate? But worse than the lies were the false promises from Boris Johnson about redirecting EU money to the NHS. How could he promise anything? The Leave team had precisely two MPs between them – Johnson and Gove – out of a parliament of six hundred and fifty. And Farage wasn't even an MP.

It was misinformation from both sides. The landlord was under the impression that we couldn't trade with Commonwealth countries like India. I knew this to be untrue from personal experience. The poppadams I'd once bought from an Asian supermarket in Blackburn had come directly from the subcontinent, along with the infestation of insects I later discovered in my kitchen drawer. He also complained that the apples in the orchard next to his pub were collected by "Lithuanian illegals". That may well have been true, but that's not an argument against the EU. It's an argument for better policing. Some Puerto Ricans work illegally in the US and they aren't in the EU.

Regardless of the heated chatter, the pub's kitchen provided a really lovely plateful of wild boar sausages, mash and gravy. The landlord told me that wild boar were local around here. After a 700-year absence they'd been reintroduced from Europe.

Bloody wild boars, coming over here, taking our acorns!

Chapter 10: The campsite of broken hearts

Kent, Greater London, the City of London, Surrey and Berkshire

The next morning I cycled into Kent and Tenterden. In the centre of town a parked car opened its door on me. I had to swerve to avoid messing up my morning. From the look I got, I suspect the driver would have been more concerned with the head-shaped hole in her door.

Tenterden achieved short-lived national fame in 2013 by switching on its Christmas lights during the first week of September. Making such a big deal about Christmas is another very British trait; most countries don't bother until a week or two before the day itself. A lot of people do the same thing with their summer holidays, booking them six months or more in advance. If the British can only remain sane by looking forward to something in the distant future, what does that say about the present?

As everyone learns in school, Kent is the garden of England. For all the food grown in the fields around here, there appears to be precious few places that sell any of it. The farther south I went, the fewer little shops and convenience store garages there were. There must be friendless, phoneless, computerless old dears in some of these houses literally starving to death. I continued on my way and cycled through a town with only half a name, Thanington Without. Without a what though? Without anywhere to buy food probably. Apparently, a local wag once exposed the truth with his graffiti. On the town's sign, after the words "Thanington Without", he'd added "Classy Birds".

It wasn't long before I rolled into Canterbury. The big attraction is obviously the cathedral and I made my way to it through a protective sheath of chain stores. Unfortunately, the cathedral itself is ringfenced by smaller buildings and this was the first megachurch of the trip so far that wouldn't even let me see its exterior without paying, which isn't very Jesus of them. I suppose those archbishops' frocks and silly hats don't come cheap.

I moved back towards the shops. In the street, a sweet-voiced young woman called Daisy Tickle was singing "Love You Better Now" accompanied by an acoustic guitar played by a bloke, perhaps Mr Tickle.

The shops became less chainy and more interesting on cobbled Burgate and the King's Mile. A coffee shop advertised "Coffee made with love". Keep your pants on, barrista. Just stick to milk.

There were lots of souvenir shops milking the Queen's recent 90th birthday. What is it about royal events that so enthuses the tea towel industry? And why do the people who claim to love her want to wipe her face all over some dirty crockery anyway?

Overall, invisible cathedral aside, Canterbury had been a pleasant place to spend an hour or so but it was time to leave. My plan had been to cycle on the Crab and Winkle trail to Whitstable. It followed the route of the world's first regular steam passenger railway, closed in 1952, but the path wanted me to do weird things, like get off and walk, which is the opposite of what a cycle path should do, and so I decided to use the roads as I always seem to end up doing. This took me up Tyler Hill, where a sign had been defaced and now said, "Please d-i-e slowly".

It wasn't long before I hit the north Kent coast and Whitstable. Near the harbour, built by Thomas Telford, a little city of market stalls sold gifts and snacks. Patriotism was in the air. A man was trying to photograph a couple's Union Flag scarf-wearing bulldog. More Britishness occurred when a Mr Whippy van's ice cream machine exploded comically and the six-strong queue all cheered raucously. That sort of thing doesn't happen in other countries. In Germany they'd just tut and say, "Ach, terrible engineering!"

Maybe the patriotism was related to the referendum, now less than a fortnight away. I was interested in what Radio Four was going to talk about once it was all over. At least seventy-five per cent of its output was related to Brexit. And the referendum's presence was here too. Boats in the harbour flew anti-EU banners. One said, "Save the fishing industry. Vote leave!" Given its unprofitability I would have thought the UK fishing industry appreciated its EU subsidies. It was heartening to see their desire to stand on their own two feet again, but the only way to save the fishing industry would be a total ban on sea-fishing for a decade or two so our waters could grow some bloody fish again.

I cycled out of the harbour, past an untidy beach with mud and small pebbles and more stalls selling shellfish, and into town. It has a pleasant, characterful main street. A man with the handsome, healthy looks of a south European ambled down the pavement wearing an Athletic Bilbao red-and-white-striped football shirt sponsored by Bimbo, the American sliced bread made chiefly of fresh air and sugar. I wonder if he knew what Bimbo means in English. It could have been worse. The Danish national football team was once sponsored by an energy company called Dong.

I transferred to a smaller coast road, through Seasalter, a village whose very name tastes of kelp. There wasn't much going on but after the traffic of Britain's south-east it was lovely to cycle peacefully beside the sea for a while. The quiet lanes terminated in Faversham and then morphed into the horribly busy A2 to Sittingbourne. It's not just the locals over on ilivehere.co.uk who like to have a dig at this town. David Baddiel once described it as the sort of place "you feel overdressed with two ears".

South of here is an area mercifully free of large roads. Lanes, often only a car wide, link ghost villages populated by huge, expensive houses but no pubs, shops or any other amenities. How does a community grow when there's nowhere to meet your neighbours? Or maybe all your neighbours are bankers and you don't want to meet them anyway.

Certainly nobody seemed to be bothering with community-building projects such as smiling or acknowledging the existence of others. Not far from the starchily-named village of Stiff Street I was nearly hit by a Ferrari because he assumed I'd move, despite his own Give Way sign. This close to London, there was clearly money here – lots and lots of it – but the area had less soul than the playlist at a zombie discotheque. Of all the places I'd seen so far in Britain, this is the last place I'd like to live. Which is just as well as it's also the last place I'd be able to afford.

The lanes took a long time to negotiate. I knew roughly where there was a campsite – in Detling – but it turned out that I knew *very* roughly. I popped into the first pub I'd seen for an hour and asked directions. The site was another three miles away, said the bloke, over the dual carriageway, down a lane and then up a massively steep dirt track. By the time I arrived, the sky was threatening rain. The female warden took pity on me and my sweaty forehead and gave me a handful of wet wipes. She then charged me half price because "there's only one of you and it's not fair", a principle I hoped would spread like a virus throughout the whole of the UK.

Unfortunately, although par for the course in the south-east, the nearest supermarket was a Tesco's another three miles away. To make matters worse, this one was down a huge hill on a nightmarish dual carriageway.

"What do you need?" she said.

"Just something for dinner."

"Hang on, I'll see if Eric is going to the chippy."

And he was! I climbed into the passenger seat of his tiny Smart car and off we shot. It started to rain, big angry drops. The windscreen wiper made a scrapey sound as it ineffectively attempted to remove the water.

"The wiper stops working when it starts to rain," Eric said.

That was handy. We screamed down the dual carriageway in the outside lane despite there being no other traffic around us. It felt faster than the speed of light, but cars always seem bowel-looseningly rapid after I've spent several months moving at ten miles an hour.

"It's alright," I said. "The wiper's working on my side. I'll let you know if you're going to hit anything."

I mentioned the lack of shops during today's ride.

"Yeah, but you're in the middle of nowhere," he replied.

But that isn't true. With 1.5 million people, Kent is the fifth most populous county in Britain. You can't really be in the middle of nowhere in the south of England, unless maybe you're sitting in the centre of Dartmoor. And apologies to any American or Australian who reads that statement. If you find a map to check the remoteness of Dartmoor you'll think I've been sniffing glue.

Back in my rainy tent I listened to the football. The European Championships had started. England was certain to do well this year, especially since more teams were competing in the competition this time, and more teams meant *worse* teams, from countries with populations smaller than that of a British town. It was as good as ours. And it started off well until England gifted Russia a point right at the first game's death and then their ungrateful fans jumped the stadium walls and beat us up.

Of all the nationalities in Europe, it's the Russians who are most similar to the British. We both can't stop drinking, we both take off our shirts as soon as the temperature reaches double figures and we both believe we still have, or should have, or will have again, an empire. I suppose it was only natural the Russians would look into the back catalogue of British attributes and pull out football hooliganism.

Anyway, England had a point against the most difficult team in our group. We were on our way to European Championship glory. What could possibly go wrong?

*

I packed up and left in a fine drizzle and then, for an hour, got lost in dark lanes heavy with foliage around Boxley. I was never more than a mile or two from a motorway – the M2 or the M20 – but I felt like I was in the middle of the Black Forest. I followed my compass northwards and hoped I'd find a road sign or maybe a trail of breadcrumbs leading me out of the woods.

I eventually arrived in Bredhurst and then, via the villages of Borstal and Thong, rode into Rochester. The town's castle looked majestic but it would've taken a long time to get around. I pressed on knowing I had to penetrate London today, and in less than ideal weather conditions. The sky was as grey as John Major's underpants, and as wet as Edwina Currie's the first time she saw them.

The ride to Gravesend took me alongside the A2, now four lanes in both directions, each car with a single, glum-looking occupant. The roar was deafening after the morning's empty lanes. This stretch of the ride had become an ordeal.

Cycling through Dartford I saw two girls at the side of the road, probably about fourteen years old, shouting at passing cars. Both wore fluffy onesies despite the drizzle. As I cycled past, the one in the camouflage print shouted, "Oi, mate, I like your legs!" #everydaysexism.

I fought my way into London with a failing smaller chain ring slipping annoyingly on the uphills. For all we're told of the wealth that nestles inside the M25, this part of London – Belvedere and Abbey Wood - felt very much like Blackburn, terraced and poor. Sure, the houses are probably worth a squintillion pounds but the quality of life looked grim, people packed liked pilchards into filthy streets.

I got lost and saw a big hill. Despite being on the outskirts of central London I couldn't get a signal for my phone, and so I couldn't go online to check the map. The correct way is always into the wind or up the big hill. I started to climb it. A black woman in a red, green and yellow shawl, carrying her baby like she was still pregnant with it, told me I was going the wrong way. I was supposed to go *down* the hill. That had never happened before. It was the highlight of my day.

After asking a couple more times for directions I stumbled across the campsite. Down a little lane on a backstreet of terraced houses, a field covered in caravans suddenly opened up, incongruous in a city like London. The land alone must have the value of a decent Premier League club, and worth far more than it could possibly earn hosting camper vans and tents at £18 a night, probably the cheapest place to sleep this close to Big Ben, aside from Primark's doorway.

A poster on the wall of the campsite's reception warned against leaving out your food or shoes. Apparently, squirrels will steal your leftovers and foxes your footwear. This was news to me.

A woman in reception had a problem. Her shoes were missing and she feared she had thrown them away. No one mentioned the foxes. She asked if someone could look in the rubbish for her missing footwear. Apparently this wasn't possible because of health and safety, the standard answer in Britain these days it seems when no one can be arsed to do something.

That evening there was thunder and lightning. While I ate dinner inside my tent, from the corner of my eye I noticed something move. I went to put down my mug and noticed the trainer I was using as a cupholder had vanished. The foxes! I quickly opened the tent flap and saw my shoe stranded in the middle of the grass, ten metres away,. Luckily for me, my shoes smelled so badly even the vermin had given up on them. What does the fox say? "How about some Odour Eaters, mate?"

*

I woke up to more drizzle. As I was leaving the campsite I saw a couple of foxes chasing each other around the field. Despite the weather they seemed happy to be outside, or maybe they couldn't go home because their den was full of boots.

With the steel grey sky this wasn't going to be the day when London looked at its finest. The route took me through Woolwich and, under the conditions, its badly attended outdoor market, and then I spent longer than I should have fruitlessly looking for the meridian at Greenwich Observatory. Disappointed, I headed to Peckham and its wonderful Rye Lane, a multicultural, multinational melting pot, its noise and colour a more vibrant version of Athens' similarly ethnic and hectic Archanon Street. If Richard Littlejohn wobbled down this road, his liver would rupture in an overproduction of anti-immigrant bile.

I'd been told I had to try an East End staple, the infamous pie, mash and liquor. As a Lancashire lad, my youth hadn't been short of pies and given the sales pitch I'd heard for this London treat I was expecting greatness.

I headed to Manzies, the spiritual home of the Cockney dish, in the centre of Peckham. The menu on its wall only contains four items, the three already mentioned plus eels.

My meal was served in the manner of a school dinner. The woman behind the counter plonked a pie on a plate, and used a large palette knife to scoop up some mash and then literally scraped it on to the side of my dish. Two more smears of potato were added and the lot was drowned in a ladleful of thick, grey, green-speckled paste. It had to taste better than it looked. And yet.

I took my plate to one of their wooden benches, sat down and tucked in. The pie was unexceptional, more crust than meat and with a pastry so tough that the whole lot collapsed when you tried to dig in. The mashed potato was just that. Nothing but mashed potato. No milk or cream or even salt and was reminiscent of the bland spuds of school lunchtimes. Surely the whole would be saved by the sauce. I took a small spoonful. Mmm. It had the consistency of Gloy and absolutely no taste whatsoever. The green speckles are supposedly parsley, which is hardly the tastiest of herbs at the best of times, but I wasn't getting a hint of even that. I suspected the two main ingredients of my liquor were cornflour and hedge trimmings.

Now, maybe Manzies was having an off-day, or maybe so long in The Smoke has dulled yer average cheeky Cockerney's taste buds to such an extent that they need to reboot them with a meal that actually tastes of something, like a northern pie, chips and gravy, because today's lunch was rank. When I mentioned this opinion on Facebook later in the day I had a London crowd question my sanity, my sense of taste and my sexuality. But, like Liverpool's scouse, there's a good reason this local speciality hasn't travelled.

Having cycled right across London on my capital city tour, I didn't particularly want to do it again. Under other circumstances I would have visited a distant corner of the county of Greater London and been happy with that. Unfortunately, since I was visiting every county, and because Britain's smallest is the City of London, I had no choice but to burrow right into the middle, like an armadillo looking for parasitic worms.

The iconic sights of the nation's capital grew as I approached – the Shard and the Gherkin – and the ride across Tower Bridge was utterly glorious as I made for The City.

While in a rainforest of tower blocks the skies opened and fat droplets poured. I decided to hide for a while. Under cover of some scaffolding I watched banker types scurry backwards and forwards from building to building like mice worried that they were made of soap. The men were anonymous in identical dark suits. At least the women had a choice of a small range of colours. What did they do all day except run from office block to coffee shop to office block? Many of the blokes had their hair slicked back, although maybe as a result of the rain rather than some stylistic choice to emulate Gordon Gekko. I tried to imagine what thoughts ran through these bankers' heads but all I could hear was a permanent loop of Vincent Price's laugh at the end of *Thriller*.

I stood there for a good twenty minutes. It's odd how invisible you are in London. Only one person, a young black lad, acknowledged my existence during the entire time. I thought about what I was watching, about these actions as actual lives being lived, and a chill ran down my spine. If the same people even noticed me they probably saw a tramp on a bike and felt the same shiver.

I carried on under spits and spots, saw St Paul's and crossed back over the Thames at Blackfriars Bridge. My plan of escape was to hog the river until Twickenham but the riverside path stopped after a kilometre or so. I tried to follow cycle path signs to Richmond but even in newly bike-friendly London that was hopeless with vague directions and dead ends.

The rain came down properly once again in some nondescript part of town and this time I cowered under the porch of another office block. Traffic streamed past me, spraying the grey-brown puddles on to the pavement for them to refill again immediately. The odd, lone walker, dressed in the muted colours of a Lowry painting, shuffled by, a glum expression of isolation and alienation fixed on her face. I was imagining all this of course. She might have been thinking about the film première she was attending tonight followed by dinner at The Ivy. But in my Radiohead version of events it wasn't going to get any better than Netflix and a frozen lasagne.

I reached Putney. London was changing, improving. I stopped for another pastry refuelling session a couple of miles short of Richmond. Signs for Twickenham, my target, suddenly dried up. Lin, Nina's sister, had said she was only a ten-minute ride from Richmond Park and so I headed in that direction and was rewarded with a hill and a great view over London. Apparently Rupert Murdoch has a place up here. He likes the high ground, though not morally speaking, obviously. I worked out where I was, crossed Richmond Bridge and pootled through St Margaret's to Lin's.

Lin has a lovely house, unassuming from the front, but clean and brightly white inside, with a huge kitchen and a garden that finishes with a small river, a tributary of the Thames. Her little boat wallowed in the water, waiting for the right conditions.

"You can only use it when the tide's coming in," Lin said. "To go for a drink, you have to set off at the right time and then you've two hours before you need to come back."

"Tides are every twelve hours," I replied. "You could stay in the beer garden for fourteen hours, surely."

We had a Guardianista snack of chorizo, hummus and some delicious, chewy-centred, crunchy-crusted home-made bread and then jumped into her little sports car and went to look at the oddity that is Eel Pie Island.

This tiny isle in the Thames was once the location of the Eel Pie Island Hotel that saw shows by The Rolling Stones,

The Who, Genesis, Black Sabbath and Deep Purple, amongst many others. It was closed by the authorities and then burnt down in a mysterious fire in the early seventies.

Sitting in the Thames, joined to the real world by a single, narrow, traffic-less iron bridge, all food has to be delivered via the water. In a land of such densely packed people and heavily planned communities, Eel Pie Island is a genuine one-off. It's how the world would look if the phrase "Planning Department" had never been invented.

Its houses are joined by a narrow lane and of every conceivable architectural style, from shacks to 1960s pebble-dashed council houses to mini-Alpine chalets. They have cute names like Wyndfall and Ripple, Wild Thyme and Piecrust. One has an interesting collection in its garden: gnomes, a canoe, a crocodile's head and a zombie escaping the soil. And then, once back over the bridge, normality returns.

We headed to the White Swan to meet a couple of Lin's friends. Its beer garden gets cut off at high tide and so you have to make sure you have enough to drink or risk getting your feet wet.

The day's final weirdness was a memorial stone from 1896 near Lin's house that seemed to have been finished in a hurry. Its inscription says "To the Glory of Cod". Maybe it was a nod to the almost fishy nature of its host street's name, Haliburton Road.

Lin cooked me a chilli and made a salad. I suddenly realised this was the first green matter I'd eaten in nine weeks, aside from that manky parsley sauce at lunchtime today. I made a resolution to improve my diet in the weeks to come that I instantly ignored.

Despite the dank weather, I'd enjoyed my ride through London. Like last time, it was a bit of a fight, but the traffic was well-behaved and no one tried to kill me. But I was glad to be escaping it for leafier places tomorrow. Samuel Johnson famously said that when a man is tired of London, he is tired of life. Or maybe he's a cyclist.

*

I said goodbye to Lin with a pack of ham and horseradish mustard sandwiches and a posh scotch egg that she'd parcelled up for me. It was already drizzling as I left London behind.

Today was certainly leafier but the countryside of Surrey continued the uninspiring theme. You'd think wealth would be attracted to Britain's scenic hotspots, but not around here. I headed out through the Elmbridge area, apparently Britain's dogging capital, and towards Box Hill to see the best of it, but the weather came down and the traffic was relentless. After sheltering from the rain first in a garage forecourt and then a bus stop I decided that once I got to Leatherhead I'd abandon sightseeing completely and turn towards Guildford. At one point I was caught between shelters and got absolutely soaked in something approaching a tropical storm. Still, it could have been worse. I could have been in an office.

Guildford wasn't looking at its best with its cobbled main street dug up just in time to greet any summer visitors and so I cycled towards a campsite that had been described as "miles from anywhere and down a mile-long rough lane". I came to a track near a small collection of houses that could have been a contender.

"Is there a campsite down here?" I asked a woman walking by.

"Oh, I don't think so."

Maybe she wasn't local.

"Are you from around here?" I asked.

"Yes, I live just there," she replied, pointing at a nearby house. "And I've lived here for years. No, there's no campsite."

Without a serious alternative I went through the lengthy

process of starting up my phone and finding the site's actual location. This was indeed the correct lane. Maybe it was a secret campsite.

I cycled down it. At the bottom was a farm house and a handsome young fella, Justin, was pottering about. His half-New Zealand, half-Thailand ancestry gave him a striking look.

The campsite was basic, with one shower and one toilet and, as far as local conveniences went, it held the record so far for being the farthest from any shop.

"The nearest place is seven miles away," said Justin. "In Godalming."

"Oh."

"But I'm popping there in the car later if you want a lift."

I set up my little home. Lin had been kind enough to wash my entire wardrobe yesterday and I suspect it was this, my new-found cleanliness, that revealed my tent had taken on the odour of an old and mildly incontinent dog. It didn't matter much. In a day or two, everything I owned would smell like that again and I wouldn't even know.

Justin was 31 but had a boyish charm. He'd been living with his girlfriend in Switzerland but she left him and seemed to get the better deal when it came to their shared belongings. She got the house and he'd returned to Britain, homeless and hard up.

Justin's van, which he kept on-site, was now also his house. He worked for the campsite's owner, a farmer, doing odd jobs, like fixing up the shower. To access the passenger seat of his tiny mobile home meant a lot of rearranging, his possessions spilling out on to a campsite table protected from the elements. Unencumbered by his worldly goods the insides of the van were revealed. His vehicle had cost £800 and he'd spent another £200 on wood to fit it out. He'd done a great job.

Justin drove me into Godalming. He described it as "proper middle-class Surrey". It seems life has always been a little better around here. While the rest of Victorian Britain was burning its children to keep warm, this was the first place in the country to have a public electricity supply and electric street lights. In 2016 it was considered the most prosperous place in the UK. I ambled around the chain-lite streets, popped to the supermarket, bought a newspaper and waited in the pub until Justin was done. At the risk of damning the place with faint praise, Godalming seemed very pleasant.

In the evening, back at the field, I sat at the covered table – Justin had repacked the van with his possessions – and chatted. Over too much wine, we were joined by Claire, in her early forties and a floaty, flowery dress. She was living in a large tent at the other end of the field with a puppy, a boisterous and shiny black spaniel called Daisy. She'd bought the dog as an emotional crutch for her seventeen-year-old daughter who'd recently chosen to have an abortion. But then she'd changed her mind and decided to keep the baby and so the puppy stayed with mum. Claire herself had recently withdrawn from a ten-year relationship.

"The only other caravan on this site is a bloke who's just been dumped too," said Justin. "It's like the campsite of broken hearts."

Justin had enjoyed a colourful life, trying to make money whenever and wherever he could. In Switzerland he'd started a pop-up crêpe business but it was closed down by the authorities for lack of a licence. He talked about one of his possible upcoming money-making ventures.

"There are a lot of people in my position," he said, rolling a cigarette. "I want to do up vans, make it possible to live in them. But I've got no money to start."

"I'm getting a van I need doing up," said Claire enthusiastically. "And I have money. We can go into business

242

together."

"Great! We can do that!"

"It has to be big enough to live in but small enough to get down the lanes of Spain and Portugal."

Everyone was on the move, or running away from their broken hearts. Justin had his own Portuguese plans. He was hoping to move there some time soon and try self-sufficiency. He'd recently come back from a fact-finding mission to see how feasible it was.

"Yeah, I visited sixteen eco-sites there, mostly run by Germans and Scandinavians."

"Was it useful?"

"Yes, but they weren't very friendly," he said. "Some were actively hostile, a lot of alpha males."

He planned to buy a cheap acre and start his own with a friend. With his soft-spoken ways perhaps Justin could be a better, non-alpha ambassador for future eco-warriors who needed advice and information.

It was lovely to sit there and have a night-long conversation after many quiet evenings in the tent. Both Justin and Claire were good company. It felt like an oasis of calm after the traffic-mad roads of Kent, Surrey and London. I hadn't had a proper day off the bike since Bristol, nearly a month ago, and so tomorrow, because I could and because I didn't have to scurry from office block to coffee shop to office block, I granted myself a holiday.

*

I awoke to a thump. What the hell was happening? My tent seemed to be collapsing from the outside.

"Sorry!" sang Claire. "It's just Daisy."

I stuck my head out of the door to be greeted by a beautiful day and a spaniel trying her best to keep balance while walking on the sloping roof of my house.

Claire invited Justin and me over to her tent for breakfast.

We each brought whatever we had. I was a part of a commune and it felt lovely.

"I don't want to go back to my house," Claire said. "I want to stay here and be free."

It had been two months since her fella had gone. She felt she needed a change. Her daughter thought she was bonkers.

Claire fried some bacon on the stove outside her tent while Daisy stole the baguette it had been intended for. Claire retrieved an unchewed half of it from the ground but Daisy made another daring burglary and the bread was gone for good.

Barry the farmer was out as well, driving his grass roller around and around the large site in an attempt to give his field the look of Wembley Stadium.

We sat there, drinking coffee and looking around us. The vast flatness of the landscape emphasised the skies. An army of clouds marched across from left to right, close to the horizon.

I lounged around for most of the day, reading and recharging my body. In the evening Justin returned to Godalming again and so I went with him, this time for a stroll down the River Wey. A middle-aged man stood at the side of the water alone, feeding the ducks. A little way down the water was a cloister, a tranquil haven built as a memorial for John George Phillips, the Titanic's radio operator, whose own broadcast had been cut short by that stray iceberg.

In the evening, back at our table, Justin set up a sheet as a screen and put on a film but we just talked all the way through it. We swapped travel stories.

"I was in India," he said, "and ate some dodgy food. I was on a coach and knew I had to be sick. We were stopped at some lights and so I stuck my head out of the window and threw up."

"It could have been worse," I said.

244

"It was. For the guy on the moped directly beneath the window."

Claire popped by but she needed an early night as she was working the next morning, and she was still nursing a hangover from the night before. And then Taz, a friend of Justin, turned up. She was a fragile-looking young woman with long, ginger hair tucked inside a woolly hat, wearing denim shorts and purple tights. Her mum had died recently and Taz was now homeless. She gave off an overwhelming air of sadness, sometimes looking like she wanted to smile but had forgotten how to. Taz was scouting for somewhere to live. Also on the site was a small boat that had been the payment to farmer Barry for some distant debt. She gave it a once over to see if she could live in it. It looked like another broken heart was moving into this lovely, little field.

*

It had been a great place for a relaxing day away from the saddle but it was time to move on. Under another blue sky I went to Justin's table to tell him I was off. He was on the phone.

"Can I call you back in a minute," he said to the person on the other end. "I need to say goodbye to a very good friend of mine."

It was very easy to like Justin. He was genuine, laid back and one of life's dreamers. I agreed to come and find him when he got to Portugal.

My route for the next week or so would be an anti-clockwise half-orbit of those counties west, north and east of London that everyone gets mixed up, probably because they are so similar. My map of British stereotypes labelled the inhabitants of these areas as either "depressing", "posh people" or "twats".

Despite sticking mostly to A-roads, around here they were quiet and mercifully flat. The route, now in Berkshire, took me through Lightwater and Ascot. A lot of Britain, especially the south, feels unloved or at least uncared for. Many roads are bumpy as hell and signs are illegible, grown over by trees as though I'd slipped into some post-apocalyptic future. Maybe no one needs signs any more if everyone has a satnav. We can just have the machines tell us where to go until the next big solar flare wipes out our electronics and then the human species can starve to death as it tries to drive home from work in huge circles.

But close to Windsor, things were different. Carriageways were wider than normal, certainly big enough to allow a car to overtake me without straying into the opposite lane. But why only here? Maybe it's like the story that the Queen thinks the world smells of paint because ten yards in front of her there's someone with a brush tarting up whatever she's visiting. Maybe she thinks Britain's roads are well-maintained because the ones near her houses get special attention.

Windsor is a very pretty place although having a naff McDonalds directly opposite the castle cheapens it. I went to look at the town's biggest draw but, in addition to my taxes, the Queen wanted twenty quid. Surely it's one or the other. I went online to see if my entry fee could go to nearby Legoland instead but they wanted even more, a whopping £50. And, as a funfair, I wasn't sure about the health and safety issues of giant rollercoasters made out of tiny, little plastic bricks.

I also wanted to see nearby Eton. Like a melon I followed the road signs and five miles later I arrived. It was only then that I saw the bridge connecting Windsor and Eton, the one that could have got me there in thirty seconds from the castle. Beneath the bridge hundreds of swans paddled in the Thames just waiting to be plucked and roasted by Lizzie.

Eton College wasn't open to us proles today and so I cycled its little streets instead. A few students wandered around in their ridiculous doorman uniforms. I wanted to see the kids playing rugby in their top hats but the sports fields were empty today. The residents of Eton clearly cared about their town. It was rich and staying rich. Local shops meant the money stayed local.

With this deep-seated desire to maintain its reputation, I was surprised by what I saw as I cycled through town, my eye inevitably drawn to Eton's Porny School. Brilliant, I thought, a place where you can actually get a GCSE in blowing your beans. But don't get excited. It's just a primary school set up by a Mr Porny in the days before his name induced mirth. By the way, that's Dick Porny.

It was early afternoon and England's second European Championship match had started. I found an incongruous-looking snack bar and had a cheeseburger and chips, once again a million times better than anything Maccy D could manage, and listened to the game on my radio. Wales scored. The Asian fellas behind the counter asked who was playing and then looked amused that England were losing.

I headed out of town. The former blue skies had been replaced by brooding clouds. It started to rain. I hid under a large tree and listened to the last few minutes of the game. England ragged a winner right at the death, an escape the inmates of Stalag Luft III would have been proud of.

Berkshire is a county of contrasts. I found a mostly peaceful route towards Maidenhead, Britain's infidelity capital. Unlike classy Windsor and Eton just down the road, Maidenhead was shabby, how I imagined nearby Slough to look, at least as portrayed on The Office, its naff architecture crying out for John Betjeman's "friendly bombs". It was hard to believe that only ten miles separated these places, like Buckingham Palace giving garden space to Steptoe's scrapyard.

Out the other side of town I headed down more lanes to

the Hurley Caravan Site. The bloke wanted £22. You'd think a place charging such outrageous fees would have some facilities, like a shop or something, but you'd be wrong. I cycled back out to the little store in Hurley village but, usefully, it closed at 5pm and it was now twenty past. A woman was going into the house next door to it. I asked her where the nearest place to buy food was. She looked blank.

"I honestly don't know," she replied.

It was a week from the referendum. According to the radio, after the former solid lead for the Remainers, the Leave campaign was seven points ahead. Everywhere I cycled, gardens displayed Leave signs. There were few Remainers doing the same. Maybe it's more difficult to get excited about voting for the status quo, those wanting Out shouting louder, more enthusiastically. But I was near Henley, a wealthy area. Money and education usually coincide and the newspapers were reporting how the better educated you were, the more likely you were to vote Remain. So what was going on around here? But Berkshire is also a very white area. When you live around people from other countries you realise they're no different to you. The whitest areas tend to be most fearful of foreigners. It was, after all, Blackburn's whitest ward that voted in the BNP. Regardless, in seven days' time the votes would be in.

Chapter 11: Fleas and fleeing

Oxfordshire, Buckinghamshire, Hertfordshire and Bedfordshire

I cycled a few miles to Henley, passing a sign for a village called Cockpole Green. Green is definitely not a great colour for a cockpole. Green was also the colour of a little car I saw that was, for reasons I'll never know, completely covered in astroturf.

Despite a sky like elephant skin Henley looked classy, like the sort of place that would be sponsored by Pimms. I pushed my bike down the side of the river and a woman in her sixties asked me if I was walking the Thames Path. She'd done it twenty-odd years ago, ten miles a day, but couldn't remember how far it was or how many days it had taken her.

"You could cycle it," she said.

"Does it go to Abingdon?" I asked, today's target.

"Yes."

"And it's a continuous track the whole way?"

"The whole way."

I was marginally excited. It would be wonderful, I thought, to ride along the riverside. But after fifty metres the path came to an abrupt end. It hadn't come as much of a surprise to be honest. I decided to stick to the roads. Besides, this would allow me to cycle through Pishill, and that appealed to the massive child inside me.

I cycled out of Henley and passed a pub with a chalkboard sign saying, "Pub open for lunch and supper." Supper? As a northerner I'd only just got used to calling my evening meal 'dinner' instead of 'tea'.

I ascended the incline towards the village of Pishill, a wee climb, and now in Oxfordshire saw a sign for Christmas Common. Someone had suggested I see this. On top of a hill grew thousands of pine trees. I passed a Christmas shop, closed now but open from the first of November. Ten months holiday a year sounds good to me. And then I hit Christmas Common the hamlet and cycled through it in thirty seconds. What was I here to see? The trees? Yep, they were alright. Perhaps better in Sweden or Norway where they aren't all aligned in rows. Or was there something else I was missing? The origins of its seasonal name aren't certain. It's either because of a nearby Christmas Day truce during the English Civil War, the local holly trees or the Christmas family, who have local connections. See, Father Christmas *does* exist.

About six miles short of Abingdon I saw a sign for a campsite. I cycled in past a toilet block surrounded by a forest of lemon balm, a plant I'd never have recognized had it not been for what I learnt looking for those fairies.

The site was directly on the Thames, boats moored up on its near-side bank. I was quickly realising that, for all its lack of drama, the south's scenic beauty depended upon its waterways, especially the Thames. The aesthetic highlights of the last two days had been on the river, in Eton, Henley and right here. It wasn't Snowdonia, but it would do until I could return to the truly awe-inspiring parts of Britain.

*

As I packed away I got speaking to Vas, a Bulgarian who'd lived in Britain for the last twelve years and was married to an English woman. Their small son toddled at his feet. He wanted to know about touring because he planned to cycle from his current home in Abingdon to Bulgaria. The exoticism of speaking to someone with an Eastern European accent felt like I was travelling abroad again. As I set off under a leaden sky, along a flat road with unattractive industry to my left, I was transported back to a day in 2012 when I'd cycled from rough-and-ready Harmanli to Plovdiv, Vas's home town and Bulgaria's second city. Back then, the ugly roadside industry had looked fascinating, possibly just because it was somewhere foreign, somewhere not Britain. This morning, England had, albeit temporarily, transformed into an exciting Otherworld. I was quickly pulled back to my British reality when my cycle path became so narrow I was stung on both hands and legs by the nettles that encroached on the neglected tarmac.

I arrived in Abingdon and reached the main square just as a troupe of Morris dancers turned up, in a variety of colours and embarrassing accoutrements like bells and clogs. They danced for a bit while a small crowd of us watched. It's really not that impressive a dance, is it? It's the sort of bodily movement made by someone outside a locked toilet door who's desperate to get inside. But after five minutes of skipping on the spot the guys had worked themselves up enough to require several beers, despite being only half ten in the morning, which I'm guessing is the entire point of the exercise. There weren't many more things to tick off my bucket list of Typically British Must-Sees. Morris dancers had been one of them. The only thing left was a street fight.

In an attempt to find a quiet route into Oxford I got lost but, as a result, accidentally stumbled upon Oxford's main campsite, which research had already told me was a 25-minute walk into town. I decided to see the rest of Oxford on foot.

I set up the tent and walked into town. It was instantly impressive. The city feels like it was designed hurriedly by someone playing a classical version of Sim City, with ancient, grand building after grand building dumped higgledy-piggledy next to each other.

Strolling down busy Cornmarket Street a session of Science Soapbox was in operation. Three individual, crate-sized platforms had a white-coated doctor on each, explaining some PhD project or other to anyone interested.

How beautifully Oxonian!

Then came a street preacher, his crappy P.A. system and nonsense thankfully drowned out by chatter from thousands of people, tourists and residents alike, of every hue. I looked at their faces. It's great the UK has so many immigrants these days, of every shade of skin. It means you can walk down a British street nowadays without thinking everyone's dying of a vitamin D deficiency.

I headed off to see something beautifully pointless. On the way a rollerblading fella came tearing down the street dressed like a combination of Captain America and that hyperactive, partially animated cockwomble from *LazyTown*. That cheered me up.

I eventually arrived at the Headington Shark, a wonderfully bonkers installation. It looks like Jaws fell out of a plane and through the roof of a terraced house. It was erected in 1986 to symbolize the isolation, alienation and helplessness felt over Chernobyl and other nuclear issues, or something. It was highly controversial to begin with. The council wanted to remove it because planning permission hadn't been sought. But the locals campaigned to save it. I'm not sure the nearby neighbours care much for it. As I took a photo one local resident crossing the road openly sneered at me, like she didn't want this sort of thing encouraged. It was too late now. The Shark is part of the Oxford furniture.

Walking back into town, I ambled down Headington Hill where a chunky lad of about nineteen, sitting on a skateboard, tore downwards, using his feet ineffectively as brakes, nearly colliding with a jogger and then a lamp post before screaming to the bottom and landing in a messy heap in the road.

Being on foot in Oxford was my first re-acquaintance with crowds since Brighton. Lots of tourists were in phone zombie mode, walking in a straight line staring at their devices until they collided with someone. That instinctive way opposing groups of walkers used to merge past each other wasn't happening any more. It was getting dangerous. It wouldn't be long before some politician suggests we can only walk around towns if we're insured to do so.

I ambled past Oriel College, part of Oxford University. I'd heard on the radio how a bunch of its students had wanted to remove the statue of Cecil Rhodes that stands outside because of his policy of enforced racial segregation in South Africa. A student tour guide was making the case to a bunch of roadside tourists. This seemed a bit short-sighted. If we were going to remove the statue of every leader who ever misbehaved then we wouldn't have any statues left. My school was called Queen Elizabeth's. Should they rename it because her hobby was murdering Catholics?

Not far from the campsite I entered a pub called The White Horse to see Aunt Sally, a game local to this area. I'd seen a scoreboard for it out in the beer garden but no one was playing. It was only a quarter to five. Maybe it was an evening thing. To play, you throw sticks at a model of a woman's head. The pub smelled of farts and the Eastern European barmaid looked unhappy. Maybe she thought it was me who'd let one off. The odour was here before I was though. It was probably her. Or maybe she was just annoyed at newcomers not knowing the rules of the game and constantly pelting her face with sticks.

*

I woke up, made some coffee and had a couple of blueberry muffins for breakfast. I hadn't seen much of Oxford yesterday – the walk to the shark had taken longer than expected – and so I decided to stay on and have a museum day. Walking out of the site I noticed a sign on the door of the facilities.

"Please do not cycle around the toilet block."

I wondered how many people had fallen off their bicycles and into the urinal before they'd felt a need to put that sign up.

I arrived at The Ashmolean. It bills itself as Britain's First Museum, which shouldn't be confused with Britain First's Museum, which is just a collection of racist arseholes.

I sought out their locker room and suddenly remembered the Devon gnomes. I put my bag into locker number 38 and vowed to act upon their numeric meal recommendation as soon as I was out of here.

There was a ton of fascinating stuff in there, from every part of the world and every period of history. I doubt you could do it justice even if you had a week. There was an impressive collection of impressionist art, including Pissarro, Renoir, van Gogh, Manet and Monet. There was also an army of sculptures from Ancient Greece, much of which had been mishandled unless old Athens had a disturbing number of well buff amputees. And it was great to see so many Buddhas and to prove finally that the unfortunate period when The Enlightened One piled on all the weight must have been swift since it wasn't captured by anyone. He's either svelte or morbidly obese. It looks like the Nirvana he found was the Nestlé ice cream variety.

It was lunch time. I nearly visited Thirsty Meeples, a café whose shtick is that, as well as your coffee and cake, you can choose from hundreds of board games. It's a great idea to trap people in your business for twelve weeks while they try to finish a single game of Monopoly. It seemed the sort of place to visit with friends at a later date rather than sitting there this lunchtime, expectantly flashing my eyes at strangers and then at my ready-to-go Hungry Hippos.

Instead I went to the Angrid Thai Canteen and chose what the gnomes had suggested. It turned out to be squid in three sauces with rice, a dish of delicious battered tentacles in a sweet chilli and ginger sauce with onions and peppers. I needed to keep up my strength. I still had more museums to see.

Next up was the Museum of the History of Science. It wasn't very big with just a couple of rooms open. A third room was closed "due to staff sickness", which I hoped meant someone was off with the flu rather than some poor sod had spilled their sample of bubonic plague in there. There were lots of telescopes and microscopes and orreries, along with medical stuff like an eerie, pre-anaesthetic amputation set and a doctor's kit with two trepanning tools, an operation their patients needed like a hole in the head.

I walked back through town via Cornmarket Street. It was now crawling with people and political stands campaigning for Leave and Remain. Around the Remain desk there were more people than Kate Moss has had hot dinners (i.e., just one person) although Leave's was teeming. The polls had narrowed in the last few days. The murder of MP Jo Cox by a right-wing nutjob had shown the darker side of British nationalism and tipped a handful of people in the other direction. The mood was getting nasty.

Not everyone was interested in the EU debate. Some people stood around and watched a tight-rope-walking leprechaun singing Irish songs and playing a fiddle. Others were so self-obsessed they weren't watching anyone but themselves. An Indian fella videoed himself with a selfie stick as he examined shop windows. He wasn't videoing the items in the windows, just his reaction to them, which, for the most part, was po-faced glumness.

My third museum of the day was the Oxford Modern Art museum. There wasn't much inside, but the little they had was nicely mental, including a piece by Sol LeWitt, an artist so lazy he merely wrote the instructions on how to create his art and left the museum to carry them out in red and black crayon. Basically it was just a few wall-sized squares with an extra line in one or two of them. The caption told me that "despite seeming to allude to a particular geometric theory" it was in fact "a highly personal formulation unconnected with mathematical logic". I love that these places take such pretension seriously. If you'd submitted that as part of your GCSE Art project you'd probably have been expelled.

There was another exhibit called Eye of Shark by Dorothy Cross. It was twelve rusty bathtubs and a shark's eye embedded in the gallery wall. She apparently "dissolves the hierarchy between living and inanimate matter to produce a sense of continuity between man and landscape". Which is nice.

I'd done my culture for the day and so headed back to the campsite. Waiting for the zebra crossing's lights on the busy Abingdon Road, two English blokes in their forties spilled out of a house on the other side. It started with raised voices and a bit of shoving and then a proper fight broke out. Oh yes, here it was, my street fight. My sticker book of British icons was complete! A woman stood in the doorway with a baby in her arms.

"Stop fightin', Kev!" she screamed.

Kev had his arms locked around the other fella's shoulders as they wrestled on the pavement.

"But he hit me first," was Kev's mature reply.

They ended up rolling around on the tarmac, grunting wordlessly like pigs in labour, their arses hanging out of their tracksuit bottoms. Nobody was coming out of this looking good.

The lights changed and I crossed the road. Their tumbling carcasses were sort of blocking my way and so I stepped around them, pretending I hadn't noticed them. The guy pinned to the floor looked up at me. I gave him a half-smile and sort of raised my eyebrows in greeting. How very British.

I stopped short of giving him a lusty "Good afternoon!" I walked back to my tent feeling a bit depressed by what I'd seen. No one was seriously hurt, but still.

*

Facebook told me that today, Monday the 20th of June, was the first day of summer as the rain hammered on the roof of my tent. I felt a bit like an old tyre, deflated, flat and I wasn't sure why.

I'd enjoyed my time in Oxford. I didn't really want to leave, especially in the rain. There were still things to see here. I knew that once I got rolling my mood would improve but the motivation to get moving wasn't there. I decided to stay in Oxford.

I went to the office to pay for another day, passing the shower block. A girl stood outside the gents' toilet door, looking at the chain partially across it. For some reason the vast majority of campsites clean their toilets between eleven and twelve in the morning, just when most people are leaving and probably need to use the facilities.

"Is it open?" she asked, pointing at the door.

"I don't know," I said. "But that's the gents anyway."

She looked at me.

"I'm a boy," he replied. "I've just got long hair."

I didn't help matters by being surprised.

"You're a boy?" I said. "Really?"

I remember being mistaken for a girl about his age. I could have handled that better.

The last museum still to see, and one that had been closed the previous day, was the Bate Collection of Musical Instruments. It didn't open until two and so I went for a wander around Christ Church Meadow. Oxford has some lovely spaces. It would be amazing to study here, surrounded by the history and the beauty.

Great Tom, the loudest bell in Oxford, sits in Tom Tower

that guards the entrance to Christ Church. Every night at five past nine it is rung 101 times, one bong for each of the original scholars of the place. It used to be the signal for the colleges to close their gates. If you had to be back home for nine each night, perhaps it wouldn't have been such a great place to learn.

I wandered aimlessly and ended up back in the centre of town. I got a newspaper and headed to St Aldate's Tavern, a dark, near-empty pub and ordered a Ginger IPA. The toilets were downstairs. The first door I came to was marked Narnia. I tried it but it was locked.

I passed the Aldate's police station, apparently where Inspector Endeavour Morse was based, and then arrived at the music museum. Unlike the grand entrances of Oxford's other museums, here you had to press a button to be let through a little door. It all felt a little bit James Bond.

There was only one other couple inside. The friendly guy in charge explained that I couldn't touch the main instruments but I could play with those on the table in front of his desk.

"And you can also play the theremin," he said.

"Wow! A theremin!" I blurted out excitedly.

Despite a youth filled with synthesizers I'd never even seen a theremin before. It's an electronic gizmo with two antennae, one each to monitor the movement of your hands. Your right hand's side-to-side motion controls the pitch while moving your left hand up and down changes the volume. It makes an other-worldly sound and has been used extensively in science fiction movies, most notably Star Trek.

I switched it on, and its amp screamed with deafening feedback. The man on the desk jumped out of his seat.

"That'll be the kids playing with the settings," he said.

He sorted out the amp and I stood for longer than I probably should, annoying him with my electro-whine while he tried to read.

An American family came in and talked to the curator. The daughter was just about to start studying music at one of the colleges here. She sat down at a harpsichord and played like Bach. I figured now would be a good time to stop dicking about on the theremin.

The museum has over two thousand instruments, mostly orchestral and some ancient pieces including a 'serpent', the black, twisty horn that was the forerunner of the sax. They even have a harpsichord they believe once belonged to Handel – he appeared with it in one of his portraits – and they're convinced enough to have insured it for a quarter of a million pounds. That said, Salvador Dalí once appeared in a self-portrait with a melted clock hanging off his 'tache.

In the evening I cooked up some food on my stove. A busy city campsite feels different to a quiet rural one. In the country, sitting in an almost empty field, I'm an intrepid explorer on the outskirts of civilisation. Here, cross-legged outside my tent, prodding the contents of my pan with a spoon, amidst the expensive caravans and camper vans, I'm a penniless cave troll. People smiled and then walked nervously by, probably scared I was going to eat their dog.

*

Cycling out of Oxford early the next morning in a cloud of fellow cyclists I was reminded of Copenhagen. According to Ed Miliband in 2009 the city was the green capital of Britain despite, only a few years earlier, said the Guardian, a day spent breathing the air of Oxford's city centre was equivalent to smoking sixty cigarettes. Even today it has five times the legal limit of pollution. Perhaps the profusion of bicycles just makes it seem clean.

I escaped town via Headington and threw myself into quiet lanes. The other roads eastwards out of Oxford had looked big and well-trafficked. My chosen route was mostly flat and beautifully peaceful. The quiet was interrupted crossing the noisy M40 and then peace descended once again, the only noise the tweeting of birds and the distant, lazy rumble of farm equipment. I'd stubbed out the supposed fag-packet air of Oxford and was now breathing in the fumes of crops gently toasting in the sun. A couple of days wandering city streets had been fun but I belonged in the countryside, like cow shit or myxomatosis.

At a junction I met another bloke on a bicycle going my way. He was off to a business meeting in the tiny village of Brill in next-door Buckinghamshire. Brill should form some sort of Positive Village alliance with Staffordshire's Flash and maybe invite Dorset's Plush along too. They could stand in direct opposition to the League of Misery, which would no doubt include the Perth and Kinross village of Dull and Hertfordshire's Nasty.

"It's more of a chat with my coach," he said. He was the head of a software company, employing fifteen. "It aids with loneliness. And it's nice to be able to start a day like this for a change."

We climbed the hill to the centre of the village and parted company. I went to see the windmill he'd recommended. It was built in 1685 and commanded great views of the surrounding flat countryside. If the city of Oxford wasn't as green as it should have been then this area certainly was. They recycled everything, including the names. Just south of here is a hamlet called Little London, while north is Muswell Hill.

Tolkien lived here in Brill for a while and used it as inspiration for the Middle Earth settlement of Bree. It felt like the sort of place you could imagine hobbits kicking around. And you'd have to go further than Oxford to find Mordor. That was apparently based on the blast furnaces and steelworks of the West Midlands.

The rurality continued. Beneath chestnut trees in the little village of Edgcott I passed the unlikely location of another prison, HMP Grendon. It is billed as a "therapeutic community prison", which almost made me want to stop and spend some time there. No one else in Britain's countryside was getting much community.

Bletchley is a town famous for one thing and one thing only and so it was a little perplexing, when arriving from the south-east, to see no evidence that the world's greatest puzzle-smashing fortress was anywhere nearby. Sure, the welcome sign to the small town mentions "The Home of the Codebreakers" but after that you're on your own. It wasn't until I was right out the other side of town, after guessing at a number of roundabouts and a couple of junctions, that I eventually found what I was looking for. Maybe if you aren't up to fulfilling this relatively simple mission you don't deserve to see the place.

The story of Bletchley Park isn't as secret as it once was. When I was there the film The Imitation Game hadn't been out long. The movie almost gives the impression the code was cracked single-handedly by Alan Turing when, although he played a pivotal role, it took a massive team. At its peak ten thousand people worked on this site. And what a pretty site it was, with great lawns and a lovely lake in the middle. A number of couples met and fell in love around this water, taking a break from decoding Nazi plans to fill the world with the type of blond-haired, blue-eyed Aryans that Hitler wasn't.

Maybe if the entire project hadn't been so secret back in the day, the British government might have turned a blind eye to Turing's homosexuality, then illegal, rather than chemically castrating the poor sod. The museum steers clear of mentioning Turing's fate in too much detail and merely says he died of cyanide poisoning without telling you it was

Turing himself who injected the lethal element into an apple and then took a bite, one explanation put forward for the reason Apple has the logo it does. In any case, it was no way to treat the man who'd helped to shorten the Second World War by an estimated two years, fooling Hitler's forces into thinking the Normandy landings were taking place farther up the coast at Pas de Calais.

The road south from Bletchley to my evening's camp took me through Stoke Hammond and once again I'd stumbled upon another Thankful Village. Given there are only 54 of them, this was a huge coincidence. Stoke Hammond is much bigger than Herodsfoot and so the chance of everyone returning home safely from the war was even more remote.

After requiring the help of nearly the entire village to find the campsite, hidden a mile out of town over one of those hump-back stone bridges that trolls live under, I set up my tent and settled down with the only newspaper that had been left in the newsagent's, a copy of The Times.

Brexit fever had infected the entire nation and The Times had broken down both camps into easy generalisations. The fact that UKIPpers and BNPeabrains were Leavers wasn't much of a shock, but Leave had a substantial lead amongst the over-sixties, the working class and unemployed, and those in the Midlands, the north-west, Yorkshire, the south-west or, in other words, almost everyone in England outside the M25. The Remainers were painted as anyone who'd been to university, the middle and upper classes, and the young. If this was the case, then the future for Britain, regardless of who won, seemed bleak. The country couldn't have been more divided, and fights on social media were becoming more frequent. Sides had been taken and the newspapers in both camps had categorized everyone involved: the thick, lazy, racist idiots versus the stuck-up, out-of-touch, elitist bastards.

*

From inside my tent the outside conditions were peaceful. There was no wind or rain to disturb my breakfast blueberry muffin. It was a disappointment then to open the tent flap and find myself sitting inside a cloud, a drizzle so fine as to be inaudible. The tent was soaked and, with the sky a uniform pencil grey, no change was likely in the next few hours. There was little point in hanging around.

I cycled back through the Thankful Village and then skirted another called Heath and Reach, which, prosaically, had once been two villages, one called Heath and the other Reach. I passed through another town whose name is less interesting than it sounds, Leighton Buzzard, and then, without even realising, came inches from the site of the Great Train Robbery at Bridego Bridge, where Ronnie Biggs helped nick the equivalent of £49 million in today's money with the help of, if memory serves, Phil Collins.

The origins of Slapton's name were more telling. It means "farm by the slippery place" and I'm fairly certain the slippery place in question is the Quantum Energy Health and Wellness Centre, an organisation in the village following the Deepak Chopra policy of tagging on to a name the word 'energy' or 'quantum', or in this case both, as though it actually adds something meaningful. The Centre offers an entire smorgasbord of nonsense, including aura chakra imaging, polarised light therapy and a platinum ionic aqua detox. The aqua detox is a particularly interesting scam. It's basically a low-voltage foot bath in which the water turns a murky brown. Look at all the toxins we've removed from your body! It's a con. The brown colour is actually caused by corrosion of the electrodes in the water bath and the liquid would discolour whether or not your feet were in it. But you'll find testimonials all over the web describing how having a session improved someone's life. So, even though it doesn't work, if you believe it works then it works. Just like religion.

But today I had some genuine magic to see and it was a few miles away in Tring. It was finally here! Today was Mexican flea day. If this were an audio book, you'd now be hearing the "Ay! Ay! Ay!" and wild trumpet of a Mariachi band.

Lionel Rothschild, a member of the family so wealthy that the internet can't even think of a number big enough to describe their riches, liked his animals. From the late 19th century he employed a team of explorers and professional collectors to amass for him one of the world's greatest zoos. It's one in which no creature suffers and the animals never hide in their dens waiting for the gawping thousands to leave. The Natural History Museum has four thousand species, expertly stuffed, and each rat, wolf and snake looks as good today as the day it died, in some cases probably better because their tongues are no longer awkwardly lolling out of their mouths.

As you know, I'd been looking forward to seeing the museum's fleas, mostly because the idea that someone would dress them was so bonkers as to be fascinating. But when I saw them and read the attached story I was even more impressed.

The museum's two fleas, tiny as they are, are viewed through a microscope. And given the limitations of the human eye I would have thought that whoever clothed these insects would have needed a microscope too. But that seems unlikely. They were dressed by a woman in Mexico in 1905, who, to kill time of an evening once the kiddies were in bed, would catch the fleas from the family dog and then make costumes for them. She would have been creating these clothes by candlelight!

Don't think this place is just about fleas. It's got every

animal you can think of and a lot more besides, including a royal antelope the size of a chihuahua and a giant – and I mean *really* giant – armadillo. You could ride the thing. Go and see it.

As I was on my way out of the door I was stopped by a student doing a survey.

"Is there any specific reason why you came here today?"

I looked at him with widened eyes.

"Yes, there was!" I said emphatically.

I left my statement hanging, expecting him to say, "Oh, obviously you mean the fleas" but he looked at me blankly.

"The fleas?" I added.

He shook his head.

"You don't know about the fleas?" I asked.

"No. What fleas?"

He'd never heard of them. The world needs to know about the fleas.

Only a few miles down the A4251 is Hemel Hempstead, which featured heavily in hit TV programme "When Road Builders Do Smack". On first approach, new town Hemel Hempstead's Magic Roundabout is horrifying. I'd come this way during the first week of my all-Europe ride but even on a second approach it's bloody awful. The first time I saw it I thought it was just a big roundabout and rode across it oblivious to the cacophony of angry car horns. This time, knowing what it really was, I was more cautious.

The sign for the roundabout is beautiful, like a simplified diagram of some ancient piece of jewellery, a series of six circles set inside a larger one, but it doesn't even hint at the confusion ahead. The first thing you notice as you approach the roundabout is that some cars appear to be going the wrong way around it. They aren't, of course. They are merely negotiating the nearest of its six mini-roundabouts. This is why it was voted the second worst roundabout in Britain. I got off and pushed.

Hemel Hempstead may get a savaging over on ilivehere.co.uk but, if you're into that sort of thing, it has Britain's classiest ghost. As well as being a new town, Hemel Hempstead is a very old town. Legend has it Henry VIII and Anne Boleyn, in the days when she still had a head, used to visit the place to hunt, sometimes having more than a swift half in the local alehouses. Tales are told of ghostly laughter in one of the hostelry's bedrooms and so some believe it to be Henry VIII. Obviously.

I got lost not far out of Hemel Hempstead. In fact I think I took the wrong exit of the 95 available options from that bloody roundabout. Eventually I stumbled across a cycle path that said it was fifteen miles to St Albans. My map told a different story. I stuck to the roads and got there in five. The campsite was out the other side of town, as campsites always are, and it was well hidden. Without my phone I'd never have found it, into an industrial estate, down a little lane and over a bridge until, along a rough track, I came to a large house beside a huge field.

I rang the bell on the pillar of the metal gates and a young Asian fella came out and walked me to the field.

"It's just twenty pounds," he said nonchalantly.

"That's expensive," I said.

"Well," he said. "It costs £20 for one or two people, £30 for three or four, and £40 for five or six. See that six-man tent there. For them it's mega-cheap. They're only paying about seven quid each."

"Yeah, that's what I paid last night near Bletchley."

What was I supposed to do? Replicate myself five times? And I couldn't believe he hadn't given the six-man tent an even better deal. It was part of a colony of about ten others.

He showed me the minimal facilities.

"And this is where you wash your pots if you have a

barbecue or something. Are you having a barbecue?" he asked.

"I can't. You've taken all my money," I said. "I was going to have venison but now I suppose it'll just be crisps."

He didn't break a smile but I know he had a sense of humour. There was a smashed up car in his driveway, probably the result of an accident caused as he laughed all the way to the bank.

Despite the size of the field I was told to limit myself to the edges because that colony of tents belonged to a Mexican frisbee team – a Belgian team would be arriving later – here for some nearby plastic-disc-throwing event.

I cycled off to do a bit of shopping and reached Radlett before I found a supermarket. I'd heard how this place had a reputation for affluence - its average house price is over a million pounds – but you'd never tell just by looking at it. What good is all that wealth if you're trapped within the M25's ring of urban misery?

Tomorrow I would begin my journey north and I couldn't wait to start.

*

It rained all night. It was like trying to sleep beneath a loud white-noise generator and so I didn't.

For a twenty-quid campsite you'd probably expect the Glastonbury-style lavs to include toilet paper. The frisbee teams certainly did, but they were out of luck. The paper was all gone. It was probably just penny-pinching on the greedy owner's part, but perhaps there was a darker explanation. Maybe the British Frisbee Association had slipped our landlord a few quid to deny their competitors the necessary facilities. Perhaps this afternoon, while the UK team was leaping and diving and catching their frisbees with gay abandon, the Mexicans and Belgians would be stumbling awkwardly around the field with gurgling stomachs and clenched buttocks.

Toilet paper wasn't the only missing feature of this site. The lazy sod hadn't even provided any bins. On any other site I'd have taken my rubbish with me but his blatant profiteering had annoyed me. I left a full carrier bag at his front gate. Maybe the Mexicans could have a root through it and find something to wipe their arses.

Today I was meeting Lucy. All I knew about Lucy was that she was going to cycle with me today. The original plan was for her to travel across Bedfordshire into Hertfordshire, but because I'd buggered up the order of my original counties – we were already in Hertfordshire – I didn't know what was going to happen now. We met at a café in the little village of Wheathampstead.

Lucy had two jobs. For half of her time she ran an HR company and for the other half she worked for Inventor Tom.

"Who the hell is Inventor Tom?" I asked.

"He won The Apprentice in 2011. He invented the curved nail file."

"Is that useful?" I asked. "It doesn't sound very useful."

"Not for me. I bite my nails."

Lucy was a good laugh and we were getting on when today's big topic raised its head. It was Thursday 23rd June – Referendum Day – after all.

"I know what your opinion will be," she said.

"Do you?"

"Yeah, you travel all around Europe. You'll be Remain. But don't try to change my mind. I've had it all from Lord Sugar."

Ah, you little name dropper, you!

"You've spoken to him about it."

"Yeah. He said it was a no-brainer, but, well..."

She didn't finish her argument. It didn't matter. She had better names to drop though. Her husband worked in security, but I don't mean he's the sort of bloke you'd find strolling around dark warehouses on the edge of town with a little torch.

"He works on films. He did the new Star Wars."

"I'm sure it wasn't his fault," I said.

She smiled.

"Yeah, he said it was rubbish too. And he's just worked with Brad Pitt. He has to keep the paparazzi at bay."

But we could only talk razzmatazz for so long. We were soon talking about cycling.

"Have you learnt anything on this trip?" she asked.

"Yeah. That I'd rather not be in the south-east."

Screw positivity!

"I know what you mean. It's not great, is it?"

Time was getting on. We'd been sitting there for half an hour.

"Shall we set off?" I asked.

"Alright."

And we did. And three miles down the road, just after a sign for a left turning, she said that this was where she was leaving me. Maybe it had never been her plan to cycle far, or maybe she hated me.

Travelling north alone, I entered Bedfordshire. I would describe it for you but I have no memories of the leg. It was entirely forgettable. But then again maybe I should have been on my toes. After all, and although possibly missing the point of how this capital thing works, in 2015 the Daily Mirror announced that the *entire county* of Bedfordshire was the murder capital of Britain. But before you make a detour and avoid the place next time you're in the vicinity, have a look at the numbers.

In a population of 617,000, the 33rd most populous county in Britain, Bedfordshire saw 12 people murdered in 2015. That's 1 in 51,400. Compare this to Washington D.C., with a similar population and, according to the most recently available numbers, 131 murders. That's 1 in 4,600.

Whatever faults Britain might have, you're unlikely to be murdered. Out of 218 countries, Britain's murder rate comes 188th. France's is a third higher. Finland's is nearly double. Little Liechtenstein's is three times as high, although that was because its population is tiny and a single person was iced. Don't trust statistics. But the numbers don't lie when they state that the US's rate is over four times that of Britain, Lithuania's six times, Russia's ten times, and Honduras, the dodgiest place in the world, has a rate nearly one hundred times higher. Sleep easy, Britons!

I cycled through Cardington, past Britain's largest aircraft hangars, the home of the HAV304, the world's longest airship, described classily by the Daily Mail as "the flying bum".

The weather was looking ominous and I wanted to stop and find somewhere to stay but I'd been told of something in Bedford I was sure to find interesting: the house of Jesus Christ. Normally you'd have to cycle all the way to Galilee to find such a place but not today. Jesus is a Bedford lad.

The Panacea Society was founded in 1919 on Bedford's Albany Road and it is number 18 on that street, an end-of-terrace house, that has been prepared for the return of Jesus after his Second Coming. Previously, the religious cult had believed the world was going to end at the turn of the millennium and that their own god, Octavia – God's daughter rather than that mangy-looking ostrich off Pipkins – was going to return, although what exactly she was going to return to if the world had ended is anyone's guess. When the year 2000 turned out to be disappointingly unapocalyptic the Society recast their predictions and decided to fit out the house with all the mod cons the Son of God might need. To begin with they hesitated to install a shower because He would have "a radiant body" but even Jesus wouldn't stay radiant for long trudging the sticky carpets of Bedford's

Wetherspoon's converting the town's sinners. I'm not sure how else the house is furnished. Obviously it'll have a sofa and stuff but it probably wouldn't have a pool table. It would be difficult to play with stigmata. The cue would keep slipping through His palms. Anyway, if you're interested, then go and ask the current tenants of "The Ark". They are on a two-month rolling lease just in case He does turn up.

The history of the Panacea Society is interesting in itself. They were the custodians of Joanna Southcott's box, which isn't as naughty as that sounds. Joanna, an 18th century mystic announced she was pregnant with the new Messiah. The box in question contains Super Jesus's satin slippers. The Society was founded by a vicar's widow who made a slogan of "Crime and Banditry, Distress and Perplexity will increase in England until the bishops open Joanna Southcott's box". But, as everyone knows, you can't get a bishop anywhere near a woman's box.

The Society once had a membership of thousands but the final two survivors were Ruth Klein and John Coghill, both now deceased, who attributed their longevity to "divine water", which "is good for all ailments while you live and, when you die, you go to Uranus to await the second coming." So presumably that's where Ruth and John are now, sitting up there on, ahem, a huge gas giant with no actual surface. Or maybe they've moved closer to Earth now. Perhaps John is that old moon fella off the John Lewis Christmas ad. In any case, they won't be around if Jesus does clock in a second time and so there'll be no one to tell the current tenants of 18 Albany Road to sod off.

There would be no room for me at Jesus's inn and so I headed out of town, passing rowers practising on the River Great Ouse, towards Willington and its Matchstick Wood campsite. Unfortunately no one in Willington knew what the hell I was talking about and the postcode of the campsite coincided with the Danish Camp, a café that definitely wasn't a campsite.

I'd already cycled around fifty miles today and so to discover the next nearest campsite was another twelve miles away was a bit annoying, especially when the skies opened and stayed open. After an hour on splashy country lanes I arrived in Henlow and was given the last available space for a whopping £25.50.

"Well done!" I said to the woman behind the desk. "You're the most expensive campsite in Britain."

"Yeah," she replied, "but we're more than just a place in a field."

And she was right. This site offered something else. It was a place in a *muddy* field.

The reason the campsite was so full was because tomorrow was the start of a special weekend. It was their music festival. For seventy quid you could watch a load of great acts. Sort of. They were tribute acts and so basically you were stumping up a wodge of tenners for glorified karaoke. If you stuck around you'd get to see pretend versions of Madonna, Mick Hucknall, Robbie Williams and Queen. I'm sure a lot of people would think otherwise but I wouldn't pay seventy quid to see their real versions. Well, maybe Queen would be interesting with a now-zombified Freddie Mercury up front.

But that was tomorrow. Tonight there was real entertainment. The referendum votes were being counted. I'm a sucker for the seemingly endless coverage of an election – I think it started with the joy of watching the Tories crumble and the smug grin on Michael Portillo's massive head collapse on a huge screen at an election party in 1997 – and so I tried to stay the distance. But by half eleven it was in the bag. Nigel Farage made a statement to say he thought the Remain campaign had shaded it. Well, if *he* had chucked in the towel, we were safe.

I fell asleep. They would talk about Brexit on the radio tomorrow and then it would all be over. It would be forgotten, a footnote to history. I snuggled into my sleeping bag content in the knowledge I could return to Spain at the end of this trip, or to anywhere else in Europe, and not suffer at the hands of a deflated pound – the kicking it had taken in the run-up to the referendum would quickly sort itself out – knowing I could live and work anywhere in the EU without hassle, that reciprocal medical arrangements would remain in place, that I could travel without a visa, that if I ever decided to continue with my studies I'd still have 28 countries' universities to choose from.

The lies of the Leavers had fallen flat. The entirely fictitious £350,000,000 a week that Boris Johnson had promised to redirect from the EU to the NHS hadn't conned anyone. All that stuff about reducing immigration had been ignored. After all, everyone knew we needed young immigrants to prop up the pension scheme, otherwise we'd lose it completely simply because we don't produce enough young of our own. The worries that a pro-EU Scotland would tug itself free of an anti-EU England had been enough to convince voters to stay EU-friendly. And Northern Ireland too was safe. It wouldn't join Scotland in leaving the union or be forced to erect some sort of border with Ireland, reintroducing the ghosts of The Troubles. We hadn't voted for some nebulous concept like "to take back control", removing the power from the generally pro-worker EU and handing it willingly to the Slytherin Tories who had, since the late seventies, generally done everything in their power to wring the working man dry. No, none of those things had happened. It was all going to be alright. I slept the sleep of a contented man.

I mulled over the coming weeks and months. I'd already

learnt Britain was a truly wonderful place. It was just that it got progressively less wonderful, at least from a cycling perspective, the closer to the south-east I got. I really couldn't wait to put the M25 behind me, with its teeming roads, impatient drivers, mediocre scenery and wild expense. My positivity had been pushed past breaking point. I really didn't want to be here. The Mexican fleas had been great, but I needed more than a couple of bugs in fancy dress to keep my spirits up. Ahead of me lay better times: the Fens, the Peak District, the hills of North Yorkshire, Northumberland, the whole of Scotland and the Lake District. I would leave the crowds behind and roll into some of the most beautiful and sparsely populated areas of Europe. There would be days when I'd cycle twenty miles without passing a single settlement, when the rain would pour and the wind would howl and drivers coming in the opposite direction would see me from the safety of their steel wombs and look at me as though I'd gone mental. And I'd be happy again. Really, really happy.

And then I woke up early the next morning, turned on the radio and heard the news. Britain was leaving Europe. Oh bloody shit!

END OF PART ONE

The story concludes with part two
Route Britannia – The Journey North

Appendix: My gear

Some readers are interested in a list of gear used by cyclists on rides like mine. Most aren't. That's why the list is tucked here at the back. This is what I took.

The Bike

My bike is a *KTM*, a manufacturer more famous for motorbikes, although now they've started to sell their bicycles in the UK. I bought mine in Austria back in 2001. I don't remember the name of the model and all the transfers that might have given me a clue have rubbed off over time. It's a great, light, strong bike that is very comfortable to ride and cost me somewhere around £800. It has 700C wheels and is made of aluminium, which means, given its age, it is soon to die. Everything except the frame, handlebars and mudguards has been replaced at least once. I can't remember how many cassettes and chains I've gone through. It has now done in excess of 35,000 miles despite living in a garage unused for eight years of its life.

The Bags

My rugged panniers are made by *Carradice*, two on the front and two on the back, and there's a handy bar bag for valuables. Despite being made of thick canvas and water-resistant, I always line them with plastic rubble sacks to keep the water out. They're very strong and durable.

The Home

The tent this time was a *Decathlon Quickhiker*. It is supposed to be a two-man tent but I wouldn't want to share it with anyone except an emaciated lover. In truth, it's a roomy one-man tent. My old German duck down sleeping bag became increasingly ineffective during the trip and so I bought a new, synthetic one that turned out to be way too hot, even during the cooler days of a British summer. The sleeping bag's stuff sack doubled as my pillow. After a few early days of freezing temperatures, my ground mat – one of those five quid foam jobbies – became two. While cycling, the sleeping bag lived in a front pannier but the tent and ground mat were encased in a rubble sack and bungeed to the back rack. Also bungeed to this was a little rucksack, which was very handy when strolling around town or going shopping.

The Kitchen

Once again I took my *Trangia 27* meths-burning stove. My advice would be to avoid going near its pans with anything metal. For want of a plastic spoon I've now de-non-sticked two of them. I took a plastic bowl but mostly ended up eating straight from the pan. I also carried a plastic cup, a fork, a spoon and a penknife.

The Wardrobe

I took three tops that would suit cycling or around-town strolling and two fleeces, one thin, one thick. I had two pairs of underwear, two pairs of socks, two pairs of cycling shorts, two around-town shorts, a sloppy pair for the campsite, two pairs of long, lightweight trousers and a rainproof jacket. I could have left behind one of the tops and one of the pairs of long trousers. Take as little as you can.

Once again, on my feet was, mostly, a great pair of super-durable *Keen* adventure sandals. After ten thousand miles they are now looking a bit shabby. This meant that, while the weather wasn't freezing, I could get away with no socks. I also had a pair of trainers for when it was cold or when walking around town in long trousers. I took a hat and gloves and, for the first, very cold weeks, a fleecy snood my mum gave me at the last minute turned out to be very useful.

The Bathroom
I took shower gel (for washing clothes too), deodorant, a toothbrush, toothpaste, *Vaseline* and a first aid kit.

Tech
In order to save weight I took my little compact camera, which was a mistake because it packed up after a week and so I was limited to taking photos on my Samsung, and, for the most part, it was switched off to maintain batteries. As a result I don't have very many photos of this trip. I also had a rechargeable battery pack and a solar panel to recharge it. This time I also took an old Acer Aspire notebook. Its battery lasts a long time but it takes ages to charge. While waiting for it to reach 100% I was frequently forced to stay in the pub for a third pint. The horror!

Bike-related
I carried various tools, a puncture repair kit, two spare inner tubes and a folding tyre, none of which was needed. My front and rear lights were also never used. I had two 750 ml water bottles and occasionally filled an additional 1.5 litre pop bottle for extra water on hot days.

Everything Else
I had a passport, although I don't remember ever needing it, lots of blood pressure medication, a dismembered road atlas of the UK that was discarded as I finished each page, a separate, tiny map book of the UK on which I plotted where I'd been at the end of each day, a sewing kit, my notebook and a few pens, a head torch and a wallet that took a greater kicking the closer I got to the south-east.

Also from Steven Primrose-Smith

The No. 1 Amazon UK Bestseller
NO PLACE LIKE HOME, THANK GOD
A 22,000 Mile Bicycle Ride around Europe

After a near fatal illness, Steven Primrose-Smith decides that life is too short to hang around. Inspired, he jumps on his bicycle to travel a road that stretches 22,000 miles across the whole of Europe.

During his ride through 53 countries, climbing the equivalent of 20 Everests, he dodges forest fires, packs of wild dogs and stray bulls, is twice mistaken for a tramp, meets a man in Bulgaria who lives under a table, discovers if ambassadors really do dish out pyramids of Ferrero Rocher at parties, transforms into a superhero after being savaged by radioactive mosquitoes near Chernobyl and comes close to death in France, Norway, Ukraine and Russia.

Such a massive challenge requires calories and Steven gets his from the more unsavoury elements of European savouries: brains, testicles, lung and spleen stew, intestine sandwiches, sausages famous for smelling of poo, a handful of maggots and even a marmot. Nobody eats marmots.

But the distance and his culinary adventures are only a part of the mission. His real objective is much more difficult. Will he be able to confirm something he has long suspected or will he, after all his searching, eventually find somewhere in Europe worse than his home town of Blackburn?

*"There are many books about cycle touring but few are as entertaining, informative and engaging as this one...The result is a funny and informative account of his travels to some of the Continent's well-known and more undiscovered corners. The writing is excellent..." - **CYCLE Magazine***

The No. 2 Amazon UK Bestseller

HUNGRY FOR MILES

Cycling across Europe on £1 a Day

After blowing all his cash on his previous long-distance bike ride (*No Place Like Home, Thank God*), Steven Primrose-Smith wants to go cycling again. Without the necessary funds, he decides to see if it's possible to travel thousands of miles on a budget of just £1 a day.

Against advice, he puts together a team of complete strangers, including a fresh-faced student, a Hungarian chef, and a man with the world's worst bike, the beard of a goblin and a fetish for goats.

While cycling from Liverpool to Gibraltar through England, Wales, France, Spain and Portugal, they plan to supplement their cash-strapped diet by fishing and foraging. It's just a pity no one knows anything about either.

People quit, nerves are strained, and faces and bikes are both smashed. Will anyone make it to Gibraltar?

Amazon reviews for *Hungry for Miles*:

"A very humorous and frank account of an extremely difficult challenge and I really enjoyed reading it."

"Another great book from this author, easily as good as No Place Like Home. You know you are reading a good book when you can't put it down and are sad when it comes to an end...good fun and highly entertaining."

"He's obviously one of life's top blokes. He can strike the balance between fact, fiction, humour, sadness and in this case famine...Thank you for sharing your intelligent wit and passion for all things good..."

The No. 1 Amazon UK Bestseller

GEORGE PEARLY IS A MISERABLE OLD SOD

Seventy-year-old British ex-pat miserymonger George Pearly lives on the Costa del Sol, all alone except for his ancient, three-legged dog, Ambrose. George hates his life and everybody in it. These feelings are mutual. Everyone hates George too.

From this unhappy equilibrium the situation quickly deteriorates. First, George discovers he is dying of a mystery illness. Then his 35-year-old ape-child nephew, Kevin, moves into George's tiny and once tranquil home with a passion for Vimto, Coco Pops and slobbing around in his greying underpants. Worst of all, George's neighbours start to disappear and all accusing fingers point towards George.

Pull up a sun lounger, grab yourself a piña colada and enjoy a murder-mystery romp on Spain's sunny southern coast.

Amazon reviews for *George Pearly Is A Miserable Old Sod*:

"A bit like Tom Sharpe on speed - ridiculous plot, outlandish characters, unbelievable situations – great. Whizzes along and is great escapist stuff and light reading."

"Loved this - George Pearly is indeed a Miserable Old Sod and very funny with it - couldn't put it down."

"This book made me laugh out loud, much to the embarrassment of my son. Original and quirky."

"Most entertaining. Easy reading, witty and worth a read."